Artificial intelligence and international security

Manchester University Press

AI
FUTURES

AI Futures presents a critical analysis of Artificial Intelligence with a particular emphasis on its implication for society. It connects research into the ethics of AI to research initiatives focused on the variegated impacts of Artificial Intelligence, including on marginalised communities and on the Global South. As such, *AI Futures* encompasses a unique range of studies into the political, socio-economic, medical, biological and environmental questions raised by the onset of this new age in global history.

To buy or to find out more about the books currently available in this series, please go to: https://manchesteruniversitypress.co.uk/series/ai-futures/

Artificial intelligence and international security

Redefining arms races and contemporary warfare

Edited by
Alena Vysotskaya Guedes Vieira,
Arshin Adib-Moghaddam
and Mohammad Eslami

Manchester University Press

Published by Manchester University Press
Oxford Road, Manchester, M13 9PL

www.manchesteruniversitypress.co.uk

British Library Cataloguing-in-Publication Data
A catalogue record for this book is available from the British Library

ISBN 978 1 5261 9616 3 hardback

First published 2026

EU authorised representative for GPSR:
Easy Access System Europe, Mustamäe tee 50, 10621 Tallinn, Estonia
gpsr.requests@easproject.com

Typeset
by Deanta Global Publishing Services, Chennai, India

Contents

Contents

Table

Contributors

Arshin Adib-Moghaddam is Professor in Global Thought and Comparative Philosophies at SOAS University of London and Fellow of Hughes Hall, University of Cambridge. At SOAS, Adib-Moghaddam is the co-founding Chair of the Centre for AI Futures. His most recent books include *The Myth of Good AI: A Manifesto for Critical Artificial Intelligence* (Manchester University Press, 2025) and *Is Artificial Intelligence Racist? The Ethics of AI and the Future of Humanity* (Bloomsbury, 2023).

Ibrahim al-Marashi is an Associate Professor of History at California State University, visiting faculty at The American College of the Mediterranean, and the Department of International Relations at Central European University. His publications include *Iraq's Armed Forces: An Analytical History* (2008), *The Modern History of Iraq* (2017) and *A Concise History of the Middle East* (2024).

Fatimah Ayad is an Assistant Lecturer in Political Science at the British University in Egypt. She received her MSc in International Relations from Loughborough University. She is currently a PhD candidate at the Faculty of Economics and Political Science at Cairo University and is specialised in International Relations. Her current research is on geopolitics with a particular focus on East Asia and the Indo-Pacific. She is also interested in the role of emerging technologies in current security and strategic discourse.

Cláudia Barbosa is a collaborative researcher at the Research Center in Political Science (CICP), University of Minho, and a Research Fellow at the Foundation for Science and Technology (FCT) in Portugal. She is also a member of the Digital Society Initiative (DSI) at the University of Zurich. Her research interest primarily focuses on the European Union (EU) cyber security governance and the EU digital policy while also including cyber operations, disinformation and artificial intelligence. She is currently working on a project encompassing aspects of cyber security, digitalisation and technological development that explores the impact of digitalisation on society and the potential of a human-centered approach to enhance societal resilience and digital policy effectiveness.

Paulo Batista Ramos is an Assistant Professor in the Department of Political Science at the University of Minho, Portugal. He holds a PhD in Political Science and International Relations from the University of Manchester. He has previously worked at the Strategic Defense Intelligence Service (SIED), the foreign strategic intelligence agency of Portugal, and is currently a policy analyst in the General Secretariat of the presidency of the Council of Ministers in Portugal.

Contributors

Lauro Borges is a PhD Researcher at the University of Nevada, Reno, and a collaborative researcher at the University of Brasilia. He has been a collaborative member of the Research Center for Political Science at the University of Minho in Portugal. His research interests revolve around air warfare, US–China military–technological competition and offence–defence theory.

Muhammed Can is a researcher at the Research Centre for Political Science (CICP) at the University of Minho in Portugal. He holds a bachelor's degree in Economics from Selçuk University, Türkiye, and he completed his postgraduate studies both at the Swansea University (International Relations) and King's College London (Espionage and Surveillance Studies), UK. He was a visiting PhD researcher at King's College London (War Studies department). His research focuses on AI, irregular warfare, intelligence and counterintelligence, special operations and Chinese politics.

Mohammad Eslami is a Max Weber Fellow at the Department of Social and Political Science at the European University Institute in Italy. He was a researcher at the Research Centre for Political Science (CICP) at the University of Minho in Portugal, where he investigated Iran's Ballistic Missile and Unmanned Combat Aerial Vehicle Programs. He was also a research fellow of the Arms Control Negotiation Academy led by the Davis Center for Russian and Eurasian Studies at Harvard University. His research interests primarily relate to international security, arms control, nuclear proliferation and Middle East studies. He has published in International Affairs, Third World Quarterly,

Review of International Studies, Geopolitics, Mediterranean PoliticsGlobal Policy, Bulletin of the Atomic Scientists, Spanish Journal of Political Science, Journal of Asian Security, Small Wars and Insurgencies and the Journal for Peace and Nuclear Disarmament, and has contributed to several edited volumes published by Springer and Palgrave Macmillan, among others. ORCID: 0000-0003-0283-1839

Bassant Hassib is an Assistant Professor of Political Science at the British University in Egypt and a former Consultant with the Atlantic Council. She became a fellow at Leicester Institute for Advanced Studies (LIAS) at the University of Leicester in 2021. She holds a PhD in Euro-Mediterranean Studies from the Faculty of Economics and Political Science at Cairo University. Her current research is on cyber security governance in Egypt and the GCC (counter)surveillance, digital rights, digital economies and sexualities, counterterrorism and civil society in Egypt, military cyber and AI capabilities and the securitisation of cryptocurrencies in MENA.

Andrea Hickerson, PhD, is Dean and Professor in the School of Journalism and New Media at the University of Mississippi. Previously, she was an associate dean in the College of Information and Communications and the director of the School of Journalism and Mass Communications at the University of South Carolina. Before that, she was the director of the School of Communication at Rochester Institute of Technology in Rochester, New York. She conducts research on journalism routines with an emphasis on technology use and adoption as well as on political communication, with an emphasis on transnational populations. Her work has appeared in a wide range of academic journals, including *Communication Theory*, *IEEE Journal of Selected Topics in Signal Processing* and the *International Journal of Communication.* She is part of an interdisciplinary research team building a deepfake detection tool for journalists. This work is supported by grants from the Knight Foundation and the National Science Foundation. She has a BA from Syracuse University in Journalism and International Relations; an MA in Journalism and an MA in Middle Eastern Studies from the University of Texas at Austin; and a PhD in Communication from the University of Washington.

Maria (Mary) Papageorgiou is a Leverhulme Early Career Fellow at Newcastle University. She was a Lecturer in Politics and International Relations at the University of Exeter, an Associate Lecturer in Research Methods at UCL, a visiting researcher in Defense Studies at King's College London, and an Associate Lecturer at UBIC, Bradford University. Prior to these roles, she was a Teaching Fellow at SOAS University. Her research interests include studies on international relations (IR) theory, Sino-Russian relations, Greek foreign policy and interstate relations in social media, with a focus on quantitative studies. She has published in a number of journals and think tanks, including *International Affairs*, *Fudan Journal of Humanities and Social Sciences*, *Journal of Chinese Political Science* and *Journal of Asian Security and International Affairs.*

Justin M. Pelletier is the Director of the Cyber Range and Training Center in the ESL Global Cybersecurity Institute at

Rochester Institute of Technology (RIT). As a component of this work, he oversees the premier worldwide offensive cyber security competition (Global Collegiate Penetration Testing Competition), which brings together the top ethical hackers from across the planet. As a Professor of Practice in the Department of Computing Security, Dr. Pelletier teaches at the undergraduate and graduate levels, trains and leads student teams to perform security assessments for partner organisations and helps to bring the Hacking for Defense initiative to RIT. He holds a PhD in Information Assurance and Security, an MBA in Entrepreneurship and a BS in Computer Science. Prior to joining academia, Dr. Pelletier was a civil servant in the intelligence community. He is a combat veteran and currently serves as a Lieutenant Colonel in the US Army Reserve.

Alessandra Russo is a researcher at the Department of Political Science within the Faculty of Political and Social Sciences at Università Cattolica del Sacro Cuore (UCSC) in Milan, Italy, where she is also a subject expert in the courses of Strategic Studies and International Relations. She is working on her project focusing on military AI and its critical and lethal applications in warfare. Her research delves into the implications of AI on warfare, exploring its transformative impact on operations, tactics and global security dynamics.

Christopher Schwartz is an American philosopher focused on counterdisinformation and cyber security. He completed his doctorate at KU Leuven's Institute of Philosophy in Belgium, and is currently a research scientist with the Rochester Institute of Technology's Department of Cybersecurity and School of

Interactive Games, where he is assisting in the development of the DeFake deepfake detector and the Jack Voltaic cyber security training wargame. Previously, he was a journalist in the former Soviet Union and Central Asia, including serving as editor-in-chief of NewEurasia Citizen Media and consultant for Factcheck.kg as well as a guest researcher at KU Leuven's Computer Security and Industrial Cryptography (COSIC) research group.

David I. Schwartz, PhD (he/him/his) has worked in the academic field of game design and development since founding the Game Design Initiative at Cornell University in 2001. In 2007, Schwartz moved to the Rochester Institute of Technology. He was part of the founding department in 2009, which became the School of Interactive Games and Media in 2011. After receiving tenure in 2011, he became IGM's Director in 2015. His current research focuses on gamification of cyber security, resilience games, geogames, digital twins and physically based animation.

Alena Vysotskaya Guedes Vieira is an Associate Professor at the University of Minho, Portugal, and an Integrated Member of the Research Centre in Political Science (CICP). She holds a PhD in Political Science from the University of Erlangen-Nuernberg and has received scholarship grants from the Chair Inbev-Baillet Latour, Hanns-Seidel-Stiftung, Haniel-Stiftung, Compagnia di San Paulo as well as from the Portuguese Foundation for Science and Technology (FCT). She published several briefing papers and reports for EU institutions and other think tanks. ORCID: 000-0002-5643-0398

Contributors

Matthew Wright is Chair and Professor of Computing Security. He graduated with his PhD from the Department of Computer Science at the University of Massachusetts in May, 2005, where he earned his MS in 2002. His dissertation work examined attacks and defences of systems that provide anonymity online. His other interests include adversarial machine learning and understanding the human element of security. Previously, he earned his BS degree in Computer Science at Harvey Mudd College. He has been the lead investigator on more than $2.7 million in externally funded projects, including an NSF CAREER award, and he has published more than one hundred peer-reviewed papers, including numerous contributions in the most prestigious venues focused on computer security and privacy.

Acknowledgments

The creation of this book was a journey that began half of a decade ago, and which first has led us to investigate arms races at the regional scale, namely, in the Middle East region. As we were delving deeper into this subject, we became increasingly drawn to the changing nature of the arms races, in which the extraordinarily rapid, and worrisome evolution of artificial intelligence (AI) plays a prominent role. The present volume presents the convergence of those initial inquiries aimed at investigating AI's transformative effect on the arms race dynamics while also discussing its implications.

This book would not have been possible without the countless hours of discussions, meetings and debates among the three editors. Each conversation brought new insights, challenged our original perspective and ultimately enriched the final product. We believe in the importance of intellectual exchange and hope that our collaborative efforts inspire others to the collective pursuit of knowledge.

We are deeply grateful for the financial support provided by the Research Center of Political Science (CICP) as well as the Portuguese Foundation of Science and Technology (FCT)

(UID/CPO/0758/2020). This support has been instrumental in bringing this project to fruition. We are also grateful to all scholars who could not join our project but who have promoted it among their colleagues, and especially to Vasilis (Bill) Kappis, Bruno Oliveira Martins, Ilaria Carrozza, Afonso Seixas Nunes and Doowan Lee.

Throughout this process, as much as it was possible, we aimed to diversify gender representation, include both young and senior established researchers and integrate scholars from both the Global North and the Global South. We are convinced that this diversity of perspectives enhances the richness and depth of the discussions presented in this book.

Lastly, we dedicate this book to our families, whose support and understanding were invaluable during this journey. Once more, we extend our deepest appreciation to them, who stood by us as we worked tirelessly to finalise this project over yet another weekend that was cut short or did not take place at all. Their patience and encouragement have been a source of strength and inspiration. For that and for everything, we dedicate this book to them.

January 2025

Abbreviations

1PV	1st Person View
4IR	4th Industrial Revolution
APT	Advanced Persistent Threat
AFTI	Advanced Tactical Fighter Integration
ATLAS	Advanced Targeted and Lethality-Aid Systems
AU	African Union
ADS	Air Defense Systems
ACONA	Arms Control Negotiation Academy
ATT	Arms Trade Treaty
AI	Artificial Intelligence
ALIS	Autonomic Logistic Information System
AWS	Autonomous Weapon Systems
BMD	Ballistic Missile Defense
CCW	Certain Conventional Weapons
CDAO	Chief Digital and Artificial Intelligence Office
CCP	Chinese Communist Party
CEP	Circular Error Probable
CIS	Commonwealth of Independent States
DARPA	Defense Advanced Research Projects Agency
EU	European Union

Abbreviations

FTC	Federal Trade Commission
FIMI	Foreign Information Manipulation and Interference
GANs	Generative Adversarial Networks
GenAI	Generative AI
ICT	Information and Communication Technology
ISR	Intelligence, Surveillance and Reconaissance
INS	Internal Navigating Systems
IAEA	International Atomic Energy Agency
IHL	International Humanitarian Law
IP	Internet Protocol
IRI	Islamic Republic of Iran
IDF	Israel Defense Force
JAIC	Joint Artificial Intelligence Center
JCOIE	Joint Concept of Operating in Information Environment
LLM	Large Language Models
LAWS	Lethal Autonomous Weapon Systems
MoD	Ministry of Defense
MTCR	Missile Technology Control Regime
MAD	Mutual Assured Destruction
NIIDT	National Innovation Institute of Defense Technology
NSA	National Security Agency
NUDT	National University of Defense Technology
NGOs	Non-Governmental Organizations
NATO	North Atlantic Treaty Organization
NPT	Nuclear Non-Proliferation Treaty
NSG	Nuclear Supplier Group
OWASP	Open Web Application Security Project

Abbreviations

PIJ	Palestinian Islamic Jihad
PLA	People's Liberation Army
PRC	People's Republic of China
PHI	Personal Health Information
PII	Personally Identifiable Information
PLC	Programmable Logic Controllers
PsyOps	Psychological Operations
REAIM	Responsible AI in Military Domain
RMA	Revolution in Military Affairs
RCV	Robotic Combat Vehicles
RAISE	Roundtable for AI Security and Ethics
RoE	Rules of Engagement
SMS	Short Message Services
TALIOS	Targeting Long-Range Identification Optronic Systems
TOAD	Telephone-Oriented Attack Delivery
URL	Uniform Resource Locator
UAE	United Arab Emirates
UNIDIR	United Nations Institute for Disarmament Research
UAVs	Unmanned Aerial Vehicles
UGVs	Unmanned Ground Vehicles
USRC	Unmanned System Research Center
VCDNP	Vienna Center for Disarmament and Non-Proliferation
WaaS	War-as-a-Service
WA	Wassenar Arrangement

AI, arms races and international security: an introduction

Alena Vysotskaya Guedes Vieira, Arshin Adib-Moghaddam and Mohammad Eslami

Arms races have been a prominent feature of international relations and international security since the nineteenth century.[1] Fuelled by competition among states to achieve and sustain military superiority, they have been historically synonymous with heightened tensions and an increased risk of conflict. In the twenty-first century, academic interest in the theme has resurged after a period of decline following the collapse of the bipolar world order.[2] This renewed attention has been fuelled by advancements in the military industry and growing investments in high-tech weaponry[3] in an increasing number of countries.[4] Over recent years, this tendency has intensified, with global military spending rising for the ninth consecutive year in 2023.[5] These shifts align with groundbreaking advancements in military technologies, such as artificial intelligence (AI) and generative AI (GenAI) and lethal autonomous weapon systems (LAWS),[6] fostering what, we argue, constitutes a qualitative arms race.[7]

The intersection of AI and warfare has emerged as a critical and urgent concern for international security.[8] As AI technology continues to advance in sophistication, surpassing human capabilities in tasks such as image classification, visual reasoning and language understanding,[9] and becomes increasingly accessible, the risk that AI-assisted wars could escalate grows, with devastating implications for human lives and global stability. AI militarisation, once dismissed as a distant prospect and even futuristic science fiction, is a new reality in modern warfare and international security,[10] as evidenced by the deployment of the first AI-driven military operations in Gaza in 2017 and a systematic employment by 2024, in addition to its ongoing use in the war in Ukraine since 2022.

The recent AI advancements, underpinned by GenAI models, offer a wide array of battlefield advantages, including the deployment of autonomous and swarm weapons, optimised logistics and improved decision-making and strategic planning. AI's capacity to process vast amounts of real-time data enhances situational awareness, threat assessment intelligence gathering and target identification. Such innovations hold the potential to significantly transform individual countries' capabilities, challenging traditional deterrence approaches and reshaping the international security landscape.[11] However, the direction of these changes remains remarkably uncertain. While AI technology is often heralded as a tool to reduce the lethality of war and bolster strategic stability, it also harbours the potential to escalate violence and destabilise global peace. Autonomous systems and machines, operating with fewer constraints than human decision-makers, may commit atrocities or provoke unintended conflict. This underexplored risk has been making several international actors, including individual states as well as private actors and non-governmental organisations (NGOs), sceptical about the employment of AI-based weapons.[12]

The concept of AI arms races has faced criticism from both academia and analysts alike, partly due to the interpretation of such a race as quantitative,[13] in which states compete to amass larger quantities of military hardware, such as tanks, missiles and aircraft, with the primary focus on sheer numbers and emphasis on outpacing adversaries through volume of weaponry, fuelling military spending and weapon proliferation, and resulting in rapid arms buildups that risk destabilising the international system.[14] We argue, however, that AI reinforces the qualitative aspects of contemporary arms races, leading to AI-driven arms races. The emphasis lies on advancing the technological sophistication of military capabilities, as states seek to gain an advantage by enhancing the effectiveness, precision and lethality of their existing weapons systems.[15]

In this vein, AI in warfare emerges as a new frontier, focused on superior quality and capabilities of AI systems to outperform human decision-making in complex and fast-paced battlefield scenarios. AI can play a transformative role in two areas: first, in the development of entirely new weapon systems, such as robotic and autonomous platforms; and second, in supporting and augmenting the operation of existing weapons and capabilities, such as unmanned aerial vehicles (UAVs), unmanned surface vessels, unmanned underwater vehicles, submarines, stealth aircraft, unguided rockets, precision-guided munitions or missile defence systems.[16]

The integration of AI into warfare brings into sharper relief a number of challenges regarding the definition of national security. Protection of critical infrastructure, data and networks assumes paramount importance. Moreover, the deployment of AI systems introduces risks such as algorithmic bias, operational errors and the risks of unintended escalation,[17] augmenting the stakes of miscalculation in high-stakes conflicts.[18] These dynamics underlie the dual-edged nature of AI-driven military innovation, offering both strategic advantages and profound risks to human well-being[19] and raising ethical concerns.[20]

AI and military affairs: towards AI-assisted wars

As military forces increasingly adopt AI-powered solutions, the technology is reshaping operations across land, sea, air, space and information warfare.[21] At the heart of this transformation is AI's unparalleled ability to process vast amounts of real-time data, driving critical advancements in intelligence gathering, situational awareness and decision-making – cornerstones of modern command and control systems. These capabilities underpin operations across domains, with AI-enhanced (geospatial) tools transforming mapping, terrain analysis and the tracking of enemy movements, as evidenced in the Ukraine war.[22] AI-driven precision targeting directly benefits from these advancements, integrating data from satellites, drones and ground-based sensors, to enable high-resolution target identification while minimising collateral damage. Systems, including reconnaissance satellites equipped with AI algorithms, provide strategic advantage across all branches of the armed forces, prompting the US Joint Chiefs of Staff to liken the power of algorithmic warfare systems to that of tactical nuclear weapons.[23]

In the air domain, the integration of AI represents the most transformative leap since the advent of stealth technology in the

1990s. By enhancing decision-making, operations efficiency and combat precision, AI has reshaped the dynamics of air power, with applications spanning advanced fighter jets, autonomous drones and swarm systems. The US Air Force has taken a leading role in this evolution, employing AI to enhance pilots' situational awareness and decision-making in fast-paced combat scenarios.[24] AI-driven autonomous flight control systems further support pilots in executing complex manoeuvres with precision, alleviating cognitive workloads and allowing them to focus on critical mission tasks.[25] Among most important examples, the American F-35 features the Autonomic Logistics Information System (ALIS), and the F-22 integrates the Advanced Tactical Fighter Integration (ATFI) system.[26] Other advanced fighter jets employing AI technologies include the Eurofighter Typhoon; the Swedish Gripen E; the Chinese J-20, J-31 and J-35 (let alone the most recent sixth generation Chengdu J-36);[27] and the Russian Su-57.[28] Furthermore, several Asian nations are developing fifth-generation fighter jets incorporating AI-assisted programs, such as Pakistan's FGFA fighter, part of the Azm project; South Korea's KAI KF-21 Boramae; India's HAL AMCA; Türkiye's Kaan fighter; Iran's Ghaher-313; and Japan's Mitsubishi X1.

These advancements highlight the global race to integrate AI into military aviation, with 2024 marking a significant milestone in the deployment of AI-enabled fighter jets capable of operating autonomously. Building on the continuous technological advancements, such as the US Air Force's Skyborg Program – which successfully tested AI-powered unmanned aircraft capable of operating alongside manned platforms in complex combat scenarios, advancing the concept of manned–unmanned teaming with collaborative combat aircraft (CCA), sharing real-time tactical information while performing high-risk missions – the Air Force is moving towards fielding a fleet of more than one thousand autonomy-supported unmanned warplanes, with the first units anticipated to become operational by 2028.[29] Designed to share real-time tactical information, execute high-risk missions and reduce pilot workload, these systems exemplify the next generation of aerial warfare. Following successful tests in May 2024, the Air Force expressed confidence in AI's ability to handle critical operational tasks, including data integration and weapon deployment under human oversight.

In parallel with these advancements, the integration of AI programs in military aviation has significantly expanded in recent decades to encompass Unmanned Aircraft Systems (UAS) and Unmanned Combat Areial Vehicle (UCAVs). While various countries are actively pursuing the development of AI-powered drones, the timeline for achieving full and effective autonomy for such systems remains uncertain.[30] AI has already enhanced military tactics across a range of applications, including kamikaze, surveillance and combat drones.[31] Increasingly, nations such as the US, China, Russia, Iran, Türkiye, the United Kingdom, France, Israel and Australia, alongside South Korea, Canada, Japan, Ukraine, the United Arab Emirates, India and several others,[32] have committed significant resources to the development and production of semiautonomous and autonomous UCAVs.[33] The pivotal role of AI-enabled drones has been especially evident in the ongoing Ukraine war, in which both Russia and Ukraine[34] have relied on such technologies for tactical and strategic purposes.[35]This reliance has also driven substantial investment in counterdrone technologies designed to mitigate new threats.[36]

AI has also made significant inroads into missile capabilities, influencing both defensive and offensive operations. AI technology can assist in identifying the distinct signature of a radio or radar signal emitted by a specific aircraft across the entire electromagnetic spectrum. Once this signature is recognised and the aircraft's precise location is determined, its signal and communication can be disrupted or its coordinates relayed to an air defence system (ADS) to eliminate the threat by intercepting the aircraft. Beyond aircraft, AI enhances the detection of strategic threats such as ballistic missiles by recognising their unique electromagnetic signature and calculating their trajectory with precision. Equipped with this data, ballistic missile defence (BMD) systems can deploy countermeasures to intercept incoming missiles.[37] While AI integration in ADS and BDM systems remains largely experimental, several countries, including China, the US, Russia, Iran, the UK, Israel and India, are actively developing platforms to enhance their missile arsenals with AI-powered target recognition and decision-making technology.

The integration of AI-assisted technology into naval operation has emerged as a key priority for major military powers, as they seek to enhance existing capabilities across a broad range of applications, from AI-powered turrets to unmanned surface vehicles (USVs).[38] Countries incorporating AI-assisted USVs in their naval forces include the US (e.g., Sea Hawk, Sea Hunter, Vanguard, Mariner and Ranger), China (e.g., Zhu Hai Yun and Sea Fly-1), Russia (e.g., KMZ Kingisepp Dandelion, Sargon), Iran (e.g., Ya Mahdi, Tir and Bavar), Ukraine (e.g., Mykola, Sonobot, Sea Baby and MaguraV5), the UK (e.g., Arcims), Israel (e.g., Protector), Türkiye (e.g., SIDA) and Australia (e.g., Mantas T-12). Stealth-designed USVs can operate undetected and be deployed from beneath the sea, alongside their associated carriers. More broadly, USVs perform various maritime missions, including surveillance, reconnaissance, mine detection, anti-submarine warfare and search and rescue operations. Their employment significantly bolsters operational capabilities, enhances maritime domain awareness and overall effectiveness in naval operations.[39]

AI-powered applications are also transforming submarine operations by introducing new capabilities that enhance stealth, operational efficiency and adaptability.[40] Nuclear-powered submarines play a crucial role in deterring war due to their capacity to withstand an initial nuclear attack and remain undetected. The current reliance on sonar technology as the means of underwater communication, which utilises sound waves for communication and detection, is associated with various drawbacks, including detectability and potential harm to marine life and humans,[41] which makes the incorporation of advanced AI especially important. Additionally, AI optimises navigation by suggesting routes to avoid detection, enhances the capabilities of both autonomous and semiautonomous submarines and enables predictive maintenance and automates routine tasks.

The revamped significance of submarines is reflected in alliances such as AUKUS, established in September 2021, which underpins Australia's acquisition of nuclear-powered submarines. Technological advancements facilitated by AUKUS highlight the potential of AI in future naval warfare,[42] particularly in enhancing stealth, predictive maintenance and ocean-floor navigation. The US has pledged to supply Australia with up to five Virginia-class submarines starting in 2032, with plans to integrate AI to aid crew members in tracking Chinese submarines more efficiently.[43] In addition to AUKUS as a prominent example of AI integration in submarine technology, other nations, including China, Russia, India, Israel, Iran, Japan and South Korea, are actively pursuing AI-powered submarine programs, indicating widespread efforts to modernise and enhance underwater military capabilities.

AI's potential on ground forces is equally significant. The evolution of AI-supported weapons and technologies, particularly when combined with robotics and biotechnology, has the potential to create significant disparities among nations.[44] The integration of AI into ground forces is not only reshaping warfare through enhanced decision-making, improved combat mission execution and the automation of logistical support, predictive maintenance and supply chain management, but it is also driving the development of advanced technologies such as exoskeletons and ground drones that augment soldiers' physical capabilities and bolster battlefield communication networks. In addition to the US ground-based AI systems, such as the robotic combat vehicle (RCV) and autonomous exoskeletons technologies; Russia's testing of unmanned ground vehicles (UVGs), such as Platform-M; China's UGVs, such as the Sharp Claw series; and India's robodog army (which was revealed in 2025), there are more recent, battle-tested examples of AI integration into ground forces. These include Russia's employment of robotic mini-tanks in eastern Ukraine;[45] Israel's employment of combat and surveillance robots in the tunnels, such as the so-called robodogs[46] and the Rooster,[47] which combines ground mobility with flying; and Ukraine's development of remotely controlled vehicles for battlefield operations. While the levels of autonomy in these systems vary, with some still in testing stages, consistent investment in their development reflects their strategic advantages. For instance, in Ukraine, a remotely controlled or autonomous vehicle is assessed to have the capability of substituting three to six soldiers in the challenging task of battlefield evacuation.[48]

AI is also central in enabling drone swarms to operate collectively and autonomously across land, sea and air domains. These systems rely on advanced algorithms, such as reinforcement learning and mesh networking, to facilitate real-time data sharing, decentralised decision-making and dynamic task allocation. By reducing operator requirements, AI allows a single technician to oversee multiple drones, enhancing scalability and minimising human intervention. Swarms are capable of integrating reconnaissance, electronic warfare and kinetic attacks, adapting dynamically to battlefield conditions even under electronic countermeasures. They have been developed by several countries, including the United States, in projects such as AI-driven Perdix drones since 2017, which focused on naval and aerial applications; as well as China's large-scale investments in naval swarms aimed at enhancing area-denial strategies. Other projects have also been developed by Israel, several European countries, including France, the Netherlands, and the United Kingdom, as well as South Korea, India, and Türkiye.[49] Russia is reportedly advancing experimental swarming, and, since 2022, Ukraine has tested swarming with AI-powered command software developed by the company Swarmer, enabling a single operator to control multiple intelligence, surveillance, reconnaissance (ISR) and first-person view (FPV) suicide drones. The integration of large, high-altitude drones, such as the US Gray Eagle, with low-cost, multi-role platforms, such as EAGLET, demonstrate the potential for multi-domain drone swarming.

AI has also become part of cyber warfare, reinforcing both offensive and defensive operations.[50] On the offensive side, AI amplifies the precision and effectiveness of tools such as self-replicating malware, capable of identifying high-value targets and adapting to network defences. AI-driven tools have allowed advanced persistent threat (APT) actors to infiltrate critical infrastructure and military supply chains, remaining undetected while compromising strategic assets. On the defensive front, AI has enhanced automated threat detection and mitigation, enabling automated systems to identify anomalies, analyse vulnerabilities and respond to cyber threats in real time. On the defensive front, AI is critical for protecting infrastructure and ensuring operational continuity in the face of sophisticated threats. For instance, Ukraine's collaboration with private companies, including Microsoft, has demonstrated the utility of AI in autonomously detecting and neutralising cyber intrusions, proving its instrumental role in safeguarding critical infrastructure and maintaining operational continuity against increasingly sophisticated cyber attacks.

AI's capacity to produce and disseminate content targeted to a particular operational theatre, without human involvement, thickens the increasingly digital fog of war. During the early stages of the Ukraine war, an AI-generated deepfake of president Zelensky falsely declaring Ukraine's surrender was widely disseminated, highlighting the potential of AI to exploit human cognitive vulnerabilities and reshape the information environment in an adversary's favour. By transforming the production of human-like and persuasive content online, particularly on social media, AI has elevated the scope and precision of disinformation campaigns. Powered by AI-powered sentiment analysis and audience targeting, such campaigns maximise the psychological impact of operations and adapt in real-time shifting societal dynamics. Examples include Russia's Doppelgänger operation targeting Ukraine, the US and Europe, or China's deployment of deepfakes and automated bots to promote state narratives. However, AI also holds significant promise as a tool for counterdisinformation efforts. Automated detection systems leveraging AI can identify disinformation, hate speech and synthetic content, enhancing the digital resilience of individual societies. In Ukraine, platforms such as Mantis Analytics,[51] which gather real-time data from social media networks, TV and online media, have been instrumental to identifying disinformation campaigns.

Governing military AI: challenges of a lacking regulatory framework

The intensifying race for technological supremacy has brought, to the forefront of global security discussions, the question on the framework to regulate the evolution of the military AI. Compounding this challenge is the influence of private actors in the development and deployment of military AI technologies, vividly demonstrated in the war in Ukraine. In early 2024, OpenAI revised its usage guidelines, removing the explicit prohibition against military and warfare applications. This has enabled partnerships with the Defense Advanced

Research Projects Agency (DARPA) on cyber security tools and collaboration with Anduril to integrate AI into counterdrone systems. Such developments have brought into sharper relief the issue of how to prevent misuse and ensure accountability, transparency and human oversight over the military AI, especially in the employment of LAWS.

International efforts to regulate these developments remain fragmented. In the absence of specific international treaties or customary laws, regulation relies on existing frameworks, such as International Humanitarian Law (IHL). Article 36 of Additional Protocol I to the Geneva Conventions mandates reviews for new weapons, but the verification challenges posed by AI technologies, such as algorithmic opacity (the 'black box dilemma') and real-time data sharing do not allow for this regulatory option (as well as for an effective arms control regime). While some argue that AI can enhance compliance with IHL by improving targeting precision and reducing collateral damage, critics point to concerns stemming from clashes with the principles of proportionality, due to its open-ended nature, and distinction. Human Rights Watch, for example, has repeatedly emphasised that current AI systems lack contextual awareness and the ability to interpret human intentions (including surrender), rendering them incapable of accurately distinguishing between civilians and combatants or adapting to the complexities of unpredictable combat scenarios, as for instance, in urban or asymmetric warfare. Issues of algorithmic bias and accountability deficits represent further points of fundamental concerns over ethical and legal implications of military AI deployment.

Despite ongoing discussions within the framework of the UN Convention on Certain Conventional Weapons (UN

CCW), progress has stalled since the adoption of the 11 Guiding Principles in 2019. This impasse reflects deep-seated global divisions, with major powers prioritising strategic advantages. The UN Secretary-General has urged the establishment of a legally binding treaty by 2026 to prohibit LAWS that lack human control and oversight, following previous initiatives and appeals, including by the European Parliament and the Campaign to Stop Killer Robots, a coalition of 250 NGOs from 70 countries. In addition, the opposition to the use of military AI seems to be significant: the 2023 Ipsos Halifax Report on AI demonstrated that 60 per cent of respondents across thirty countries are concerned about AI-based defence systems becoming a threat to humanity due to the loss of human control, with this percentage remaining stable since 2019.

Given the improbability of a full ban on LAWS, and complexity associated with the extension via reinterpretation of the existing rules and principles in IHL that could have provided a regulatory framework,[52] attention has shifted towards alternative regulatory approaches. In addition to promoting voluntary commitments and encouraging national self-regulation, one widely discussed legal approach involves applying rules of engagement (ROE) as a means to address key regulatory challenges associated with military AI. ROE provide a balance of specificity, flexibility and legal compliance by translating political and legal objectives into actionable guidelines, specifying conditions under which military force can be used.

Although not constituting a formal regulatory framework, ROE play an important role in shaping customary law by identifying the interpretation of existing rules.[53] Their adaptability allows them to be tailored to the specific characteristics of AI systems, establishing guidelines on human oversight, permissible autonomy levels and acceptable margins for error. ROE can rely on technology as a form of regulation, with the algorithm of the LAWS programmed not only in alignment with the Geneva Conventions and their additional protocols but also additional operational constraints, such as limiting AI operations to specific (not densely populated) areas.[54] Relying on ROE, human control and intervention can be maintained at all levels of command, define the extent of human involvement (whether direct, shared or supervisory), specify the tasks AI systems are authorised to perform and prevent AI from autonomously making critical decisions, such as target selection. ROE also provides mechanisms for managing unexpected situations by setting protocols for escalation and alerting operators to anomalies, ensuring that human oversight remains central even in dynamic combat environments. Furthermore, they reinforce compliance with IHL by mandating legal reviews when AI capabilities evolve and requiring commanders to seek legal counsel before engaging in operations in which AI involvement raises ethical or legal concerns.

What are the characteristics of the AI-driven qualitative arms races?

The contemporary qualitative arms race, driven by advanced militarised AI, although displaying differences when compared with arms races more generally, creates a range of implications for global security. Countries strive to gain a military edge through the use of AI, be it in autonomous weapons systems, cyber warfare capabilities or advanced sensors and communications systems, all of them holding the promise to enhance their military capabilities and, eventually, project power and influence. However, when compared to arms races in more general terms, the AI-assisted arms race displays a number of differences.

The first defining feature of the contemporary arms races is the unprecedented pace of the evolution of AI underpinned by exponential growth in data, advances in computing power and machine learning. Since 2010, this acceleration has been further fuelled by massive investment into AI,[55] especially by the US and China, alongside significant contributions from countries such as India, the UK, Germany, France, Canada, Israel, Japan, South Korea and Australia. The dual-use nature of most AI applications makes the general pace of technological evolution critically relevant to maintain technological supremacy or superiority. This dynamic has already been exemplified by the swift advancement of LAWS, highlighting the strategic imperative for continuous innovation to stay ahead in the evolving landscape of AI-driven military capabilities.

The second key characteristic of the current arms races is its global reach.[56] While the US–China competition for AI supremacy and technological leadership, reinforced by the massive Chinese investment into AI since 2017, dominates headlines, it is by no means its only expression.[57] Countries across the economic and ideological spectrum are increasingly investing in military AI applications and adapting their defence structures. Thus, despite varying economic capacities and normative positions on militarised AI, states recognise the strategic imperative of AI in modern warfare. However, achieving meaningful military AI capabilities requires substantial resources, specialised expertise and significant organisational adaptation.[58] The resulting aspiration adds to the race to harness AI's full potential, shaping the global defence landscape by influencing strategic calculations and military modernisation efforts.

The third important feature of the AI-driven arms race is the significant uncertainty surrounding its very development and actual capabilities. The advancement of AI-assisted military technologies is often conducted in secrecy, making it challenging for other countries to monitor or accurately assess these capabilities. This opacity is compounded by complexity of military AI applications, which can only be fully evaluated in conjunction with a state's broader military capacity within specific realms.[59] As a result, the true extent of a country's AI military capacity may remain unknown until the actual armed confrontation, challenging the established notion of deterrence and complicating strategic planning. The new ensuing dimensions of risk and unpredictability in military strategy require novel approaches to intelligence gathering, defence posturing and international cooperation to avoid potential miscalculations and unintended escalations.

Finally, the contemporary arms race is distinguished by its comprehensiveness, as AI is not confined to a single domain of warfare but is being integrated across all domains, including land, sea, air, space and information operations. This requires countries to develop a comprehensive approach to AI-enabled military capabilities, which allows for seamless functioning across operational environments.[60]

The characteristics of the AI-assisted arms race raise questions about the evolving balance of power and the key facets of AI that will shape future warfare. AI technologies can be used to optimise and enhance existing weapons systems, making older military equipment more effective and relevant, such as in drones, or by equipping aged fighter jets or helicopters with AI-assisted radars and AI-powered guided rockets and missiles. This allows even the nations with limited resources to upgrade their military capabilities and possibly contribute to fostering arms races.

Finally, an important feature of the AI-driven arms races is the lack of international norms and standards governing the responsible use of AI in warfare.[61] As mentioned, the process of establishing international norms and regulations for responsible use of AI, especially in conflict situations, which restrains the ongoing high-tech arms race in more general terms, has proved to be extremely challenging, in spite of the constant appeals, adopted statements and declarations,[62] campaigns proposals[63] and recommendations.[64] The European Union's (EU) AI Act, adopted in late May 2024,[65] is an important step in this regard, even though it is limited to areas within EU law, and even though it provides exemptions such as for systems used for military and defence. The resulting lacuna allows countries to continue developing and deploying AI technologies without meaningful restrictions, exacerbating risks associated with unintended consequences or heightening the escalatory dynamics. More importantly, the resulting increased instability and great power rivalry in AI stemming from the AI-enhanced arms races results in a dangerous dehumanisation in the military domain that reduces humans to data and technology.

What does this edited volume offer?

The rapid evolution of military AI, and its recent deployment in conflicts such as Ukraine and Gaza, urge deeper investigation. However, this task is particularly complex due to the novelty of AI as a research theme as well as the scarcity and the nature (often classified) of the available data.

The present edited volume aims to contribute to the ongoing debate on AI and its implications for international instability and insecurity. While issues such as the legal and ethical dimensions of military AI, its role in the evolution of military affairs and the influence of private sectors and tech giants on AI-driven conflicts have been extensively investigated, this book seeks to break new ground by delving into the underexplored domains of quantum computing, cyber warfare, deepfakes and AI-assisted nuclear arms races. Through a collection of six meticulously crafted contributions, it examines the AI-assisted arms races from diverse and innovative perspectives, offering fresh insights into how these emerging technologies are reshaping the dynamics of global security. Drawing on theories and analytical frameworks from international security and political philosophy, and incorporating interdisciplinary approaches, the chapters provide a comprehensive and original examination of the challenges posed by the weaponisation of AI, with a particular focus on the intersections of quantum, cyber and AI technologies in shaping the future of warfare.

The first chapter, written by Papageorgiou, is developed from an international security perspective. The main argument highlights the dual nature of AI as a force multiplier for both economic and military capabilities, thereby enhancing a country's overall power. Specifically, the chapter examines military–technological capabilities and the balance of power among major states, particularly the US, China and Russia. Additionally, it explores the integration of AI into their national security strategies, budget allocations and research centres dedicated to AI advancement. This analysis underscores the emergence of an AI-driven arms race driven by qualitative innovation and shifts in warfare capabilities, with significant implications for international security and the current tense geopolitical landscape.

Chapter 2, by Barbosa, Vysotskaya Guedes Vieira and Ramos, examines the employment and weaponisation of AI in cyber space. The authors show that the integration of AI into warfare represents a significant evolution from early cyber-assisted operations to the deployment of autonomous systems that enhance precision, automation and situational awareness while reducing human risk. However, AI advancements also introduce vulnerabilities, including exposing critical infrastructure to new threats. The AI–cyber nexus, which is still characterised by ambiguity in terms of its impact and potential, is analysed in the context of the ongoing war in Ukraine. In addition to demonstrating the importance of cyber resilience and strategic cooperation in maintaining essential state functions under persistent digital threats, the authors show how AI has enabled advanced offensive and defensive capabilities in the cyber realm, including adaptive cyber attacks, self-replicating malware and AI-driven disinformation campaigns such as Doppelgänger. The use of AI in information warfare also raises ethical concerns, particularly regarding disinformation and the exploitation of human vulnerabilities, highlighting the need for robust governance frameworks to protect cognitive integrity, human rights and societal stability.

The third chapter, written by Can and Yonder, delves into the potential of quantum computing and its implications for the future of the internet. However, its development remains an intricate and ongoing process, with widespread adoption and practical application of these technologies still on the horizon. Drawing on the analogy that contemporary technological advancements mirror the early stages of human civilisation, the chapter exposes the evolving landscape of emerging technologies and their far-reaching consequences. The authors identify a range of threats stemming from a constant evolution and the production of new types of outputs facilitated by emerging technologies: disinformation, potent influence campaigns and AI-based social engineering attacks. These elements are now becoming central to modern psychological operations, reshaping the dynamics of information warfare and geopolitical strategy.

The contribution of Schwartz, Pelletier, Schwartz, Wright and Hickerson addresses the issue of AI and arms races by exploring deepfakes as a means to augment the (multi-vectoral) narrative warfare. Deepfakes are investigated from a comparative perspective by focusing on the approaches of three major powers, namely Russia, China and the US, and their individual military traditions as well as contemporary military doctrines. Tracing the evolution from the historically and strategically significant events (including the retreat of the Jin Dynasty from the Central Plains (316), the Battle of Red Cliffs (208–09), the Battle of Yorktown (1781), the Qing Dynasty's initial response to the Taiping Rebellion (1850–64), the battles of

Borodino (1812) and Gettysburg (1863), the Chinese Communist Party (CCP)'s manoeuvres during the Chinese Civil War (1927–49) and the Second Sino-Japanese War (1937–45), the battle of Midway (1942), the Soviet defence of Stalingrad (1942–43), the battle of Normandy (1944) while also incorporating the analysis of military strategies and strategic concepts (*maskirovka* (маскировка); *wu wei* (無爲), or 'non-action'), the battle of Inchon (1950) and the Operation Desert Storm (1991)), it demonstrates the alignment between China's and Russia's 'ways of war', which allows for the wholesale embracing of deepfakes, contrary to the US 'ways of war' and the ensuing reluctance to rely on deepfakes. The contribution urges caution towards deepfakes that can be viewed as 'atomic bombs' of narrative warfare. The authors offer concrete ideas for how the US might either deploy weaponised deepfakes in a manner consistent with democratic values or refrain from deploying them at all.

Chapter 5 unpacks how and to what extent AI-assisted systems can affect the world's nuclear security and whether the most recent AI advancements can lead to an escalation of the nuclear arms race, primarily focusing on four roles of AI in the nuclear domain: production, targeting, testing and safeguarding. Eslami, Al-Marashi, Borges and Russo demonstrate that, in the production cycle, AI can optimise performance, innovate and reduce costs associated with the development and production of nuclear material. In the testing domain, AI-based technologies and their advances in the simulation of nuclear detonations lead to a decrease in nuclear tests and their security and environmental consequences. In the targeting domain, AI can create an autonomous nuclear weapon system, augmenting intelligence, surveillance and reconnaissance; automated target recognition and terminal guidance; and delivery and defence systems used against nuclear attacks. Finally, in the realm of safeguarding, AI can detect technical disorders in the enrichment and production process through its collaborative analysis platform and, therefore, lower the dangers associated with the development of nuclear warheads. The chapter demonstrates how the analysed AI technology and applications eventually affect strategic decision-making, autonomous weapons systems and enhanced target recognition capabilities, therefore fuelling a new nuclear arms race.

Finally, Chapter 6, by Hassib and Ayad, centres on AI development, the testing of AI-based weapons in contemporary warfare – using the Gaza war (2023) and the Russian invasion of Ukraine (2022) as key examples – and the regulatory challenges associated with AI development and deployment. It highlights the rapid militarisation of AI, emphasising ethical dilemmas, the accountability gap and challenges in regulating autonomous systems. The chapter also explores how states and private technology companies collaborate to develop autonomous weapons while sidestepping international norms, resulting in heightened civilian casualties and ethical concerns. It discusses the impediments of existing governance regimes to establish a global regulation, such as the absence of agreed definitions, trust, enforcement mechanisms and export control regimes. Furthermore, it critiques the use of conflict zones as experimental grounds for AI technologies, exposing the risks of unchecked innovation. The chapter concludes by advocating for multi-stakeholder engagement that ensures compliance with international humanitarian law, urging the global community to address these challenges and establish effective regulation before

AI-driven warfare escalates further. As the world moves into the mid-2020s, the governance of AI, particularly in the realm of military ethics and norms, struggles to keep pace with technological advancements. The manifest diffusion of AI technology in armed forces is evident in integrating AI-driven platforms and weapons across various conflict zones, such as the Ukraine and Gaza wars. Given AI's extraordinary battlefield advantages, particularly in cyber and information warfare, a complete ban on its use is neither feasible nor realistic. However, the pressing need for constraints on military AI calls for urgent attention, prompting further academic engagement, especially concerning the dehumanising impact and reliability of AI systems. In response to these challenges, the present edited volume seeks to explore the underlying ideas driving the AI-driven arms race, drawing on the latest research. It aims to contribute to the ongoing dialogue and, as we hope, stimulate further investigation in the realm of ethical, legal and strategic dimensions of military AI.

Notes

1 Joe Maiolo, *Cry Havoc: The Arms Race and the Second World War, 1931–41* (London: Hachette UK, 2010); Mohammad Eslami and Alena Vysotskaya Guedes Vieira (eds), *The Arms Race in the Middle East: Contemporary Security Dynamics* (Cham: Springer International Publishing, 2023); Mohammad Eslami and Alena Vysotskaya Guedes Vieira, 'Introducing the arms race in the Middle East in the twenty-first century: A "powder keg" in the digital era?' in Mohammad Eslami and Alena Vysotskaya Guedes Vieira (eds), *The Arms Race in the Middle East: Contemporary Security Dynamics* (Cham: Springer International Publishing, 2023), 3–13.

2 Amitav Acharya, *An Arms Race in Post-Cold War Southeast Asia: Prospects for Control* (Vol. 8, Institute of Southeast Asian Studies, 1994) https://www.iseas.edu.sg/ (accessed 4 February 2026); Talia Blatt,

‘Anti-satellite weapons and the emerging space arms race’, *Harvard International Review* 41:3 (2020), 29–34; Jon Brook Wolfsthal, ‘Why arms control?’, *Daedalus* 149:2 (2020), 101–115. https://doi.org/10.1162/daed_a_01792

3 Maria Papageorgiou, Muhammed Can and Alena Vieira, ‘China as a threat and balancing behavior in the realm of emerging technologies’, *Chinese Political Science Review* 9:4 (2024), 441–482.

4 Paul Scharre, ‘Killer apps: The real dangers of an AI arms race’, *Foreign Affairs* 98:3 (2019), 135–144.

5 Nan Tian, Diego Lopes da Silva, Xiao Liang and Lorenzo Scarazzato, *Trends in World Military Expenditure* (Stockholm: SIPRI, 2024). https://doi.org/10.55163/BQGA2180

6 Shayne Longpre, Marcus Storm and Rishi Shah, ‘Lethal autonomous weapons systems & artificial intelligence: Trends, challenges, and policies’, *MIT Science Policy Review* 3:1 (2022), 47–56.

7 Mohammad Eslami, Alena Vieira, Arshin Adib-Moghaddam, Lauro Borges, Maria Papageorgiou, Fabio Cristiano, Ibrahim Al-Marashi, Tom Sauer and Christian Kaunert, ‘The geopolitics of AI-driven arms races’, *Geopolitics* (2025), 1–43.

8 Heather M. Roff and Richard Moyes, ‘Meaningful human control, artificial intelligence and autonomous weapons’, Briefing Paper prepared for the informal meeting of experts on Lethal Autonomous Weapons Systems, UN Convention on Certain Conventional Weapons (2016).

9 Ray Perrault and Jack Clark, Artificial Intelligence index report. Stanford University Human-Centered Artificial Intelligence (2024). https://aiindex.stanford.edu/wp-content/uploads/2024/04/HAI_2024_AI-Index-Report.pdf (accessed 4 February 2026).

10 Amandeep Singh Gill, ‘Artificial intelligence and international security: the long view’, *Ethics & International Affairs* 33:2 (2019), 169–179. https://doi.org/10.1017/S0892679419000145

11 James Johnson, *AI and the Bomb: Nuclear Strategy and Risk in the Digital Age* (Oxford: Oxford University Press, 2023).

12 Maximilian Hoell and Sylvia Mishra, ‘Artificial intelligence in nuclear command, control, and communications: Implications for the nuclear non-proliferation treaty’, in Julia Berghofer, Andrew Futter, Clemens Häusler, Maximilian Hoell and Juraj Nosál (eds), *The Implications of Emerging Technologies in the Euro-Atlantic Space: Views from the Younger Generation Leaders* (Cham: Springer International Publishing, 2023), 123–142.

13 Charles L. Glaser, 'The causes and consequences of arms races', *Annual Review of Political Science* 3:1 (2000), 251–276. https://doi.org/10.1146/annurev.polisci.3.1.251
14 John McFarland, 'The development of hypersonic weapons in the US, China and Russia: An incipient arms race', *The RUSI Journal*, 168:1–2 (2023), 10–18; Iftikhar Ali and Jatswan S. Sidhu, 'Strategic dynamics of the arms race in South Asia', *Journal of Asian and African Studies* 58:8 (2023), 2284–2302. https://doi.org/10.1177/00219096231153150
15 Nicholas Emery-Xu, Andrew Park and Robert Trager, 'Uncertainty, information, and risk in international technology races', *Journal of Conflict Resolution* 67:8–9 (2023), 1339–1370. https://doi.org/10.1177/00220027231214996
16 Justin Haner and Denise Garcia, 'The artificial intelligence arms race: Trends and world leaders in autonomous weapons development', *Global Policy* 10:3 (2019), 331–337. https://doi.org/10.1111/1758-5899.12713
17 Arshin Adib-Moghaddam, *Is Artificial Intelligence Racist? The Ethics of AI and the Future of Humanity* (London: Bloomsbury Publishing, 2023).
18 Scharre, 'Killer apps'.
19 Mariarosaria Taddeo and Luciano Floridi, 'Regulate artificial intelligence to avert cyber arms race', in Luciano Floridi (ed.), *Ethics, Governance, and Policies in Artificial Intelligence* (Cham: Springer International Publishing, 2021), 283–287.
20 Forrest E. Morgan, Benjamin Boudreaux, Andrew J. Lohn, Mark Ashby, Christian Curriden, Kelly Klima and Derek Grossman, *Military Applications of Artificial Intelligence: Ethical Concerns in an Uncertain World* (Santa Monica, CA: RAND Corporation, 2020). https://www.rand.org/pubs/research_reports/RR3139-1.html (accessed 4 February 2026).
21 Peter Asaro, 'Autonomous weapons and the ethics of artificial intelligence', in S. Matthew Liao, *Ethics of Artificial Intelligence* (Oxford: Oxford University Press, 2020), 212–236.
22 Ukraine's defence ministry refers to Clearview AI to verify identities of dead soldiers and combatants and combat misinformation, leveraging vast databases scraped from social media, while GIS Arta integrates satellite data with decentralised targeting networks. This is in addition to other systems, such as the US-developed 'Delta' battle management system, ARTEMIS (Aerial Reconnaissance Tactical Edge Mapping

Imagery System) – providing real-time mapping and imagery capabilities, complementing satellites in atmospheric conditions unsuitable for traditional reconnaissance – and Griselda, processing information from satellites, UAVs, social media and hacked resources.

23 Roy Lindelauf, Herwin Meerveld and Marie Postma, 'Leveraging decision support in the Russo-Ukrainian war', *Atlantisch Perspectief* 47:1 (2023), 36–41.

24 Peter Layton, 'Fighting artificial intelligence battles: Operational concepts for future AI-enabled wars', *Joint Studies Paper Series 4* (Canberra: Department of Defence, 2021).

25 Joshua Rountree, Patrick Hipelius, Brian Dienst, Jonathan Aronoff, Ryan Neely, Robert Steigerwald, Skylar Griffis, David de Schweinitz, Chiawei Lee and Ryan Hefron, 'Testing artificial intelligence in high-performance, tactical aircraft', in *2021 IEEE Aerospace Conference (50100)* (IEEE, 2021), 1–15.

26 Clay Wilson, 'Artificial intelligence and warfare', in Maurizio Martellini and Ralf Trapp (eds), *21st Century Prometheus: Managing CBRN Safety and Security Affected by Cutting-Edge Technologies* (Cham: Springer International Publishing, 2020), 125–140.

27 Jesse T. Knight, *Future Kill Chains: Harnessing Emerging Technology to Improve Marine Corps Warfighting* (Command and Staff College, Academic Year 2019–20). https://apps.dtic.mil/sti/pdfs/AD1178021.pdf (accessed 4 February 2026).

28 Jinglong Wan and Zhili Tang, 'The research progress and prospect of key technologies in the interior weapon cabin', in *Proceedings of the 5th China Aeronautical Science and Technology Conference* (Springer Singapore, 2022), 413–425.

29 Mark Gunzinger and Lukas Autenried, 'Understanding the promise of Skyborg and low-cost attritable unmanned aerial vehicles', *Mitchell Institute Policy Paper* 24 (2020); Caitlin Lee and Mark Gunzinger, *The Next Frontier: UAVs for Great Power Conflict: Part I: Penetrating Strikes* (Arlington, TX: The Mitchell Institute for Aerospace Studies, 2022). https://mitchellaerospacepower.org/wp-content/uploads/2022/12/The-Next-Frontier-UAVs-for-Great-Power-Conflict-FINAL.pdf (accessed 9 March 2023).

30 James Rogers, 'Future threats: Military UAS, terrorist drones, and the dangers of the second drone age', in *Drone Warfare: Trends and Emerging Issues* in *A Comprehensive Approach to Countering Unmanned Aircraft Systems* (The Joint Air Power Competence Centre, 2021), 481–505.

31 Mohammad Eslami, 'Iran's drone supply to Russia and changing dynamics of the Ukraine war', *Journal for Peace and Nuclear Disarmament* 5:2 (2022), 507–518. https://doi.org/10.1080/25751654.2022.2149077

32 Including Pakistan, Yemen, Lebanon, Brazil and South Africa, as well as several European countries, including through collaborative projects.

33 Mohammad Eslami and Lauro Borges, *The Drones Race and International Security* (Cham: Springer International Publishing, 2025).

34 David Axe, 'Russia sent its new A.I. drone-killer to Ukraine. A Ukrainian drone blew it up', *Forbes* (2024). https://www.forbes.com/sites/davidaxe/2024/01/13/russia-sent-its-new-ai-drone-killer-to-ukraine-a-ukrainian-drone-blew-it-up/ (accessed 4 February 2026); Alena Vysotskaya Guedes Vieira, 'Arms sales as an instrument of Russia's foreign policy and the shifting security dynamics of the Middle East', in Mohammad Eslami and Alena Vysotskaya Guedes Vieira (eds), *The Arms Race in the Middle East: Contemporary Security Dynamics* (Cham: Springer International Publishing, 2023), 241–256.

35 Dominika Kunertova, 'The war in Ukraine shows the game-changing effect of drones depends on the game', *Bulletin of the Atomic Scientists* 79:2 (2023), 95–102. https://doi.org/10.1080/25751654.2022.2149077

36 Yildirim, Goksel, 'Turkish defense giant Aselsan begins to export anti-drone system IHTAR', *AA AKADEMI* (2023). https://www.aa.com.tr/en/turkiye/turkish-defense-giant-aselsan-begins-to-export-anti-drone-system-ihtar/2867970 (accessed 4 February 2026); Isabel van Burgen, 'Russia deploying new AI-powered anti-drone devices', *Newsweek* (2024). https://www.newsweek.com/russia-artificial-intelligence-ai-drones-ukraine-1895424 (accessed 4 February 2026).

37 Mohammad Eslami, 'Iran's ballistic missile program and its foreign and security policy towards the United States under the Trump administration', *Revista Española de Ciencia Política* 55 (2021), 37–62. https://doi.org/10.21308/recp.55.02

38 Chia-Ming Tsai, Yi-Horng Lai, Jau-Woei Perng, I-Fong Tsui and Yu-Jen Chung, 'Design and application of an autonomous surface vehicle with an AI-based sensing capability', in *2019 IEEE Underwater Technology (UT)* (IEEE, 2019), 1–4.

39 Xiangen Bai, Bohan Li, Xiaofeng Xu and Yingjie Xiao, 'A review of current research and advances in unmanned surface vehicles', *Journal of Marine Science and Application* 21:2 (2022), 47–58. https://doi.org/10.1007/s11804-022-00224-8

40 Natasha Bajema, 'Will AI steal submarines' stealth? Better detection will make the oceans transparent – and perhaps undermine nuclear deterrence', *IEEE Spectrum* 59:9 (2022), 36–41. https://doi.org/10.1109/MSPEC.2022.9881233

41 Bryan Clark and Timothy A. Walton, *Fighting into the Bastions: Getting Noisier to Sustain the US Undersea Advantage* (Washington, DC: Hudson Institute, 2023).

42 Nick Childs, 'The AUKUS anvil', *Horizons: Journal of International Relations and Sustainable Development* 25 (2024), 100–113.

43 Quina Baterna, 'Here's how the US Navy is planning to use AI in submarines', *Clash Gear* (2023). https://www.slashgear.com/1477021/how-us-navy-plans-to-use-ai-submarine-warfare/ (accessed 4 February 2026).

44 Stavros Atlamazoglou, 'AbramsX: The U.S. Army super duper tank of the future or waste of cash?', *The National Interest* (2024). https://nationalinterest.org/blog/buzz/abramsx-us-army-super-dupa-tank-future-or-waste-cash-210306 (accessed 4 February 2026).

45 David Axe, 'The Russians sent a platoon of grenade-hurling robotic mini-tanks into battle. The Ukrainians blew up the "bots in the usual way: with drones"', *Forbes* (2024). https://www.forbes.com/sites/davidaxe/2024/03/31/the-russians-sent-a-platoon-of-grenade-hurling-robotic-mini-tanks-into-battle-the-ukrainians-blew-up-the-bots-in-the-usual-way-with-drones/ (accessed 4 February 2026).

46 Assaf Gilead, 'Israel recruits robot dogs for Gaza fighting', *Globes* (2023). https://en.globes.co.il/en/article-israel-recruits-robot-dogs-for-gaza-fighting-1001465142 (accessed 4 February 2026).

47 Arie Egozi, 'Rooster: The new hybrid drone of Israel Defence Forces', *Defence Industry Europe* (2024). https://defence-industry.eu/rooster-the-new-hybrid-drone-of-israel-defence-forces/ (accessed 4 February 2026).

48 Amos Chapple, 'Ground drones: The next frontier of unmanned combat in Ukraine', *Radio Free Europe* (2024). https://www.rferl.org/a/ground-drones-war-russia-invasion-ukraine/32911118.html (accessed 4 February 2026).

49 Zachary Kallenborn, 'The plague beckons: On the proliferation of drone swarms', in Rajeswari Pillai Rajagopalan and Sameer Patil (eds), *Future Warfare and Critical Technologies: Evolving Tactics and Strategies* (New Delhi: ORF and Global Policy Journal, 2024), 12; Dominika Kunertova, 'The war in Ukraine shows the game-changing effect

of drones depends on the game', *Bulletin of the Atomic Scientists* 79:2 (2023), 95–102. https://doi.org/10.1080/25751654.2022.2149077

50 James Johnson, 'The AI-cyber nexus: Implications for military escalation, deterrence and strategic stability', *Journal of Cyber Policy* 4:3 (2019), 442–460. https://doi.org/10.1080/23738871.2019.1701693

51 Cyril Tregub, 'Critical thinking: The AI frontier – Ukraine's role in the future of warfare', *Friends of Europe* (2024). https://www.friendsofeurope.org/insights/critical-thinking-the-ai-frontier-ukraines-role-in-the-future-of-warfare/ (accessed 4 February 2026).

52 Mark Klamberg, 'Regulatory choices at the advent of gig warfare', *Journal of International Humanitarian Legal Studies* 15:1 (2023), 115–141. https://doi.org/10.1163/18781527-20230005

53 Tobias Vestner, 'Rules of engagement: Developing a regulatory framework for military artificial intelligence', *Lieber Institute West Point* (2024). https://lieber.westpoint.edu/rules-engagement-regulatory-framework-military-artificial-intelligence/ (accessed 4 February 2026).

54 Klamberg, 'Regulatory choices'.

55 Regina Surber, 'Artificial intelligence: Autonomous technology (AT), lethal autonomous weapons systems (LAWS) and peace time threats', *ICT4Peace Foundation and the Zurich Hub for Ethics and Technology (ZHET)* 1 (2018), 21.

56 Jeremy Julian Sarkin and Saba Sotoudehfar, 'Artificial intelligence and arms races in the Middle East: The evolution of technology and its implications for regional and international security', *Defense & Security Analysis* 40:1 (2024), 1–23. https://doi.org/10.1080/14751798.2024.2302699

57 Mohammad Eslami, Nasim Sadat Mosavi and Muhammed Can, 'Sino-Iranian cooperation in artificial intelligence: A potential countering against the US hegemony', in Paulo Duarte, Francisco Leandro and Enrique Galán (eds), *The Palgrave Handbook of Globalization with Chinese Characteristics: The Case of the Belt and Road Initiative* (Singapore: Springer Nature Singapore, 2023), 543–559; Muhammed Can and Alena Vysotskaya Guedes Vieira, 'The Chinese military-civil fusion strategy: A state action theory perspective', *The International Spectator* 57:3 (2022), 85–102. https://doi.org/10.1080/03932729.2022.2080262; Maria Papageorgiou, Muhammed Can and Alena Vysotskaya Guedes Vieira, 'China as a threat and balancing behavior in the realm of emerging technologies', *Chinese Political Science Review* 9:4 (2024), 441–482. https://doi.org/10.1007/s41111-024-00248-0

58 Ajey Lele, 'Disarmament, arms control and arms race', in Ajey Lele and Radha K. Sharma (eds), *Disruptive Technologies for the Militaries and Security* (2019), 217–229; Heather M. Roff, 'The frame problem: The AI "arms race" isn't one', *Bulletin of the Atomic Scientists* 75:3 (2019), 95–98. https://doi.org/10.1080/00963402.2019.1604812

59 Bassant Hassib and Fatimah Ayad, 'The challenges and implications of military cyber and AI capabilities in the Middle East: The geopolitical, ethical, and technological dimensions', in Mohammad Eslami and Alena Vysotskaya Guedes Vieira (eds), *The Arms Race in the Middle East: Contemporary Security Dynamics* (Cham: Springer International Publishing, 2023), 49–65.

60 Jeppe T. Jacobsen and Tobias Liebetrau, 'Artificial intelligence and military superiority: How the "cyber-AI offensive-defensive arms race" affects the US vision of the fully integrated battlefield', in Fabio Cristiano, Dennis Broeders, François Delerue, Frédérick Douzet and Aude Géry (eds), *Artificial Intelligence and International Conflict in Cyberspace* (London: Routledge, 2023), 135–156.

61 Hendrik Huelss, 'Norms are what machines make of them: Autonomous weapons systems and the normative implications of human-machine interactions', *International Political Sociology* 14:2 (2020), 111–128. https://doi.org/10.1093/ips/olz023

62 US Department of State, 'Political declaration on responsible military use of artificial intelligence and autonomy' (2023). https://www.state.gov/political-declaration-on-responsible-military-use-of-artificial-intelligence-and-autonomy/ (accessed 4 February 2026).

63 UNESCO, *Recommendation on the ethics of artificial intelligence* (2023). https://unesdoc.unesco.org/ark:/48223/pf0000381137 (accessed 4 February 2026).

64 Denise Garcia, *The AI Military Race: Common Good Governance in the Age of Artificial Intelligence* (Oxford: Oxford University Press, 2024); CNN, 'China has adopted legal rules on algorithmic recommendation systems, deep fakes, or generative AI', *CNN* (2022). https://english.www.gov.cn/news/topnews/202201/04/content_WS61d3f8fbc6d09c94e48a31d1.html (accessed 4 February 2026).

65 European Council, 'Artificial intelligence (AI) act: Council gives final green light to the first worldwide rules on AI', *Council of the European Union* (2024). https://www.consilium.europa.eu/en/press/press-releases/2024/05/21/artificial-intelligence-ai-act-council-gives-final-green-light-to-the-first-worldwide-rules-on-ai/ (accessed 4 February 2026).

1

Unveiling a new spiral of insecurity: AI capabilities and the international military balance of power

Maria (Mary) Papageorgiou

Introduction

The post-Cold War period has witnessed a defining new feature in military technologies: the introduction of artificial intelligence (AI). For some, AI is a critical technology that is poised to become the 'new oil' of world politics,[1] initiating 'the biggest geopolitical revolution in human history'.[2] It is often likened to the advent of the nuclear bomb – an event that fundamentally altered the course of history and revolutionised military affairs and strategic decision-making.[3] However, what distinguishes AI from the development of nuclear weapons is that it can be solely researched and developed within the civilian sector.

Like other Fourth Industrial Revolution (4IR) technologies, AI is firmly rooted in the civilian domain, with the majority of research emanating from the commercial science and technology (S&T) sector, involving private technology firms and research institutes.[4] This dual nature of AI acts as a vital force multiplier for both economic/societal and military capabilities,[5] constituting a crucial addition to a nation's aggregate power.[6] As such, AI has provided certain countries with the advantage of pursuing these technologies, distinguishing them from others unable to keep up with technological developments or finance research costs.

In the military domain, AI is expected to bring significant changes to warfare. Unlike conventional military systems, AI advancements are expected to rely more on innovation and quality rather than sheer quantity.[7] The focus on continuous technological advancements, which not only surpasses traditional weapons development but also enhances operational accuracy, efficiency and speed, has already generated an arms race between many countries, leading to a significant potential source of instability and acting as a catalyst for great power strategic rivalry. Bans and export restrictions on sensitive technology, such as semiconductors essential for AI applications, have intensified tensions between countries, especially the United States (US) and China, which regard technological advancements in the military as a defining feature of their competition.[8] What is different in this emerging arms race, however, is that the US does not have a monopoly or even a first-mover advantage in this technology, and even medium powers are able to access benefits of AI for commercial purposes and then integrate them in their military affairs.[9] Still, after a certain level, the costs, patents and financing benefit only the most powerful countries.[10]

Furthermore, several states, such as the US, China and Russia, view the development of AI as a crucial strategy to enhance national competitiveness and maintain national security. They have even adjusted their military doctrines to account for such advancements, infusing their technological policies with narratives of national superiority, leadership aspirations and their status as great powers. This new realm of competition has heightened geopolitical tensions and threat perceptions, with AI seen as a challenge to national security that is likely to fuel strategic competition and distrust, thus reinforcing power dynamics and significantly influencing the balance of power in the international system.[11]

Yet, some consider that both the benefits and the risks of this type of technology are exaggerated.[12] Historically, developments in AI have seen cycles of sudden progress and heightened expectations that were later followed by disillusionment and divestment referred to as 'AI winters'.[13] Critics also contend that AI's impact may ultimately resemble the incremental changes seen by previous technological advancements rather than a revolutionary breakthrough and that without balanced perspectives on what it can deliver or acknowledging the importance of human–machine collaboration, the focus may shift to an overhyped discourse.[14]

Therefore, this chapter will seek to answer how states' prioritisation and funding of AI development for military purposes contributes to the potential emergence of arms races and the reconfiguration of the balance of power. These implications are argued to have generated a competition between great powers that has given place to a new spiral of insecurity by elevating AI developments into an issue of national security and as a source of threat perceptions. To address such considerations, this chapter starts by examining whether there is a transformative impact of AI on military affairs and why it is regarded as a revolutionary force. Subsequently, it examines the incorporation of AI technologies in three great powers' national security strategies along with the budgets and AI centres developed to support its advancement. The next section discusses the emergence of an AI arms race, while the last section address implications in international security. The conclusion summarises key points, and it evaluates the impact of AI under the contemporary geopolitical context marked by intensified competition and a new spiral of insecurity.

Artificial intelligence as revolution in military affairs

Technological developments have always influenced military affairs, not only in the development of artillery but also on military command and military concepts. The field of artificial intelligence has advanced at an ever-increasing pace over the past two decades, and it is widely acknowledged as a revolution in military affairs (RMA).[15,16,17] AI has changed the military landscape in numerous ways, offering advancements in detecting, precision strikes, issues with recruitment, monitoring, intelligence gathering and strategic planning.[18] It has been utilised in automating turrets, drones, aircraft, spacecraft and submarines, as well as in missile defence systems, surveillance, cyber security, logistics, modelling and simulations, along with intelligence collection and analysis, while also offering the potential for military systems (drones) to fight as a 'swarm'.[19] AI has significantly revolutionised war operations in the area of logistics by reducing requirements such as food supply, fuels, replacements and navigational constraints[20] and has also helped in reducing the overall cost of military operations.[21]

Still, the importance of AI is more evident in decision-making, in which AI algorithms swiftly process vast data, predict enemy movements and enhance situational awareness, aiding commanders in making informed combat decisions.[22] AI's ability to effectively remove emotions from strategy is a capability that was not attainable with previous advancements. Nevertheless, removing the human factor and, essentially, moral judgement, which is essential to consider especially when deploying autonomous systems, underscores the necessity for robust ethical frameworks and oversight mechanisms to ensure responsible and accountable use of AI in military contexts.[23]Accordingly, many countries have developed their own positions on the use of autonomous and semiautonomous systems, trying to ensure that they operate only with meaningful human control.[24]

AI has started being used widely in 'various military domains and in support of various processes, e.g., Intelligence, Surveillance and Reconnaissance (ISR), Command and control (Observe/Orient/Decide/Act – OODA loop), or Targeting'.[25] Targeting can be defined as 'the process of analysing and evaluating potential threats and targets for engagement (attack)'.[26] Traditionally, targeting has relied on human intelligence that has slower processing capabilities as well as cognitive constraints.[27] Nevertheless, targeting is not a singular process but best represented as a 'targeting cycle, i.e., the set of steps and assessments commanders apply before assigning force'.[28] These steps include '*find, fix, track, target, engage and assess*', which AI capabilities enhance by undertaking target analysis, determining choice of weapons, assessing weapon capabilities, estimating collateral damage and risk mitigation, developing mission strategy, planning for contingencies, adapting manoeuvres in the battlefield and continuous impact assessment.[29]

Therefore, AI has managed to process data much faster, recognise patterns, learn from experience and make data-driven predictions, resulting in identifying and prioritising targets more effectively while being able to minimise potential collateral damage.[30] In particular, the ability to reproduce accurate targeting and increase the distance of engagement and the location of targets has redefined remote warfare with drone warfare at the forefront.[31]

Therefore, the integration of AI in military engagement systems has enhanced targeting accuracy, speed and precision by analysing data from multiple sources, such as sensors, unmanned aerial vehicles (UAVs) and satellites, for target identification and tracking.[32] Examples of such systems include Project Maven, the Athena AI Defense target classifier, the Pleora project, the Advanced Targeting and Lethality Aided System (ATLAS) AI targeting system and the Targeting Long-range Identification Optronic System (TALIOS) system that can process sensor and image data and work with machine learning and cloud computing for automatic targeting detection, classification and recognition.[33] China has significantly invested in improving targeting in its systems such as the HN-1 unmanned undersea glider, the JARI unmanned surface vehicle and the targeting intelligence of its cruise and ballistic missiles.[34] Two prominent examples of the military using data and AI to target include COVID-19 testing in 2020 in Liverpool and the US's Security Assistance Group-Ukraine amidst the Ukraine war in 2022, both of which highlight the critical issue of data availability and the risk of corrupted or poisoned data.[35] Especially amidst the war in Ukraine, the Palantir software that integrates several platforms and channels of data gathering and processing has been primarily used for most of the targeting in Ukraine's military engagement.[36]

Another crucial domain in which AI exerts significant influence is cyber security, playing a pivotal role in detecting and responding to cyber threats, particularly vital in countering hybrid, grey-zone and information warfare operations by certain states abroad, making AI-driven cyber security indispensable in national security strategies while also serving as offensive capabilities for gathering intelligence.[37] This strategic perspective highlights that AI is not merely employed as a supportive feature but, rather, as an independent tool for a new type of war.[38] Therefore, it is imperative for militaries to adapt their strategies to accommodate the capabilities driven by AI.[39]

Overall, AI literature from both academics and practitioners is categorised into enthusiasts, pragmatists and sceptics, each presenting differing perspectives on its potential to transform warfare.[40] Consequently, authors argue, these changes have led to a new 'artificial intelligence-driven RMA' wave with multiple implications in weapons, training, military doctrines, battle management and operational capabilities.[41] AI is expected to reshape warfare, influence decision-making during international crises and redefine concepts such as nuclear deterrence and strategic stability. However, others argue that military AI technologies are more widely perceived as 'enablers and amplifiers' of established systems that continuously evolve, thus reflecting an evolution rather than a revolution in military affairs.[42] Finally, others have cautioned against exaggerated claims on current AI capabilities.

AI national strategies

In recent years, many countries have begun to emphasise the role of AI as a cornerstone in both their national strategies and military doctrine. Given that strategy constitutes a plan defined by a national state to achieve systemic and long-term objectives,[43] states set up their AI objectives as part of a comprehensive framework aimed at leveraging AI technologies to advance their military, economic, social and security interests while addressing ethical and regulatory considerations. Accordingly, AI has evolved into a strategic priority, recognised for its pivotal role in driving economic growth and enhancing competitiveness and military superiority.[44] Moreover, within this context, there is a discernible emphasis on the AI resources and capabilities towards achieving broader objectives, reflecting the notion of 'the calculated relationship of means to large ends', as articulated by Gaddis 2009.[45] Thus, the emphasis placed on AI in states' national defence strategies reflects policymakers' perceptions on the impact of this technology.[46]

China has strategically integrated AI into its national agenda through key documents such as Made in China 2025 and the New Generation Artificial Intelligence Development Plan, and due to the importance of these two documents, it has created a spillover effect with other countries since publishing its strategy on AI, with Russia and the US following suit.[47] The Made in China 2025 document, published in 2015, explicitly sets out China's ambitions to enhance Chinese industrial power and reshape dynamics in global markets but also indicates geopolitical ambitions.[48] This underscores the government's recognition of AI's importance for economic growth and China's national dream of rejuvenation. In addition, with this document, China moves away from an economy entirely based on manufacturing and copycat characterisations, moving towards embracing high technologies.[49] Although this document does not explicitly refer to AI, the references to technology/-ical (79 references), innovate/-ion (95 references) and research and design (R&D) (23 references) showcase China's focus on becoming a technology powerhouse by leveraging emerging technologies such as AI.[50]

Nevertheless, it was the publication of the New Generation Artificial Intelligence Development Plan issued by the State Council of China on July 20, 2017 that outlines China's strategy to build an AI industry: to become a leading AI power and a global AI innovation centre by 2030.[51] Since then, AI has gained prominence in China's domestic industry use and has become a national priority for monetisation, amounting to a trillion-yuan ($150 billion) industry, aligning with President Xi Jinping's grand vision for China.[52] The plan states that AI has become a new focus of international competition and that 'AI is a strategic technology that will lead in the future; the world's major developed countries are taking the development of AI as a major strategy to enhance national competitiveness and protect national security'[53] seen as promoting messages of national superiority.[54] Simultaneously, China aims to position itself as the leading authority in establishing ethical norms and standards for AI.[55] These objectives reflect China's determination to play a significant role in shaping

AI regulations rather than merely adhering to Western conventions.

Regarding the application of AI to the military domain, the 2017 document states that the government will 'promote two-way conversion and application for military and civilian scientific and technological achievements and co-construction and sharing of military and civilian innovation resources; form an all-element, multi-domain, highly efficient new pattern of civil-military integration'[56] and 'strengthen a new generation of AI technology as a strong support to command and decision-making, military deduction, defense equipment, and other applications'[57] and finally 'promote all kinds of AI technology to become quickly embedded in the field of national defense innovation'.[58] The document also recognises that AI has become a new focus of international competition and an important strategy to advance national competitiveness. It, nevertheless, acknowledges that 'there is still a gap between China's overall level of development of AI relative to that of developed countries'[59] in various domains.[60] Overall, the document indicates that becoming a global science and technology power will help the country 'achieve the two centennial goals and the great rejuvenation of the Chinese nation'.[61] Thus, it emphasises the country's geopolitical ambitions in maintaining competitiveness, achieving major breakthroughs and establishing China as the world's innovation centre by 2030.[62]

The Ministry of National Defense and the Academy of Military Science drive AI advancements for military purposes, aligning with China's commitment to modernise defence capabilities and reflect the pursuit of asymmetric capabilities by Chinese officials, which could offer a crucial advantage in warfare.[63] Chinese military leaders consider that warfare is evolving from today's 'informatised' (信息化) to 'intelligentised' (智能化) warfare[64] and that AI can contribute to China's broader geopolitical objectives, such as monitoring, surveying and controlling the South China Sea with the use of manned and unmanned teaming operations.[65]

Furthermore, China's 13th Five-Year Science and Technology Military–Civil Fusion Special Plan,[66] issued by the Ministry of Science and Technology and the CMC Science and Technology Commission, focuses exclusively on the military–civil fusion of AI technology and reflects on the importance of this strategy to China's economic and military power.[67] Overall, as seen in these documents, China's quest for leadership and predominance in AI is central in its national strategy and is placed in an antagonistic framework with other countries, mainly the US, viewing it as an opportunity to challenge and even surpass American military hegemony.[68]

Conversely, the 2018 formulation of the AI strategy adopted by the US Department of Defense (DoD) underscores the pivotal role of AI in shaping the country's security and economic landscape. It identifies competition with other global powers, especially China and Russia, highlighting concerns over their substantial investments in AI for military applications. The document highlights the competition with other countries, notably stating, 'other nations, particularly China and Russia, are making significant investments in AI for military purposes, including in applications that raise questions regarding international norms and human rights. These investments threaten to erode our technological and operational advantages and destabilise the free and open international order'.[69] This acknowledgement signals the US's recognition of the shifting geopolitical dynamics and the emerging importance of AI in maintaining global influence. The reference to the stability and prevalence of the US-promoted international order and its accompanying norms also highlights a normative dimension and ideological considerations, generating a distinction between the US and others: 'our adversaries and competitors are aggressively working to define the future of these powerful technologies according to their interests, values, and societal models'.[70] Moreover, the strategy advocates for collaboration with US allies, emphasising the collective adoption of AI technologies to maintain strategic positions and uphold the existing international order, stating that 'the United States, together with its allies and partners, must adopt AI to maintain its strategic position, prevail on future battlefields, and safeguard this order'.[71] This call for multi-lateralism acknowledges the interconnectedness of global AI development and the importance of cooperative efforts in shaping its future trajectory.

The Executive Order on AI issued by President Donald Trump on February 11, 2019,[72] as outlined in the title, seeks to maintain 'American leadership in artificial intelligence' and considers AI 'of paramount importance to maintaining the economic and national security of the United States and to shaping the global evolution of AI in a manner consistent with our Nation's values, policies, and priorities'.[73] The order sets ambitious goals for 'scientific discovery, economic competitiveness, and national security'. Overall, the document has multi-faceted targets and blends normative and operational approaches while recognising a growing threat by highlighting the importance of 'protecting our critical AI technologies from acquisition by strategic competitors and adversarial nations'.[74] However, in this document, China and Russia are not named. Additionally, the document emphasises an ideological dimension, aiming to advance American innovation while upholding civil liberties, privacy and American values. This aspect will be a defining feature for the competition between techno-democracies and techno-autocracies.[75]

A more recent document, the 2023 Data, Analytics, and Artificial Intelligence Adoption Strategy,[76] published by the DoD underscores further the urgency of

> accelerating adoption of data, analytics, and AI technologies will enable enduring decision advantage, allowing DoD leaders to prioritise investments to strengthen deterrence; link cross-cutting campaign outcomes that counter our competitors' coercive measures; and deploy continuous advancements in technological capabilities to creatively address complex national security challenges in this decisive decade.[77]

This reflects a recognition of the evolving and changing nature of modern warfare in the AI era.

The Kremlin has mobilised state support to foster AI technological development. The first major Russian government AI proposal was the Russian Ministry of Defence's (MoD) ten-point statement issued in March 2018, which brings together various institutes to organise a

> full-scale account of long-term and medium-term trends in the development of artificial intelligence, as well as monitoring changes taking place in the field of artificial intelligence in other countries, should organise research on the entire range of issues related to the development of Artificial Intelligence, including social and scientific ones.[78]

The document, which was military-specific, explicitly called for a new MoD research campus on the Black Sea to provide the armed forces with innovative AI-driven solutions, yet it lacked information regarding collaboration with the private sector and, instead, proposed that government entities lead AI development in Russia.[79] This approach is further emphasised in the Russian National AI strategy published in 2019,[80] which states that 'state corporations, state companies, joint-stock companies with state participation, strategic documents of other organizations in the part related to the development of artificial intelligence'.[81] Regarding competition in AI, the document calls for monitoring global AI development but does not indicate a rising competition or a threatening domain.

In addition, the document delineates a comprehensive set of objectives aimed at advancing various facets of Russian society and economy, fortification of national security and the cultivation of competitiveness within the global landscape in the realm of AI. The strategy astutely acknowledges the fierce international competition surrounding AI technologies, characterising them as a pivotal battleground for supremacy in the global arena and accounts for specific challenges such as 'import of advanced microelectronics technologies, the attraction of qualified specialists in the field of artificial intelligence from other States, as well as the introduction of restrictions on the free dissemination of technologies'.[82] Further, it associates these challenges as emanating from nations perceived as adversarial, which in the text, are characterised as 'unfriendly',[83] highlighting the geopolitical dimensions of AI competition.[84] An interesting element is that the Russian government recognises the impact of international sanctions on its technological progress and also acknowledges that the leading countries in the field are China and the US.[85] Further, it underscores the importance of a domestic imperative for the 'promotion of Russian ethical standards in the field of artificial intelligence at the global level'[86] that asserts the country's national identity and values. It also aims to shape the broader discourse surrounding AI ethics worldwide, positioning Russia as a key player in shaping the ethical framework of AI development and deployment. Moreover, Russia considers that the successful implementation of the strategy's objectives will solidify its position as a global AI leader by joining 'the group of world leaders in the development and implementation of artificial intelligence technologies and, as a result, the country's technological independence and competitiveness'.[87]

When comparing approaches to AI in military strategy, the US emphasises wargame simulations, operational concepts and psychological operations, China focuses on scaling AI-enabled capabilities across the DoD and Russia prioritises electronic warfare tactics. Both China and Russia also leverage AI for cyber attacks and propaganda, and the US emphasises defensive data monitoring, operations security, military deception and electronic warfare.[88]

Budget

The AI advancements by the US, China and Russia hold significant influence, providing insights into global AI competition and its impact for international security.[89] The three states have devoted big parts of their annual budgets to AI research and development. In US, the defence-related spending on AI was around $4 billion in 2020.[90] The latest DoD's fiscal budget in 2024 request includes $1.8 billion for AI, $1.4 billion for Joint All-Domain Command and Control initiatives and a total of $67.4 billion for cyber, IT and electronic warfare capabilities, making it the largest DoD budget ever in these technologies.[91] In 2020, China is estimated to have spent $70 billion on AI, but the specific amount of defence AI R&D is unknown, as no official figures exist.[92] In 2021, different estimates placed the People's Liberation Army's (PLA) annual military AI spending between $1.6 billion and $2.7 billion, though much of China's AI R&D is conducted in universities and civilian sectors;[93] one estimate suggests that China spent around $25 billion on military-related R&D outside the official budget in 2019.[94]

Among the three countries, Russia stands out as the one adhering strictly to a traditional top-down, state-driven approach in developing AI for military purposes.[95] Major defence enterprises and companies in Russia are funded or subsidised by the state to varying degrees, with the MoD acting as their primary client.[96] Since the war in Ukraine, the Kremlin has increased its defence budget at significant rates both in 2023 and 2024, though data on how much it spends specifically on AI developments in the military are not available. However, there has been a significant increase in AI development allocation in 2024 to 5.2 billion rubles ($54.05 million).[97] Examining the 2024–26 Russian Federal budget draft,[98] the Applied R&D in 2023 stood at 406,046,[99] which decreased to 396,233 in 2024 and again to 324,966 in 2025, then increasing slightly to 345,510 in 2026. An interesting category is the military–technical cooperation that saw a continuous increase in each of the three years. This category is important, as it accounts for cooperation with other countries. Given Russia's ties with China and its statements that support joint research and development,[100] technological transfer raises concern whether it includes or excludes AI.[101] Just like China, Russia is not focused on simply outspending the US but, rather, leveraging AI as a means to achieve significant advancements in military technology and potentially surpassing the US while also promoting the development of asymmetric capabilities.[102]

AI national centres

Starting with China, Beijing has undertaken significant efforts in this regard, with the MoD setting up two research institutions: the Artificial Intelligence Research Centre and the Unmanned Systems Research Centre, which concentrate on research and development in AI and unmanned systems, signifying a substantial investment in enhancing military capabilities.[103] Additionally, the National Innovation Institute of Defense Technology (NIIDT), a subsidiary of the National University of Defense Technology (NUDT), has founded two Beijing-based research organisations focused on exploring the military potential of AI, namely the Unmanned Systems Research Center (USRC) and the Artificial Intelligence Research Center (AIRC) that have rapidly expanded since their inception in early 2018, boasting research teams of more than one hundred experts each and positioning themselves among the world's largest government-funded AI research institutions.[104]

Meanwhile, Russia has pursued an ambitious AI development strategy, exemplified by the establishment of the

Era Technopolis in Anapa in 2018. The technopolis' aim is 'the creation of military artificial intelligence systems and supporting technologies'.[105] This initiative is based on collaboration between the military–industrial complex, the civilian sector and various research institutions with more than one hundred entities, including leading arms manufacturers (including Kalashnikov, Sukhoi and Sozvezdie) and universities,[106] highlighting its scale and scope. Furthermore, the Russian MoD announced the establishment of a specialised department for AI development within its ranks in April 2021,[107] further emphasising the country's commitment to advancing AI capabilities in the military sphere.

The US, recognised as the global leader in AI development, has made significant strides in advancing its AI technologies within the military domain. The DoD's establishment of the Joint Artificial Intelligence Center (JAIC) played a pivotal role in funding and coordinating AI research across various military services; in 2022, it was integrated into the Chief Digital and Artificial Intelligence Office (CDAO), which now oversees the department's strategy on data, analytics and AI adoption. Additionally, the National Security Agency (NSA) also established an Artificial Intelligence Security Center, underscoring the importance of AI in national security efforts. The goal of these centres is to focus on the overreaching strategy of 'the three P's; the imminent period of intense competition with the People's Republic of China (PRC); the need for persistent engagement with public–private partners; and the critical role that the next generation of people will have in providing the United States with a competitive advantage against its adversaries'.[108]

By examining the establishment dates of the centres, as well as their respective aims, it becomes evident that each country has adopted distinct approaches and strategic priorities in harnessing AI for national security and defence. China's strategy focuses on collaboration with specific leading companies, the army, universities and research centres, establishing numerous new AI research centres at premier institutions. In contrast, the US has mobilised its DoD and various military centres, supported by developments from the private sector. Meanwhile, Russia's AI efforts are predominantly controlled and promoted by the Kremlin. Notably, while AI initiatives in the US are primarily undertaken by private corporations, in Russia, they are solely led by state-owned firms, whereas China has involved both state-owned and private entities such as Alibaba and Tencent.[109] Moreover, the design of these centres, the period in which they were established and their set goals reflect the intense competition and insecurity surrounding AI. Each country, thus, aims to either maintain its advantage (the US), surpass existing capabilities (China) or disrupt the status quo (Russia).[110]

A new AI arms race?

Accounting for the dual nature of AI technologies, the competition between states is more multi-faceted, and it has been emphasised both in the civil and military sector. Many countries have recognised the competitive nature of these technologies, and particularly for great powers, it has emerged as another area of strategic competition.[111] As noted by the US government

> we must win the AI competition that is intensifying strategic competition with China. China's plans, resources, and progress should concern all Americans. It is an AI peer in many areas and an AI leader in some applications. We take seriously China's ambition to surpass the United States as the world's AI leader within a decade.[112]

Similarly, Chinese President Xi Jinping, in one of his speeches at the CPC Central Committee in 2017, stated that 'in the situation of increasingly fierce international military competition, only the innovator wins',[113] and Russian President declared that 'AI is a resource of colossal power [...] those who will own it will take the lead and will acquire a huge competitive edge'.[114] In another comment during the 2022 edition of the Artificial Intelligence Journey international conference, he stated that 'with the fierce rivalry between countries, Russia's place in the world, our sovereignty, security, and viability depend on the results we achieve'.

Several countries have invested in various aspects of AI developments, and the competition is not limited to only to great powers. It is evident that they score differently in different categories, and even though the US has the overall advantage and stands in the primary position, it does not have the highest score in all of the available indicators. These differences in scoring in each category emphasise the comparative advantages of states on the one hand but also their investments in specific areas on the other hand. When it comes to China, the fact that it stands second in ranking confirms US officials' concerns that the speed of China's developments in AI could lead to the US losing its quantitative and qualitative advantage. Specifically, developments by Chinese companies, such as SenseTime (specialising in computer vision and deep learning) and DJI (specialising in UAVs), are evidence of China catching up with the US in many indicators.[115] Finally, Russia is not a leader in commercial and academic AI research, despite the Kremlin's ambitions.[116]

Autonomous weapons systems and lethal autonomous weapons systems

When it comes to military application of AI, autonomous weapons systems (AWS) seem to be the priority of states' military complexes, which have demonstrated a clear interest in developing weapon systems that operate with the support of AI,[117] increasingly integrating autonomous and automated features into these systems.[118]

As competition intensifies, states initially prioritise quantity due to cost efficiency, but a strategic shift occurs as they recognise the importance of possessing technologically advanced and qualitatively superior arsenals in the AI-driven landscape, driving increased investment in research and development to maintain military superiority,[119] further seeking to establish more autonomous properties in their weapon systems. Currently, China is the world's top exporter of combat drones, while the US is for surveillance drones. China has also taken advantage of US restrictions on exporting certain systems that use AI, such as certain types of drones, to infiltrate important geopolitical theatres and forge closer relations with the US's traditional allies.[120]

All three – China, Russia and US – have developed and attached autonomous capabilities to their weapons, and continuous advancements have raised significant concerns about their lethal potential, even being characterised as lethal autonomous weapons systems (LAWS), referring to those that 'can independently select and attack targets, i.e., with autonomy in the "critical functions" of acquiring, tracking, selecting and attacking targets and lead to the decision to take a human life'. These type of weapons constitute in themselves a revolution that makes them more 'maneuverable and attritable (i.e., cheaper and relatively expendable) enough to fulfil key missions in wartime' and 'improve battlefield decision making and minimise unnecessary loss of life'.[121] Each country has developed various autonomous weapons systems, as listed in Table 1.1. The most significant category of AWS integrating AI technology encompasses UAVs, which are capable of facilitating various operations across land, air and sea.

There are diverging perspectives on the effectiveness of UAVs, with some emphasising their predominant role in air and maritime warfare, particularly in less cluttered environments, such as the air and underwater domains.[122] One operation of UAVs that has been of particular interest in states' militaries is the ability to form autonomous drone swarms that are capable of launching, flying, targeting and striking enemies without human intervention. The use of swarms has been tested and employed by all three states, with the US Army indicating that 'they have the potential to overwhelm defenses at a very low-cost point to the adversary'[123] and they have tested TSM-800 to attack a designated target.[124] Although China has extensively used swarm drones in exhibitions, it has not publicly released plans for drone swarm doctrine, strategy or research and development,[125] while Russia has also used it during the war in Ukraine.[126]

Table 1.1 Examples of AWS and LAWS

Country	*Land*	*Air*	*Sea*
United States	High-speed anti-radiation missile	X47-B autonomous flying systems	Tomahawk Anti-Ship Missile (TASM)
		MQ-9 Reaper	LRASM
		GAAS Avenger and the MQ-9 Reaper, CH-4	CLAWS
			X-47B[a]
China	Sharp Claw I	DF-ZF stealth craft	Jinghai USV
	Sharp Claw II	Blowfish A3	DF-21D
	Mule-200	BZK005 unmanned reconnaissance aircraft	HN-1 glider
	CH-901	Cruise Missile	JARI, multi-purpose unmanned surface vessel
	SeaFly	DF-ZF craft	
		Sky Eye	'Sea Iguana' (or Marine Lizard, 海蜥蜴), unmanned surface vehicle (USV)
		Sharp Sword (Lijian)	
		Wing Loong (Pterodactyl)	
		WZ-8 hypersonic surveillance drone	
		TYW-1 and ASN-216	

Russia	Russia's Uran-9	Galtel	Poseidon
	Nerekhta	Okhotnik-B (Hunter-B)	
	T-14 Armata	KUB-LA kamikaze drone	
	Marker		
	S-350 Vityaz mobile surface-to-air defence missile system		

Sources: Author's compilation from various sources: Lance Y. Hunter, Craig D. Albert, Christopher Henningan and Josh Rutland, 'The military application of artificial intelligence technology in the United States, China, and Russia and the implications for global security', *Defense & Security Analysis* 39:2 (2023), 207–232, https://doi.org/10.1080/14751798.2023.2210367, Gloria Shkurti Özdemir, *Artificial Intelligence Application in the Military the Case of United States and China* (SETA Foundation, June 2019); Elsa Kania, *AI Weapons in China's military innovation.* https://www.brookings.edu/articles/ai-weapons-in-chinas-military-innovation/?utm_source=chatgpt.com

'X-47B[a] UCAS Makes Aviation History … Again!' Northrop Grumman, April 22, 2015. https://www.northropgrumman.com/Capabilities/ X47BUCAS/Pages/default.aspx

Implications for international security

The escalating competition among states in the field of AI has profound implications for international security. It has triggered a new arms race and a spiral of insecurity broadly impacting great power dynamics, alignment shifts, ideological divisions and institutional structures, as well as raising significant ethical concerns.

The new emerging AI arms race has more extensive implications than just a question of quantity of the weapons, as it can severely impact regional stability and create new geopolitical theatres of confrontation with the Middle East at the forefront. An AI-driven arms race is developing in the Middle East, with countries such as the US, China and Russia selling intelligent weapons; with China, in particular, capitalising on US restrictions to sell drones to the region, increasing its export of intelligent armaments to Saudi Arabia and the United Arab Emirates by 365 per cent and 169 per cent, respectively, between 2016 and 2020.[127]

Autonomy in military systems has also become a focal point of such competition. The integration of AI in command-and-control systems has enabled faster detection, enhanced precision and more effective response patterns. However, it also introduces risks of unintended errors, miscalculations and misperceptions that could increase the likelihood of rapid unwarranted escalation.[128] In a competitive environment, misperception of one's technological capabilities and intentions is higher than ever.[129]

The growing 'militarisation of AI',[130] as evidenced by the references and goals in states' national security documents, increased R&D budgets and the development of autonomous systems primarily reinforces existing global hierarchies and benefits greater powers that already dominate in the international system.[131] This trend exacerbates power disparities among states.[132] As most AI military developments are concentrated in a few powerful states, this dynamic is likely to accentuate bandwagoning tendencies.[133] Smaller powers lacking investments in AI capabilities and know-how may pursue hierarchical alliances with patron states for security.[134] Geopolitical fragmentation is also exacerbated with the uneven distribution of capabilities among countries, which can impact regional security and stability,[135] especially in regions of heightened great power competition, where smaller states might seek to align themselves under a great power's 'AI umbrella'.[136] Besides, the US–China competitive strategies are designed to divide and dominate networks of allies and partners,[137] further fuelling a bipolar dynamic and the return of geopolitical blocs.[138]

On the other hand, particularly for China and Russia, AI technology is arguably particularly important for signalling great power status but also the promotion of a multi-polar world.[139] Moreover, in regions with more advanced economies, such as the European Union (EU), intensified competition could deepen divisions, potentially reestablishing a 'multiple-speed' EU, with certain countries, particularly those in Eastern Europe and the Balkans, lagging behind. In addition, North Atlantic Treaty Organization (NATO) members face increased pressure to keep pace with technological advancements in warfare, potentially leading to a two-speed or two-tier alliance structure, dividing technologically advanced states from those lagging behind and straining internal relations.[140]

Notably, nuclear-armed states, such as China, France, Russia, the United Kingdom and the US, are increasingly seeking to integrate AI, mainly AI models and large language models, into their nuclear command, control and communication (NC3) systems.[141] This integration has the potential to destabilise nuclear deterrence by creating mutual uncertainty while also increasing miscalculations.[142] AI can disrupt traditional escalation management and limit decision-makers' flexibility – especially regarding concerns over second-strike deterrents – and may inadvertently escalate conflicts and narrow options for effective management, as automation aids in disseminating launch orders could lead states to automate nuclear procedures for coercive advantages.[143] Therefore, its integration in NC3 could disrupt national systems by interfering with launch activation (jamming), corruption, deception, false alarms or deliberate misinformation, cultivating insecurity and fear of compromised systems, potentially driving nuclear nations towards adopting more offensive nuclear postures, thus increasing the risk of nuclear escalation.[144]

Moreover, the ambiguous nature of AI, coupled with states' reluctance to establish clear definitions or impose stringent regulations on the development and use of LAWS, has given rise to an ideological divide between 'techno-democracies' and 'techno-autocracies',[145] representing both 'a political and ideological fight that tests the strength of liberal democracy as a model of government'. The two sides promote alternative models, with China advocating for a more state-driven regulatory approach that prioritises effectiveness and ease of enforcement, gaining approval from numerous governments worldwide, particularly in regimes with similar governance structures in Africa and the Middle East, while the US and the Western world endorse a model that acts as an extension of liberal values.[146] This is evident in official discourse, with the US Secretary of State Anthony Blinken openly accusing China and Russia of techno-authoritarianism and engaging in malicious cyber activities such as the SolarWinds intrusion.[147] Nevertheless, as the diverging approaches and cognitive biases become ingrained in future AI-powered weapons, they may exacerbate underlying mistrust, suspicion and misperceptions between the US and China.[148] The division among ideological groups in AI also impacts alignment formation, with a trend towards like-minded countries aligning. The US, for instance, advocates collaboration with allies to collectively adopt AI technologies and uphold existing international norms. However, this approach, exemplified by the Political Declaration launched in February 2023 at the Responsible AI in the Military Domain Summit at the Hague,[149] which aimed to establish a normative framework for responsible AI use in the military domain, excluded major countries such as China, Russia, India and Middle Eastern countries, reinforcing competition and undermining international cooperation and stability.

Finally, AI technology has also led to significant ethical and regulatory concerns, particularly regarding its military applications, notably autonomous weapons systems. The rapid advancement of AI technology has spurred ethical and regulatory concerns regarding autonomous weapons systems. The position of the three states is as follows: China has shown openness to negotiating a ban within the UN Convention on Certain Conventional Weapons (CCW), though it defines such systems in a narrow way;[150] the US advocates for a normative framework for responsible AI use but stops short of supporting an outright ban and has even highlighted the potential humanitarian benefits of integrating further autonomy into weapon systems;[151] Russia[152] opposes any legally binding treaty regarding AWS development and use, arguing that such a move would be both premature and unnecessary, citing that their use is covered by existing international law.[153] Thus, the lack of a regulatory framework persists due to resistance from great powers; challenges such as the need for hard law and extensive verification regimes; the rapidly evolving and changing technological landscape; and the unsuitability of incorporating autonomous and intelligent systems to existing arms control or non-proliferation agreements.[154]

Conclusion

In conclusion, this study examines AI's impact on great power politics and international security, highlighting its multi-faceted implications beyond mere weapon development. AI technology has fuelled a new type of arms race that focuses on upgrading conventional weaponry production, integrating intelligent systems in command and control and developing fully autonomous weapons systems. These profound changes have been argued to have led to a revolution in military affairs similar to the one attributed to nuclear weapons or have been dismissed as an overhyped trend that has not reached neither the capacity nor ambitions attributed to it.

As evidenced in this study, AI has a key position within states' national security strategies, being embedded as a crucial component of national power, leadership aspirations, great power status and even security and survival. The national strategies of the US, China and Russia reveal that there is ongoing competition when it comes to AI innovation in both civil and military developments, which eventually amplifies threat perceptions and mistrust. Moreover, the budget allocated to AI development highlights its significance but also each state's different management approach – Russia employs a more top-down model led by the government and state-owned business, while the US and China take a two-way approach that also relies on non-state actors, such as private companies alongside state defence companies, with, of course, the differences in the functions and roles private companies play in US and China.

In addition, the establishment of numerous institutes and centres also underscores the emphasis in exploring AI's potential contributions to weapons development, protection systems, surveillance and decision-making. The development of AI-driven weapons has also exacerbated the divide between those possessing and those lacking such technology, prompting alignment choices driven by fear and insecurity with smaller states bandwagoning with great and middle powers, trying to catch up with developments. Moreover, there is also an ideological division in the uses of AI, between techno-democracies and techno-autocracies, further indicating a polarisation in the international system; however, there are no dramatic changes in the current balance of power, with the US leading, China on its tail, Russia lagging behind both and other states further behind. Thus, accounting for AI polarity, this could be characterised as 'open bipolarity', which, although it features two main powers leading, also leaves space for others.

The difference between AI and conventional military capabilities, which is similar to that of nuclear weapons, is that you do not need to reach someone else's capacity to compete, but quality and innovation can offer more benefits and give one the advantage. The development of autonomous weapons by the US, China and Russia that cover land, air and sea further fuels a geopolitical competition, given that geographical limitations are rendered insignificant with the use of AI. At the same time, China and Russia are employing asymmetric capabilities that are enhanced with the use of AI (cyber attacks) to cause disruption and change. Yet, despite growing concerns surrounding the deployment of autonomous lethal weapons, all major powers are actively investing in their development and circumventing outright bans. This underscores the criticality of AI as a cornerstone of modern military capabilities, driving strategic decisions and shaping geopolitical landscapes. All these developments clearly indicate a spiral of insecurity or a new security dilemma that sees AI advancements leading to fear, restrictive policies, misconceptions and potential escalation.

Acknowledgement

I gratefully acknowledge the financial support provided by the Leverhulme Trust, which made this research possible.

Notes

1 Joseph S. Nye Jr., 'Power and interdependence with China', *The Washington Quarterly* 43:1 (2020), 7–21. https://doi.org/10.1080/0163660X.2020.1734303

2 Kevin Drum, 'Tech world: Welcome to the digital revolution', *Foreign Affairs* (2018). https://www.foreignaffairs.com/articles/world/2018-06-14/tech-world (accessed 4 February 2026).

3 Katarzyna Zysk, 'Struggling, not crumbling: Russian defence AI in a time of war', *RUSI Commentary* (2023), 20. https://www.rusi.org/explore-our-research/publications/commentary/struggling-not-crumbling-russian-defence-ai-time-war (accessed 4 February 2026).

4 Richard A. Bitzinger and Michael Raska, 'Chinese and Russian military modernization and the Fourth Industrial Revolution', in Sarah Kirchberger, Sebastian Sinjen and Nils Wörmer (eds), *Russia-China Relations: Global Power Shift* (Cham: Springer, 2022). https://doi.org/10.1007/978-3-030-97012-3_7

5 Elsa B. Kania, *Battlefield Singularity: Artificial Intelligence, Military Revolution, and China's Future Military Power* (Washington, DC: Center for a New American Security, 2017).

6 Michael C. Horowitz, Gregory C. Allen, Elsa B. Kania and Paul Scharre, *Strategic Competition in an Era of Artificial Intelligence* (Washington, DC: Center for a New American Security, 2022).

7 Jianjun Li, 'Artificial intelligence technology and China's defense system', *Journal of Indo-Pacific Affairs* 5 (2022). https://www.airuniversity.af.edu/JIPA/Display/Article/2980879/artificial-intelligence-technology-and-chinas-defense-system/ (accessed 4 February 2026).

8 Maria Papageorgiou, Muhammed Can and Alena Vysotskaya Guedes Vieira, 'China as a threat and balancing behavior in the realm of emerging technologies', *Chinese Political Science Review* 9:4 (2024), 441–482. https://doi.org/10.1007/s41111-024-00248-0; Eric Schmidt, 'Innovation power: Why technology will define the future of geopolitics', *Foreign Affairs* 102, 38 (2023). https://www.foreignaffairs.com/united-states/eric-schmidt-innovation-power-technology-geopolitics (accessed 4 February 2026); Sugio Mori, 'US technological competition with China: The military, industrial and digital network dimensions', *Asia-Pacific Review* 26:1 (2019), 77–120.

9 Thomas X. Hammes, 'Will technological convergence reverse globalization?', *Strategic Forum* 297:1 (2016).

10 Michael C. Horowitz, 'Artificial intelligence, international competition, and the balance of power', *Texas National Security Review* 1:3 (2018), 37–57. https://doi.org/10.15781/T2639KP49

11 Papageorgiou et al., 'China as a threat and balancing behavior in the realm of emerging technologies', 441–482; Kenneth Payne, 'Artificial intelligence: A revolution in strategic affairs?', *Survival* 60:5 (2018), 7–32. https://doi.org/10.1080/00396338.2018.1518374

12 Kevin LaGrandeur, 'The consequences of AI hype', *AI and Ethics* 4:3 (2024), 653–656. https://doi.org/10.1007/s43681-023-00352-y; Simone Natale and Andrea Ballatore, 'Imagining the thinking machine: Technological myths and the rise of Artificial intelligence', *Convergence* 26:1 (2020), 3–18. https://doi.org/10.1177/1354856517715164

13 Julia Ciocca, Michael C. Horowitz and Lauren Kahn, 'The perils of overhyping artificial intelligence: For AI to succeed, it first must be able to fail', *Foreign Affairs* (2021). https://www.foreignaffairs.com/united-states/perils-overhyping-artificial-intelligence (accessed 4 February 2026).

14 Nathan G. Woo, 'Explainable AI in the military domain', *Ethics and Information Technology* 26:2 (2024), 1–13. https://doi.org/10.1007/s10676-023-09682-1; Maj Ryan Ratcliffe, 'AI and international order', *Marine Corps Gazette* (2023), 10 WE. https://www.mca-marines.org/wp-content/uploads/Ratcliffe-Oct23.pdf (accessed 4 February 2026); Martin Ciupa, 'Is AI in jeopardy? The need to under-promise and over-deliver – the case for really useful machine learning', *Computer Science & Information Technology* 7:3 (2017), 59–70. https://doi.org/10.5121/csit.2017.70407

15 Alex Neads, Theo Farrell and David J. Galbreat, 'Evolving towards military innovation: AI and the Australian Army', *Journal of Strategic Studies* 47:5 (2024), 669–698. https://doi.org/10.1080/01402390.2023.2200588

16 Michael Raska, 'The sixth RMA wave: Disruption in military affairs?', in Michael Raska, Katarzyna Zysk and Ian Bowers (eds), *Defence Innovation and the 4th Industrial Revolution: Security Challenges, Emerging Technologies, and Military Implications* (London: Routledge, 2022), 6–29.

17 Richard A. Bitzinger, 'The 4th Industrial Revolution, military-civil fusion, and the next RMA', *Insight Turkey* 24:3 (2022), 11–22. https://doi.org/10.25253/99.2022243.2

18 Christian Brose, 'The new revolution in military affairs: War's sci-fi future', *Foreign Affairs* 98:3 (2019), 122–134. https://www.foreignaffairs

.com/united-states/new-revolution-military-affairs (accessed 4 February 2026).

19 Reuben Steff and Kamal Abbas, 'Artificial intelligence and the military balance of power: Interrogating the US–China confrontation', in Reuben Steff, Joe Burton and Simona Soare (eds), *Emerging Technologies and International Security: Machines, the State, and War* (London: Routledge, 2020), 65–82.

20 Mohammad Eslami and Lauro Borges, *The Drones Race and International Security* (Cham: Springer International Publishing, 2025).

21 Brose, 'The new revolution in military affairs'.

22 Pradeep Kumar Mallick, 'Artificial intelligence, national security and the future of warfare', in Roy Kaushiki Sanyal (ed.), *Artificial Intelligence, Ethics and the Future of Warfare: Global Perspectives* (London: Routledge India, 2024), 30–70; Abdul Rashid, Anirban Kausik, Abdullah Al Hassan Sunny and Mohammad H. Bappy, 'Artificial intelligence in the military: An overview of the capabilities, applications, and challenges', *International Journal of Intelligent Systems* 2023:1 (2023). https://doi.org/10.1155/2023/8676366

23 Paule Scharre, *Army of None: Autonomous Weapons and the Future of War* (New York: W.W. Norton & Company, 2018).

24 Human Rights Clinic and Human Rights Watch, Background Briefing Review of the 2023 US Policy on Autonomy in Weapons Systems February 2023 (2023). https://humanrightsclinic.law.harvard.edu/wp-content/uploads/2023/02/Review-of-the-2023-US-Policy-on-Autonomy-in-Weapons-Systems.pdf (accessed 4 February 2026).

25 Anne-Claire Boury-Brisset and Jean Berger, 'Benefits and challenges of AI/ML in support of intelligence and targeting in hybrid military operations', *Proceedings of the NATO Science & Technology Organization Meeting Proceedings* (STO-MP-IST-190) (2020), 9-2. https://www.sto.nato.int/publications/STO%20Meeting%20Proceedings/STO-MP-IST-190/MP-IST-190-09 (accessed 4 February 2026).

26 Magdalena Pacholska, 'Military artificial intelligence and the principle of distinction: A state responsibility perspective', *Israel Law Review* 56:1 (2023), 3–23. https://doi.org/10.1017/S0021223722000188

27 Clifford A. Baxter, 'Enhancing tactical level targeting with artificial intelligence', *Field Artillery Journal* 2024:1 (2024), 15–22. https://www

.fieldartillery.org/news/enhancing-tactical-level-targeting-with-artificial-intelligence (accessed 4 February 2026).

28 Tomasz Zurek, Jonathan Kwik and Tom van Engers, 'Model of a military autonomous device following international humanitarian law', *Ethics and Information Technology* 25:1 (2023), 15. https://doi.org/10.1007/s10676-023-09682-1

29 Sarah Grand-Clément, *Artificial Intelligence Beyond Weapons: Application and Impact of AI in the Military Domain* (Geneva: UNIDIR, 2023).

30 Tobias Vestner, 'The law of targeting's mechanisation and objectivisation through the use of artificial intelligence', in Irene Couzigou (ed.), *International Law and Technological Change: Testing the Adaptability of International Law* (Cheltenham: Edward Elgar Publishing, forthcoming); Rashid et al., 'Artificial intelligence in the military'; Giga Gogua, 'A revolution in military affairs and modern armaments in the Russia–Ukraine war of 2022–2023', *Future Human Image* 20 (2023), 35–45. https://doi.org/10.29202/fhi/20/4

31 Ash Rossiter, 'AI-enabled remote warfare: Sustaining the Western warfare paradigm?', *International Politics* 60:4 (2023), 818–833. https://doi.org/10.1057/s41311-021-00337-w

32 Clifford A. Baxter, 'Enhancing tactical level targeting with artificial intelligence', *Field Artillery Journal* 2024:1 (2024), 15–22. https://www.fieldartillery.org/news/enhancing-tactical-level-targeting-with-artificial-intelligence (accessed 4 February 2026).

33 Vestner, 'The law of targeting's mechanisation and objectivisation'.

34 Owen J. Daniels, 'The "AI RMA": The revolution has not arrived (yet)', *The Andrew W. Marshall Papers* (2022). https://www.andrewwmarshallfoundation.org/wp-content/uploads/2022/11/AIRMA_FINAL.pdf (accessed 4 February 2026).

35 Anthony King, 'Digital targeting: Artificial intelligence, data, and military intelligence', *Journal of Global Security Studies* 9:2 (2024), ogae009. https://doi.org/10.1093/jogss/ogae009

36 Viktoriya Fedorchak, 'The use of artificial intelligence (AI) and unmanned platforms in Ukraine in the air domain', *Luftled* 1 (2024), 15–22. https://luftled.info/ai-and-unmanned-platforms-in-ukraine/ (accessed 4 February 2026).

37 Nigel Inkster, 'China in cyberspace', *Survival* 52:4 (2010), 55–66. https://doi.org/10.1080/00396338.2010.506820

38 Rod Thornton and Marina Miron, 'Towards the "Third Revolution in Military Affairs"', *The RUSI Journal* 165:3 (2020), 12–21. https://doi.org/10.1080/03071847.2020.1765514

39 Michael C. Horowitz, 'The algorithmic battlefield: AI in the age of irregular warfare', *Texas National Security Review* 3:4 (2020), 1–16.

40 Michael Raska and Richard A. Bitzinger, 'Introduction: The AI wave in defence innovation', in Michael Raska and Richard A. Bitzinger (eds), *The AI Wave in Defence Innovation: Assessing Military Artificial Intelligence Strategies, Capabilities, and Trajectories* (London: Routledge, 2023), 1–11.

41 Raska, 'The sixth RMA wave'; Joshua Glonek, 'The coming military AI revolution', *Military Review* 104:3 (2024), 88–99. https://www.armyupress.army.mil/Journals/Military-Review/English-Edition-Archives/May-June-2024/MJ-24-Glonek/ (accessed 4 February 2026).

42 Lester W. Grau and Charles K. Bartles, *The Russian Way of War: Force Structure, Tactics, and Modernization of the Russian Ground Forces*, Foreign Military Studies Office (2016), 378–379. https://www.armyupress.army.mil/Portals/7/Hot%20Spots/Documents/Russia/2017-07-The-Russian-Way-of-War-Grau-Bartles.pdf (accessed 4 February 2026).

43 Daniel Barreiros and Ítalo Barreto Poty, 'The US strategy for short-term military artificial intelligence development (2020–30)', *AUSTRAL: Brazilian Journal of Strategy & International Relations* 10:19 (2022). https://doi.org/10.22456/2238-6912.97219

44 Leo S. F. Lin, 'An analysis of the role of artificial intelligence in China's grand strategy: Perception, means and ends', *Scientia Moralitas: International Journal of Multidisciplinary Research* 6:1 (2021), 48–63. https://doi.org/10.5281/zenodo.5135194

45 J. Lewis Gaddis, 'What is grand strategy?', *Karl Von Der Heyden Distinguished Lecture, Duke University* (2009). https://www.iicseonline.org/Grand_Strategy1.pdf (accessed 4 February 2026).

46 Anna Nadibaidze and Nicolò Miotto, 'The impact of AI on strategic stability is what states make of it: Comparing US and Russian discourses', *Journal for Peace and Nuclear Disarmament* 6:1 (2023), 47–67. https://doi.org/10.1080/25751654.2023.2205552

47 Lauro Borges, Nicholas Ross Smith and Mohammad Eslami, 'State capacity, military modernisation, and balancing: A conditional model of state capacity neoclassical realism', *Review of International Studies* (2025), 1–20; Lauro Borges, Mohammed Eslami and Peter Layton, 'The return of expendable mass to air warfare: attrition versus manoeuvre in air operations', *Defense & Security Analysis* (2025), 1–24.

48 Jinghan Zeng, *Artificial Intelligence with Chinese Characteristics: National Strategy, Security and Authoritarian Governance* (London: Palgrave Macmillan, 2022).

49 Rafael A. Elias, 'US national artificial intelligence strategy against the Made in China 2025 policy', *Contemporary Chinese Political Economy and Strategic Relations* 7:1 (2021), 447–480. https://doi.org/10.22495/cjpesr_v7_i1_p447

50 Author's calculations from Notice of the State Council on the Publication of 'Made in China 2025' 国务院关于印发《中国制造2025》的通知, 10 March 2022. CSET. Notice of the State Council on the Publication of 'Made in China 2025' | Center for Security and Emerging Technology. georgetown.edu (accessed 4 February 2026).

51 China's State Council, 'New generation artificial intelligence development plan', in Graham Webster, Rogier Creemers, Paul Triolo and Elsa Kania (trans), *New America* (2017). https://www.newamerica.org/cybersecurity-initiative/digichina/blog/full-translation-chinas-new-generation-artificial-intelligence-development-plan-2017/ (accessed 4 February 2026).

52 Lin, 'An analysis of the role of artificial intelligence'.

53 China's State Council, 'New generation artificial intelligence development plan', trans. Webster et al., *New America*, 2.

54 Thomas Christian Bächle and Jascha Bareis, '"Autonomous weapons" as a geopolitical signifier in a national power play: Analysing AI imaginaries in Chinese and US military policies', *European Journal of Futures Research* 10:1 (2022). https://doi.org/10.1186/s40309-022-00202-w

55 Huw Roberts, Josh Cowls, Jessica Morley, Mariarosaria Taddeo, Vincent Wang and Luciano Floridi, 'The Chinese approach to artificial intelligence: An analysis of policy, ethics, and regulation', in Luciano Floridi and Josh Cowls (eds), *Ethics, Governance, and Policies in Artificial Intelligence* (Cham: Springer, 2021), 47–79.

56 China's State Council, 'New generation artificial intelligence development plan', trans. Webster et al., *DigiChina* (2017), 5. https://digichina.stanford.edu/work/full-translation-chinas-new-generation-artificial-intelligence-development-plan-2017/ (accessed 4 February 2026).

57 China's State Council, 'New generation artificial intelligence development plan', trans. Webster et al., *DigiChina*, 21.

58 China's State Council, 'New generation artificial intelligence development plan', trans. Webster et al., *DigiChina*, 21.
59 China's State Council, 'New generation artificial intelligence development plan', trans. Webster et al., *DigiChina*, 4.
60 Including 'Basic theory, core algorithms, key equipment, high-end chips, major products and systems, foundational materials, components, software and interfaces', China's State Council, 'New generation artificial intelligence development plan', trans. Webster et al., *DigiChina*, 4.
61 China's State Council, 'New generation artificial intelligence development plan', trans. Webster et al., *DigiChina*, 4.
62 Huw Roberts, Josh Cowls, Elizabeth Hine, Jessica Morley, Vincent Wang, Mariarosaria Taddeo and Luciano Floridi, 'Governing artificial intelligence in China and the European Union: Comparing aims and promoting ethical outcomes', *The Information Society* 39:2 (2023), 79–97. https://doi.org/10.1080/01972243.2023.2182345
63 Roberts et al., 'The Chinese approach to artificial intelligence'.
64 Elsa B. Kania, 'Artificial intelligence in China's revolution in military affairs', in Michael Raska, Katarzyna Zysk and Ian Bowers (eds), *Defence Innovation and the 4th Industrial Revolution: Security Challenges, Emerging Technologies, and Military Implications* (Abingdon: Routledge, 2022), 65–92.
65 James Johnson, 'Artificial intelligence and future warfare: Implications for international security', *Defense & Security Analysis* 35:2 (2019), 147–169. https://doi.org/10.1080/14751798.2019.1600800
66 PRC Ministry of Science and Technology, 'The "13th Five-Year" Special Plan for S&T Military-Civil Fusion Development', *Center for Security and Emerging Technology* (2017), trans. Etcetera Language Group, Inc. https://cset.georgetown.edu/publication/the-13th-five-year-special-plan-for-st-military-civil-fusion-development/ (accessed 4 February 2026).
67 Kania, *Battlefield Singularity*.
68 Gülay Şahin Özdemir, *Artificial Intelligence Application in the Military: The Case of United States and China* (Ankara: SETA, 2019).
69 Department of Defense, *Summary of the 2018 Department of Defense Artificial Intelligence Strategy: Harnessing AI to Advance Our Security and Prosperity* (Washington, DC: Department of Defense, 2018), p. 5.
70 Department of Defense, *Summary of the 2018 Department of Defense Artificial Intelligence Strategy*, 17.

71 Department of Defense, *Summary of the 2018 Department of Defense Artificial Intelligence Strategy*, 5.
72 Donald J. Trump, 'Executive Order on Maintaining American Leadership in Artificial Intelligence', *The White House* (2019). https://trumpwhitehouse.archives.gov/presidential-actions/executive-order-maintaining-american-leadership-artificial-intelligence (accessed 4 February 2026).
73 Trump, 'Executive Order', Section 1.
74 Trump, 'Executive Order', Section 1, Article A.
75 Anu Bradford, *Digital Empires: The Global Battle to Regulate Technology* (New York: Oxford University Press, 2023).
76 Department of Defense, *Data, Analytics, and Artificial Intelligence Adoption Strategy: Accelerating Decision Advantage* (Washington, DC: Department of Defense, 2023). https://www.defense.gov/News/News-Stories/Article/Article/3578219/dod-releases-ai-adoption-strategy/ (accessed 4 February 2026).
77 Department of Defense, *Data, Analytics, and Artificial Intelligence Adoption Strategy*, 3.
78 Ministry of Defense of the Russian Federation, 'Artificial intelligence: Problems and their solutions, Article 6', *MOD* (2018). https://mil.ru/conferences/is-intellekt.htm (accessed 3 February 2023).
79 Stephanie Petrella, Chris Miller and Benjamin Cooper, 'Russia's artificial intelligence strategy: The role of state-owned firms', *Orbis* 65:1 (2021), 75–100. https://doi.org/10.1016/j.orbis.2020.12.003; Samuel Bendett, 'Here's how the Russian military is organizing to develop AI', *Defense One* (2018). https://www.defenseone.com/ideas/2018/07/russian-militarys-ai-development-roadmap/149900/ (accessed 4 February 2026).
80 Vladimir Putin, 'Decree of the President of the Russian Federation on the Development of Artificial Intelligence in the Russian Federation', *President of the Russian Federation* (2019). http://www.kremlin.ru/acts/bank/44731 (accessed 4 February 2026).
81 Putin, 'Decree of the President of the Russian Federation', Article 3.
82 Putin, 'Decree of the President of the Russian Federation', Article 179.
83 Putin, 'Decree of the President of the Russian Federation'.
84 Xiangning Wu, 'Technology, power, and uncontrolled great power strategic competition between China and the United States', *China International Strategy Review* 2:1 (2020), 99–119. https://doi.org/10.1007/s42533-020-00040-0

85 Samuel Bendett, Mathieu Boulègue, Richard Connolly, Margarita Konaev, Pavel Podvig and Katarzyna Zysk, *Advanced Military Technology in Russia* (London: Chatham House, 2021). https://www.chathamhouse.org/sites/default/files/2021-09/2021-09-23-advanced-military-technology-in-russia-bendett-et-al.pdf (accessed 4 February 2026).
86 Putin, 'Decree of the President of the Russian Federation'.
87 Putin, 'Decree of the President of the Russian Federation', Article 17.
88 Lance Y. Hunter, Charles D. Albert, James Rutland, Karen Topping and Christopher Hennigan, 'Artificial intelligence and information warfare in major power states: How the US, China, and Russia are using artificial intelligence in their information warfare and influence operations', *Defense & Security Analysis* 40:2 (2024), 235–269. https://doi.org/10.1080/14751798.2024.2321736
89 Andrew Radin, Andrew Scobell, Elina Treyger, J. D. Williams, Logan Ma, Howard J. Shatz, Sean M. Zeigler, Eugeniu Han and Clint Reach, *China-Russia Cooperation: Determining Factors, Future Trajectories, Implications for the United States* (Santa Monica, CA: RAND Corporation, 2021). https://www.rand.org/pubs/research_reports/RR3067.html (accessed 4 February 2026).
90 Jon Harper, 'Analysts say $25 billion needed for AI', *National Defense* (2020). https://www.nationaldefensemagazine.org/articles/2020/2/3/analysts-say-$25-billion-needed-annually-for-ai (accessed 4 February 2026).
91 Jon Harper, 'Pentagon requesting more than $3B for AI, JADC2', *DefenseScoop* (2023). https://defensescoop.com/2023/03/13/pentagon-requesting-more-than-3b-for-ai-jadc2/ (accessed 4 February 2026).
92 Ashwin Acharya and Zachary Arnold, 'Chinese public AI R&D spending: Provisional findings', *Center for Security and Emerging Technology* (2019). https://cset.georgetown.edu/publication/chinese-public-ai-rd-spending-provisional-findings/ (accessed 4 February 2026).
93 Muhammed Can and Ana Vieira, 'The Chinese military-civil fusion strategy: A state action theory perspective', *The International Spectator* 57:3 (2022), 85–102. https://doi.org/10.1080/03932729.2022.2080262
94 John Lee, 'Overtaking on the curve? Defense AI in China', in Jack Clark, Anusha Narayanan and Paul Scharre (eds), *The Very Long*

Game: 25 Case Studies on the Global State of Defense AI (Cham: Springer Nature Switzerland, 2024), 465–486.

95 Katarzyna Zysk, 'Defence innovation and the 4th industrial revolution in Russia', *Journal of Strategic Studies* 44:4 (2021), 543–571. https://doi.org/10.1080/01402390.2020.1856090

96 Andrew Radin, Lynn E. Davis, Edward Geist, Eugeniu Han, Dara Massicot, Michael Povlock, et al., *The Future of the Russian Military: Russia's Ground Combat Capabilities and Implications for U.S.–Russia Competition* (Santa Monica, CA: RAND Corporation, 2019). https://www.rand.org/pubs/research_reports/RR3099.html (accessed 4 February 2026).

97 TASS, 'Russian authorities budget around $54.05 mln for AI development in 2024 – PM', *TASS* (2023). tass.com/economy/1680865 (accessed 4 February 2026).

98 Julian Cooper *Another Budget for a Country at War: Military Expenditure in Russia's Federal Budget for 2024 and Beyond* (Stockholm: SIPRI, 2023). https://www.sipri.org/publications/2023/sipri-insights-peace-and-security/another-budget-country-war-military-expenditure-russias-federal-budget-2024-and-beyond (accessed 4 February 2026).

99 In millions of rubles.

100 Maria Papageorgiou and Alena Vysotskaya Guedes Vieira, 'Assessing the changing Sino–Russian relationship: A longitudinal analysis of bilateral cooperation in the post-Cold War period', *Europe–Asia Studies* 76:4 (2024), 632–658. https://doi.org/10.1080/09668136.2023.2276677

101 Liu Zhen, 'Russia and China compare notes on "military use of artificial intelligence"', *South China Morning Post* (2024). https://www.scmp.com/news/china/diplomacy/article/3250893/russia-and-china-compare-notes-military-use-artificial-intelligence (accessed 5 February 2026).

102 Roberts et al., 'The Chinese approach to artificial intelligence', 47–79.

103 Jing Li, 'Artificial intelligence technology and China's defense system', *Journal of Indo–Pacific Affairs* 5:2 (2022), 45–67. https://www.airuniversity.af.edu/JIPA/Display/Article/2980879/artificial-intelligence-technology-and-chinas-defense-system/ (accessed 5 February 2026).

104 Gregory C. Allen, *Understanding China's AI Strategy: Clues to Chinese Strategic Thinking on Artificial Intelligence and National Security* (Washington,

DC: Center for a New American Security, 2019). https://www.cnas.org/publications/reports/understanding-chinas-ai-strategy (accessed 5 February 2026).

105 *President of the Russian Federation*, 'Presentation of era innovation technopolis' (2018). http://en.kremlin.ru/events/president/news/56923 (accessed 5 February 2026).

106 Katarzyna Zysk, 'Struggling, not crumbling: Russian defence AI in a time of war', *Royal United Services Institute* (2023). https://rusi.org/explore-our-research/publications/commentary/struggling-not-crumbling-russian-defence-ai-time-war (accessed 5 February 2026).

107 *Ria Novosti*, 'The Ministry of Defense will create a department for artificial intelligence' (2021). https://ria.ru/20210426/minoborony-1730064599.html (accessed 5 February 2026).

108 *National Security Agency*, 'Gen. Nakasone offers insight into future of cybersecurity and SIGINT' (2023), paragraph 2. https://www.nsa.gov/Press-Room/News-Highlights/Article/Article/3533425/gen-nakasone-offers-insight-into-future-of-cybersecurity-and-sigint/ (accessed 5 February 2026).

109 Petrella, Miller, and Cooper, 'Russia's artificial intelligence strategy'.

110 Mohammad Eslami, Alena Vieira, Arshin Adib-Moghaddam, Lauro Borges, Maria Papageorgiou, Fabio Cristiano, Ibrahim Al-Marashi, Tom Sauer and Christian Kaunert, 'The geopolitics of AI-driven arms races', *Geopolitics* (2025), 1–43.

111 Mohammad Eslami and Alena Vysotskaya Guedes Vieira, 'Introducing the arms race in the Middle East in the twenty first century: A "powder keg" in the digital era?', in Mohammad Eslami and Alena Vysotskaya Guedes Vieira (eds), *The Arms Race in the Middle East: Contributions to International Relations* (Cham: Springer, 2023), 3–13. https://doi.org/10.1007/978-3-031-32432-1_1

112 Eric Schmidt et al., *National Security Commission on Artificial Intelligence: Final Report* (Washington, DC: National Security Commission on Artificial Intelligence, 2021), 2. https://assets.foleon.com/eu-central-1/de-uploads-7e3kk3/48187/nscai_full_report_digital.04d6b124173c.pdf (accessed 5 February 2026).

113 *Chinese Government Network*, 'Scientific and technological innovation, a powerful engine for moving towards a world-class army – The CPC Central Committee with Comrade Xi Jinping as the core leads and promotes the strengthening and rejuvenation of the army' (2023). https://www.gov.cn/xinwen/2023-10/04/content_6901234.htm

114 *President of the Russian Federation*, 'Conference on artificial intelligence' (2019). http://en.kremlin.ru/events/president/news/62003 (accessed 5 February 2026). AI is, thus, at the centre of Russia's great power aspirations. A. Vieira, 'Arms sales as an instrument of Russia's foreign policy and the shifting security dynamics of the Middle East: Contemporary security dynamics', in Mohammad Eslami and Alena Vysotskaya Guedes Vieira (eds), *The Arms Race in the Middle East* (Cham: Springer, 2023). https://doi.org/10.1007/978-3-031-32432-1_15

115 Amandeep Singh Gill, 'Artificial intelligence and international security: The long view', *Ethics and International Affairs* 33:2 (2019), 169–179.

116 Petrella, Miller, and Cooper, 'Russia's artificial intelligence strategy'; Keith Dear, 'Will Russia rule the world through AI? Assessing Putin's rhetoric against Russia's reality', *The RUSI Journal* 164:5–6 (2019), 36–60. https://doi.org/10.1080/03071847.2019.1694227

117 Ingvild Bode, Hendrik Huelss, Anna Nadibaidze, Guangyu Qiao-Franco and Tom F. A. Watts, 'Prospects for the global governance of autonomous weapons: Comparing Chinese, Russian, and US practices', *Ethics and Information Technology* 25:5 (2023). https://doi.org/10.1007/s10676-023-09678-x

118 Vincent Boulanin and Maaike Verbruggen, *Mapping the Development of Autonomy in Weapon Systems* (Stockholm: SIPRI, 2017). https://www.sipri.org/sites/default/files/2017-11/siprireport_mapping_the_development_of_autonomy_in_weapon_systems_1117_1.pdf (accessed 5 February 2026).

119 Özdemir, *Artificial Intelligence Application.*

120 Maria Papageorgiou, 'China's growing presence in the Middle East's arms race and security dynamics', in Mohammad Eslami and Alena Vysotskaya Guedes Vieira (eds), *The Arms Race in the Middle East: Contemporary Security Dynamics* (Cham: Springer International Publishing, 2023), 257–272; International Committee of the Red Cross, *Autonomous Weapon Systems: Technical, Military, Legal and Humanitarian Aspects* (Geneva, ICRC, 2014), 3. https://www.icrc.org/en/document/report-icrc-meeting-autonomous-weapon-systems-26-28-march-2014 (accessed 5 February 2026); Mohammad Eslami and Maria Papageorgiou, 'China's increasing role in the Middle East: Implications for regional and international dynamics', *Georgetown Journal of International Affairs* 24:2 (2023), 45–58; Mohammad Eslami, Nasim Sadat Mosavi and Muhammed Can, 'Sino–Iranian

cooperation in artificial intelligence: A potential countering against the US hegemony', in Paulo Duarte, Francisco Leandro and Enrique Galán (eds), *The Palgrave Handbook of Globalization with Chinese Characteristics: The Case of the Belt and Road Initiative* (Singapore: Springer Nature Singapore, 2023), 543–559.

121 Forward Defense Experts, 'What does the future of autonomous warfare look like? Four critical questions, answered', *Atlantic Council* (2022). https://www.atlanticcouncil.org/content-series/automating-the-fight/what-does-the-future-of-autonomous-warfare-look-like-four-critical-questions-answered/?utm_source=chatgpt.com (accessed 5 February 2026).

122 Jürgen Altmann and Frank Sauer, 'Autonomous systems and strategic stability', *Survival* 95:5 (2017), 123–138. https://doi.org/10.1080/00396338.2017.1375263; A. King, 'Robot wars: Autonomous drone swarms and the battlefield of the future', *Journal of Strategic Studies* (2024), 1–29. https://doi.org/10.1080/01402390.2024.2302585

123 *US Department of Defense*, 'Applied radar develops next-generation radar systems for counter-drone technology' (2023), 2. https://www.sbir.gov/sites/default/files/documents/RI-Applied_Radar-DoD-cleared.pdf (accessed 5 February 2026).

124 Jen Judson, 'US Army to demo offensive drone swarms in next Project Convergence', *Defense News* (2022). https://www.defensenews.com/smr/project-convergence (accessed 5 February 2026).

125 Eric B. Stewart, 'Survey of PRC drone swarm inventions', *China Aerospace Studies Institute, Air University* (2023). https://www.airuniversity.af.edu/CASI/Display/Article/3543399/survey-of-prc-drone-swarm-inventions/ (accessed 5 February 2026).

126 Oleksandr Kozhukhar, 'Russia and Ukraine launch swarm of drones at each other's territory', *Reuters* (2023). https://www.reuters.com/world/europe/russia-says-it-downs-33-ukraine-launched-drones-over-russian-regions-2023-12-17/ (accessed 5 February 2026).

127 Jeremy Julian Sarkin and Saba Sotoudehfar, 'Artificial intelligence and arms races in the Middle East: The evolution of technology and its implications for regional and international security', *Defense & Security Analysis* 40:1 (2024), 97–119.

128 James Johnson, 'Inadvertent escalation in the age of intelligence machines: A new model for nuclear risk in the digital age', *European Journal of International Security* 7:3 (2022), 337–359. https://doi.org/10.1017/eis.2021.23

129 Nadibaidze and Miotto, 'The impact of AI on strategic stability'.
130 Eugenio Garcia, 'The militarization of artificial intelligence: A wake-up call for the Global South', *SSRN Electronic Journal* (2019). https://doi.org/10.2139/ssrn.3452323
131 Stephane Baele, Iqraa Bukhari, Christopher Whyte, Scott Cuomo, Benjamin Jensen, Kenneth Payne and Eugenio V. Garcia, 'AI IR: Charting international relations in the age of artificial intelligence', *International Studies Review* 26:2 (2024), viae013. https://doi.org/10.1093/isr/viae013
132 Barry Pavel, Ivana Ke, Michael Spirtas, James Ryseff, Lea Sabbag, Gregory Smith, Keller Scholl and Domenique Lumpkin, 'AI and Geopolitics: How might AI affect the rise and fall of nations?', *RAND* (2023). https://www.rand.org/pubs/perspectives/PEA3034-1.html (accessed 5 February 2026).
133 Baele et al., 'AI IR: Charting international relations'.
134 Pierre-Emmanuel Thomann, 'Geopolitical competition and the challenges for the European Union of countering the malicious use of artificial intelligence' in Evgeny Pashentsev (ed.), *The Palgrave Handbook of Malicious Use of AI and Psychological Security* (Cham: Palgrave Macmillan, 2023). https://doi.org/10.1007/978-3-031-22552-9_17
135 Bitzinger, 'The 4th Industrial Revolution'.
136 Johnson, 'Artificial Intelligence and future warfare'.
137 Sarkin and Sotoudehfar, 'Artificial intelligence and arms races in the Middle East'; Hyun Ji Rim, 'The US–Chinas strategic competition and emerging technologies in the Indo–Pacific region: Strategies for building, dominating, and managing networks', *Asian Perspective* 47:1 (2023), 1–25. https://dx.doi.org/10.1353/apr.2023.0000
138 Baele et al., 'AI IR: Charting international relations'; Zeno Leoni and Sarah Tzinieris, 'The return of geopolitical blocs', *Survival* 66:2 (2024), 37–54. https://doi.org/10.1080/00396338.2024.2332056
139 Suzanne Loftus, 'The rise of China and the China-Russia relationship', in Suzanne Loftus (ed.), *Russia, China and the West in the Post-Cold War Era: The Limits of Liberal Universalism* (Cham: Springer International Publishing, 2023), 93–128.
140 Simona R. Soare, *Innovation as Adaptation: NATO and Emerging Technologies* (Washington, DC: German Marshall Fund of the United States, 2021). http://www.jstor.org/stable/resrep33488 (accessed 5 February 2026); Alice Saltini, *AI and Nuclear Command, Control and*

Communications: P5 perspectives (London: The European Leadership Network, 2023). https://europeanleadershipnetwork.org/wp-content/uploads/2023/11/AVC-Final-Report_online-version.pdf (accessed 5 February 2026).

141 Rabia Akhtar and Manpreet Sethi, 'Emerging technologies and Southern Asian nuclear deterrence', *The Washington Quarterly* 47:4 (2023), 99–116. https://doi.org/10.1080/0163660X.2024.2435161

142 James Johnson, 'Revisiting the "stability–instability paradox" in AI-enabled warfare: A modern-day Promethean tragedy under the nuclear shadow?' *Review of International Studies* (2024), 1–19. https://doi.org/10.1017/S0260210524000767; Pavel Sharikov, 'Artificial intelligence, cyberattack, and nuclear weapons – A dangerous combination', *Bulletin of the Atomic Scientists* 74:6 (2018), 368–373. https://doi.org/10.1080/00963402.2018.1533185

143 Mark Fitzpatrick, 'Artificial intelligence and nuclear command and control', *Survival* 61:3 (2019), 81–92. https://doi.org/10.1080/00396338.2019.1614782; Vincent Boulanin (ed.), *The Impact of Artificial Intelligence on Strategic Stability and Nuclear Risk: Volume 1, Euro-Atlantic Perspectives* (Stockholm: SIPRI, 2019), 53–62. https://www.sipri.org/publications/2019/research-reports/impact-artificial-intelligence-strategic-stability-and-nuclear-risk-volume-i-euro-atlantic (accessed 5 February 2026).

144 Akhtar and Sethi, 'Emerging technologies and Southern Asian nuclear deterrence', in Vincent Boulanin (ed.), *The Impact of Artificial Intelligence on Strategic Stability and Nuclear Risk: Volume 1, Euro-Atlantic Perspectives* (Stockholm: SIPRI, 2019), 53–62. https://www.sipri.org/publications/2019/research-reports/impact-artificial-intelligence-strategic-stability-and-nuclear-risk-volume-i-euro-atlantic (accessed 5 February 2026).

145 Bradford, *Digital Empires.*

146 Hin-Yan Liu, 'The power structure of artificial intelligence', *Law, Innovation and Technology* 10:2 (2018), 197–229. https://doi.org/10.1080/17579961.2018.1527480; Bhaso Ndzendze and Tshilidzi Marwala, 'Liberalism and artificial intelligence', in B. Ndzendze and T. Marwala (eds), *Artificial Intelligence and International Relations Theories* (Singapore: Palgrave Macmillan, 2023). https://doi.org/10.1007/978-981-19-4877-0_5

147 Antony J. Blinken, 'Secretary Antony J. Blinken at the National Security Commission on Artificial Intelligence's (NSCAI) Global

Emerging Technology Summit', *US Department of State* (2021). https://2021-2025.state.gov/secretary-antony-j-blinken-at-the-national-security-commission-on-artificial-intelligences-nscai-global-emerging-technology-summit/ (accessed 5 February 2026).

148 Johnson, 'Artificial intelligence and future warfare'.

149 Bureau of Arms Control and Nonproliferation, 'Political declaration on responsible military use of artificial intelligence and autonomy', *US Department of State* (2023). https://www.state.gov/political-declaration-on-responsible-military-use-of-artificial-intelligence-and-autonomy/ (accessed 5 February 2026).

150 *Government of China*, 'Working paper submitted to the Convention on Conventional Weapons Group of Governmental Experts on Lethal Autonomous Weapons Systems, April 11' (2018). https://reachingcriticalwill.org/images/documents/Disarmament-fora/ccw/2018/gge/documents/GGE.1-WP7.pdf (accessed 5 February 2026).

151 Kelley M. Sayler, 'Defense primer: US policy on lethal autonomous weapon systems', *Congressional Research Service* (2023). https://crsreports.congress.gov/product/pdf/IF/IF11150 (accessed 5 February 2026).

152 Government of Russia, 'Statement to the Convention on Conventional Weapons Group of Governmental Experts on Lethal Autonomous Weapons Systems' (2019). https://conf.unog.ch/digitalrecordings/index.html?guid=public/61.0500/70E5CC90-B100-4658-95BA8E8C0D4D581E_15h14&position=2576 (accessed 5 February 2026).

153 Bode et al., 'Prospects for the global governance'; *Human Rights Watch*, 'Stopping killer robots: Country positions on banning fully autonomous weapons and retaining human control' (2020). https://www.hrw.org/report/2020/08/10/stopping-killer-robots/country-positions-banning-fully-autonomous-weapons-and#_ftn68 (accessed 5 February 2026).

154 Gill, 'Artificial intelligence and international security'.

2

Bloodless warfare: rethinking cyber operations in the age of AI

Cláudia Barbosa, Alena Vysotskaya Guedes Vieira and Paulo Batista Ramos

Introduction

For more than two decades, a silent yet relentless conflict has been waged in the concealed recesses of cyber space. Unlike conventional battlefields, this domain is marked by intangibility – no blood is shed, no territory is seized and no clear beginning or end of the conflict is foreseen. Even so, as elusive as its contours might be, the impact of the cyber struggle is undeniable. Policymakers and military leaders alike persistently caution that cyber warfare[1] is no longer a distant threat but an active reality of our daily lives.[2]

The prospect of a catastrophic cyber incident, soon described as a potential 'Pearl Harbor', has loomed in policy discourse since, at least, the 1995 Oklahoma City bombing, which claimed 168 lives when a truck bomb was detonated outside the Alfred P. Murrah Federal Building. Exposing vulnerabilities in critical infrastructure, the incident also fuelled concerns of similar large-scale disruptions in the digital realm. In a 1996 testimony before the US Senate, then-Deputy Attorney General Jamie Gorelick warned that it was only a matter of time before a major cyber attack targeted critical infrastructure in the US, which would be, in her words, the 'cyber equivalent of a Pearl Harbor', emphasising the urgency of stronger cyber defences and international cooperation in this new conflict arena.[3]

However, the warnings have failed to produce a 'cyber shock', changing the collective perception and mobilising international action regarding security in cyber space. An incident of anticipated devastating scale and consequence has never happened for reasons that ranged from the amorphous nature of cyber weapons to the limits of human foresight and the lack of technical skills. Unlike atomic bomb and the nuclear threat, which prompted robust arms control regimes and disarmament during the Cold War, the absence of a comparable watershed moment has hindered international regulation of cyber weapons. Public concerns about 'cyber peace', analogous to nuclear disarmament, remain conspicuously absent, reflecting the intangibility and abstraction of the cyber conflict.

The need for a galvanising 'cyber shock' has not, however, influenced the rapid evolution of network-centric warfare, with cyber space as a pivotal arena of conflict. Twenty-first-century warfare revolves around unprecedented connectivity between and within three distinct battlefields: physical, informational and cognitive. Cyber space, the fifth domain of warfare,[4] is an inherently hybrid realm, encompassing not only the 'information technology space' but also the 'cognitive space' and the 'physical space' of the modern battlefield,[5] bridging all six domains of warfare.

Bloodless warfare

Network-centric warfare has also brought into sharper relief a long-standing military dream, namely a battlefield in which machines, not soldiers, bear the brunt of combat. While this vision remains only partially realised, cyber operations have accelerated their progress by deploying remotely operated weapon systems, such as unmanned aerial vehicles (UAVs), and allowing the development of autonomous weapons systems (AWS), with soldiers increasingly removed from the dangers of the front lines.

Building on this momentum, could artificial intelligence (AI) enhanced cyber operations fulfil the centuries-old dream of military commanders? Long regarded as a revolutionary technology, even before the advent of the generative AI (GenAI) spring, AI is increasingly recognised as the true revolution in military affairs (RMA) capable of reshaping the nature of military conflict. According to the acclaimed technology entrepreneur Kai-Fu Lee, AI constitutes the 'third revolution in warfare' following gunpowder and nuclear weapons.[6] The ongoing transition from human-driven to machine-driven warfare, marked by the integration of AI-enhanced technologies into the arsenals of both democratic and autocratic states, signifies a profound transformation of military power. Yet, despite their strategic relevance, the implications of this transformation in the cyber realm and AI-driven cyber operations remain a relatively underexplored field of academic inquiry.

Even though the challenges of researching cyber operations are well-known, such as state secrecy involving cyber activities, the technical complexity of tracing cyber attacks and the opacity surrounding tactical and operational realities more generally, among other aspects,[7] there is a scarcity of literature on the

AI–cyber nexus and AI-enabled cyber operations that contrasts with the academic focus on the geopolitical and military implications of AI-driven strategic competition.[8] This chapter aims to address this gap by exploring how AI is transforming cyber operations in contemporary, network-centric warfare. It contends that, although the evolution of the AI–cyber nexus has yet to experience a watershed moment, it has progressed incrementally. Evidence of this evolution can be identified in the context of the ongoing war in Ukraine.

The analysis is organised in four sections. The first section examines the distinctive characteristics of the AI–cyber nexus in modern warfare in the context of the race towards technological supremacy. The subsequent section discusses offence and defence in AI-enhanced cyber operations. The third section analyses the manifestations and the potential of AI-powered cyber operations in the context of the Ukraine war, followed by the conclusions that synthesise the findings and reflect upon the broader implications of AI-driven cyber warfare.

The AI–cyber arms race: chasing technological supremacy

AI and cyber share a common technological foundation that underpins (offensive and defensive) cyber operations.[9] While some of the earliest AI-enhanced algorithms took the form of malicious software (malware), early AI developments encompassed self-replicating and propagative cyber weapons, such as viruses, worms, spyware and chatbots. The boundary between AI and cyber is growing increasingly indistinct, as AI principles and techniques drive advancements in cyber operations and warfare. The latter, defined as the use of digital technologies to disrupt or damage an adversary's networks or systems for strategic, political or military purposes, encompasses several types of cyber attacks, including hacking, cyber espionage (e.g., stealing intellectual property), sabotage (e.g., provoking damage and disruption in critical infrastructures), theft of sensitive data (e.g., personal files), disinformation or even electronic warfare.

The AI–cyber nexus is especially critical in hybrid warfare, in which cyber operations are a key component of combined military and non-military strategy. In 2014, during the annexation of Crimea, Russia provoked surprise with its audacious and effective use of a combination of military and non-military force, bringing the concept of hybrid warfare to the forefront of the Western debate on the invasion. While hybrid warfare is characterised by a blend of a wide range of overt and covert military, paramilitary and civilian measures employed in a highly integrated manner, cyber operations have become a central component of the measures short of war portfolio, alongside sanctions, information operations and democracy promotion.[10]

Despite their growing importance, cyber operations pose the challenge of identifying, monitoring and assessing often intangible cyber arsenals. Several analysts argue that the buildup of (AI–)cyber weapon arsenals and the generation of (AI–)cyber forces do not align with the traditional definition of an arms race,[11] expressing scepticism toward the notion of AI arms race as a catchphrase for strategic competition among great powers within a digital realm in which distinctions between allies, adversaries, winners and losers are blurred.[12] Critics further contend that the concept of an AI arms race misrepresents the competition going on among countries in cyber space,[13] as AI is a technology rather than a strategic weapon, making it ill-suited to the arms race framework.[14]

However, this scepticism does not undermine the validity of concerns regarding AI's impact on the defence and military sectors. The proliferation of AI applications and the need for their responsible use by states and non-state actors remain pressing issues. Unlike the non-lethal dimension of cyber weapons, AI's technological advantages have the potential for causing significant human harm. Over the past decade, AI tools and lethal autonomous weapons systems (LAWS) have not only proliferated but were also deployed on behalf of states. Whether this constitutes an arms race,[15] there is a clear AI-driven push towards the 'killing fields', efforts to develop tools capable of identifying, detecting and neutralising enemies while reducing risks to soldiers on the battlefield – a reality that demands a critical reevaluation of how international organisations, governments, tech corporations, media, civil society and academia frame and address the military use of AI.[16]

Moreover, AI has been recognised as a decisive factor in shaping global power dynamics, with US–China strategic competition in AI emerging as a defining feature of contemporary international politics.[17] This intensifying rivalry in deep-tech fields is driving the ongoing global race for military technological dominance, reflected in the actions of the People's Liberation Army (PLA) actively preparing for a future of what it refers to as 'intelligentised warfare', or in Russian President Vladimir Putin's rhetoric that the nation leading in AI 'will rule the world',[18] echoing Mackinder's discourse and suggesting a cyber 'heartland'.[19]

Against this backdrop, and with a broader definition in mind, AI–cyber arms races can be understood as competitive military build-ups aimed at achieving technological supremacy. Evidence of such arms races can be seen in the growing recognition by great powers of the pivotal role of AI in cyber warfare, which is driving efforts to enhance their cyber capabilities.[20] Simultaneously, these powers are engaging in both offensive and defensive cyber operations to counter adversaries and secure strategic advantages. The motivations of regular armies to acquire such arsenals are connected to their ability to reduce the risks to human soldiers while simultaneously increasing the likelihood of military success.

The AI–cyber arms race can also be seen as a continuity of the often overlooked 'cyber weapons race', which has quietly unfolded within the corridors of cyber commands and defence ministries. The cyber arms race went unacknowledged due to the early cyber tech supremacy of the United States. Washington's strategic advantage precluded the creation of a cyber arms control regime to counterproliferation.[21] However, today, the technological contest has evolved into a new 'great tech game', encompassing multiple critical technologies and actors, all striving to secure geostrategic advantage. These actors, or 'cyber warriors', include civilian and military intelligence units, often operating as advanced persistent threats (APTs), as well as cyber professionals and criminals moonlighting on behalf of nation-states. In addition, numerous malign actors, such as cyber mercenaries, patriotic hackers, hacktivists and hackers-for-hire, align themselves with the strategic interests of states, further complicating the understanding of the cyber landscape.

Framing this atypical and unprecedented AI–cyber arms race remains a challenge. This unconventional race generates psychological pressures and behavioural effects among political and military policymaking elites, such as those observed in past escalation processes involving conventional or nuclear weapons. The perception that the adversary is already ahead in the race for a militarised cyber space is real. In this sense, the AI–cyber arms race is undeniably driving and fostering the emergence of rival global techno-military spheres of influence. While the end destination remains uncertain, we are witnessing a blurred and fuzzy race, marked by the development of stealthy – and at times, imaginary – AI–cyber weapons, which, despite their intangible nature, produce tangible consequences for national and global security.[22]

This is why there is a heightened sense of urgency to establish international regulation of AI, compounded by the complexity of the task. The multi-lateral response to AI has consistently lagged behind technological innovation and practice. Advances in AI raise critical concerns, particularly the risk of conflicts in cyber space, the compromise or misuse of LAWS and the erosion of human oversight during the shift towards fully autonomous systems.[23] Despite existing soft law initiatives, these issues remain unresolved. Recent initiatives include the Bletchley Declaration,[24] endorsed by twenty-eight governments at the AI Safety Summit in November 2023, and the joint acknowledgement by the UK, US, European Union (EU), Australia and China that AI poses a potentially catastrophic threat to humanity.[25] The G7 Digital and Tech Ministers initiative in March 2024 further underscored this point,[26] as it sought to align rules for AI to secure supply chains. Another landmark step was the adoption of a UN Resolution on March 21, 2024, aimed at promoting safe and reliable AI systems to enhance global regulation and support the sustainable development of AI technology.[27] Nevertheless, the establishment of a comprehensive AI international regime has been marked by competition between China and the US. This competition is reflected in China's Global AI Governance Initiative, released in October 2023, which offers a version of AI governance that prioritises development and well-being while notably omitting references to the protection of human rights and freedoms.

The AI–cyber nexus: redefining offensive and defensive cyber operations

The 1991 Gulf War offered a striking glimpse into the future of warfare, with Iraqi soldiers surrendering not to human combatants but to remotely operated UAVs – a groundbreaking moment in military history. Faced with UAVs hovering overhead, Iraqi troops waved white cloths in an almost surreal, movie-like scene. These soldiers, fully aware that their actions were being observed in real-time by remote operators via live-streamed footage from cameras mounted on the UAVs, sought to signal their intent to surrender. Remotely controlled via cyber networks and information and communication technologies (ICT), the UAVs enabled operators to interpret soldiers' gestures with precision.

This prompts a vital question: how will such a scenario unfold with the decision-making process of today's LAWS? Unlike human-controlled UAVs, AI-operated systems lack contextual understanding, emotional recognition or empathy. Instead, they act strictly in accordance with the protocols embedded in their software. In an unanticipated situation akin to the Gulf War, it is unlikely that a fully autonomous system would recognise a gesture of surrender. Instead, it would likely follow its predefined operational directives: detect, identify and eliminate enemy targets.

This shift from human-controlled UAVs to fully autonomous systems epitomises a broader transformation in warfare, parallelled by the evolution of cyber operations. The mid-1990s marked the onset of a long and covert cyber war characterised by the growing sophistication of autonomous and self-propagating cyber weapons. A defining moment in this evolution was the deployment of the Stuxnet worm in 2010, which infiltrated Iran's Natanz nuclear power plant. Widely regarded as one of history's boldest and most consequential cyber operations, Stuxnet targeted the system's programmable logic controllers (PLC) that managed centrifuges used for uranium enrichment. By manipulating the PLCs, Stuxnet caused extensive damage to the centrifuges, significantly impairing Iran's nuclear programme. As the first known cyber weapon to cause real-world physical destruction, Stuxnet redefined the strategic logic of cyber warfare, demonstrating the capacity of autonomous digital weapons to disrupt critical infrastructure without direct human intervention.

However, the effects of Stuxnet extended far beyond its intended target. Exposed to more than 100,000 internet protocol (IP) addresses, it caused more than 40,000 infections across cyber space. This global diffusion transformed Stuxnet from a surgical cyber strike into a global cyber security incident. Its inadvertent spread triggered a cycle of tit-for-tat cyber escalation with Iranian actors, exposing the risks of the deployment of digital weapons.[28]

Far from being an anomaly, Stuxnet became a manifestation of a new reality with cyber operations as integral tools of statecraft. These operations serve both offensive and defensive purposes, requiring states to master both attack and defence manoeuvres. Over time, cyber weapons have evolved into threat multipliers, force generators, enablers of information warfare and tools for accessing adversary networks and classified data. As a result, cyber warfare undermines the capacity of armed forces and societies to respond to conventional threats. It also assumes that sensitive state information is secured within internal networks or intranets, making it increasingly difficult for adversaries to extract classified information. This shift is also underpinned by the assumption that a state's secrets are stored within internal networks or intranets, posing new challenges for adversaries seeking access to high-value information.[29]

Cyber operations are, by nature, one of the state's most clandestine tools, typically conducted via the deep web and shielded by encryption-based camouflage. These operations rely on secrecy, limiting visibility and external access. By contrast, AI requires extensive access to vast datasets from both classified and unclassified sources, employing large-scale data analysis to enhance national security decision-making and operational efficiency. This fundamental distinction between cyber operations and AI reveals a core paradox: while cyber operations prioritise secrecy and isolation, AI demands openness and unrestricted access, data integration and expansive analysis of diverse datasets. To meet the demands of AI, states require infinite data access, high-performance computing, data storage capacity and integration of classified and unclassified data.

This imperative has accelerated (military) data migration to cloud-based infrastructure, compelling armed forces to establish public–private partnerships and adopt a war-as-a-service (WaaS) model, leveraging industry AI solutions to automate military actions and enhance cyber capabilities. Eventually, the principles underpinning cyber security (confidentiality, integrity and accessibility) collide with those with the data-sharing requirements of AI. This tension embodies the conflict between the 'need to share' and 'need to know' principles, reflecting deeper contradictions in information security. And while AI is seen as a solution to persistent cyber security challenges, such as threat detection, anomaly identification and rapid incident response, its adoption comes with strategic costs. The evolution of cyber warfare into a state of 24/7, perpetual engagement, in which autonomous agents continuously detect, counter and mitigate threats, introduces new, ethical, legal and operational dilemmas for military planners.

The most evident implication of AI's integration into cyber operations is its potential to create new generations of cyber attack tools and malware that are more sophisticated, adaptive and infectious than previous models.[30] AI-driven capabilities are likely to trigger a surge in cyber espionage and intelligence-gathering efforts,[31] as well as the development of malware that is far more target-specific and precise (tailored to infiltrate specific systems, extract high-value information and neutralise adversarial networks) than conventional, kinetic weapons that inflict indiscriminate physical damage.[32] Microsoft has already confirmed that hostile state actors are using large language models (LLMs) and GenAI to enhance their offensive cyber attacks,[33] providing clear evidence of a significant escalation in the sophistication of offensive cyber operations.

Cyber warriors are poised to exploit AI's capabilities to attack both soft and hard targets of adversaries. This can follow multiple pathways, with AI-powered malware being both highly customised and scalable. AI-generated malware can learn the nuances of individual users' behaviour and language by analysing their email and social media interactions. Armed with this knowledge, AI can replicate a user's writing style, generating messages that are nearly indistinguishable from authentic communications. This development poses a severe threat, as it renders even the most cyber-aware individuals vulnerable to sophisticated spear-phishing attacks. By mimicking authentic communications, such easily deployable AI-driven spear-phishing campaigns would significantly heighten user vulnerability, ultimately creating a more enduring and evasive cyber threat environment.

Sophisticated threat actors employ APTs, which are known for their ability to maintain a long-term, undetected presence within target environments. These actors operate with caution and precision, employing stealth tactics to evade traditional security controls. Their operations are often highly targeted, focusing on specific individuals, organisations, or sectors of strategic interest. With the integration of AI, their tactics are set to become far more advanced. AI-driven malware can learn and adapt to a system's dominant communication channels, ports and protocols, allowing it to blend seamlessly with routine network activity. This capacity for disguise enables AI-based malware to spread more efficiently within a digital environment, compromising a larger number of devices with greater stealth than ever before.

Moreover, AI-enhanced malware can process and analyse vast datasets at machine speed, quickly distinguishing high-value targets from irrelevant ones. By accelerating this process, AI-driven malware will facilitate faster, more efficient lateral movement within systems, significantly enhancing its ability to navigate and propagate across networks. This reduces the operational burden on human attackers, making advanced, large-scale cyber intrusions faster, more effective and more difficult to counter.

Traditionally, sophisticated cyber attacks require skilled technicians to execute complex tactics, techniques and procedures (TTPs). However, AI has the potential to achieve comparable levels of sophistication in a fraction of the time and on a much larger scale. Unlike human operators, AI is constantly evolving, learning from past interactions and becoming increasingly resistant to threat classification, categorisation and detection – a process that remains central to the *modus operandi* of legacy security approaches and that increases the need for AI-driven cyber defences beyond the reliance on past classifications of known threats.

A particularly insidious dimension of AI proliferation lies in its role in the creation of tailored disinformation campaigns aimed at creating digital chaos within adversarial societies. These modern foreign information manipulation and interference (FIMI) operations are essential components of the hybrid war arsenal, as they expand the scope of information, and psychological operations aim to destabilise the political environment,[34] erode public trust and undermine the credibility of legitimate information sources. AI allows for the automatisation of these campaigns, amplifying their sophistication, speed, reach and precision that would be far more difficult, if not impossible, to achieve through traditional means.[35]

The advent of deepfakes, created through generative adversarial networks (GANs), has made it possible to manipulate voice, images and video content with unprecedented precision. These technologies allow for the creation of highly realistic synthetic content, including videos, photos and audio files (e.g., phone calls or fingerprint scans), convincingly mimicking human behaviour and communication and enabling malicious actors to evade traditional authentication systems and security controls. Resulting in complex and difficult-to-dismantle operations, such technological advances can distort perceptions of reality and raise concerns about cognitive security as they exploit human cognitive vulnerabilities.[36, 37]

Cyber space reconnaissance is another vital component of cyber warfare with significant potential for AI integration, involving mapping adversary networks, command and control systems and infrastructures. These efforts aim at collecting intelligence on adversary capabilities, vulnerabilities and operational strategies. Cyber space reconnaissance targets the adversary's command, control, communications, computers, intelligence, surveillance and reconnaissance (C4ISR) systems, electronic warfare and weapons command systems. When enhanced by AI-driven tools, such operations enable a more efficient data analysis and tracking of adversary's activities, increasingly transforming cyber space reconnaissance into a strategic enabler of preattack preparation.

In sum, offensively, information gathering is a critical pillar of any military campaign, serving as the intelligence screen for 'fire action'. In this context, intelligence, surveillance and reconnaissance (ISR) operations represent an ideal domain for data-driven AI systems. Cyber means, such as spyware and man-in-the-middle (MITM) attacks, are already common on the battlefield and are increasingly used to intercept and manipulate communications. Through the integration of AI into cyber operations, all five intelligence-gathering disciplines – human intelligence (HUMINT), signals intelligence (SIGINT), geospatial intelligence (GEOINT), measurement and signature intelligence (MASINT) and open-source intelligence (OSINT) – can be operated through AI–cyber systems. This integration can produce a highly comprehensive, real-time picture of the battlefield, revealing the enemy's intentions, movements and operational plans. AI's unparalleled ability to process and interpret vast datasets enables faster, more accurate and deeper intelligence analysis, significantly enhancing military operations and saving millions of human working hours, especially in time-critical wartime scenarios.

As AI becomes a standard tool in the cyber warrior's arsenal, adversaries will be compelled to respond in kind.[38] The only viable countermeasure to an AI-weaponised intelligence system is to deploy AI-based defensive systems.[39] This dual-edged nature of AI is captured by the capability–vulnerability paradox, a concept introduced by Jacquelyn Schneider.[40] The paradox reveals that the very AI capabilities that enhance military power and provide strategic superiority also expose new vulnerabilities and crucial weaknesses that adversaries with equal technological prowess can exploit.[41]

In terms of defence, AI–cyber systems have the potential to enhance network visibility and strengthen defence-in-depth strategies, enabling faster, more accurate and more efficient monitoring, detection and analysis of network activity. These systems could even establish a 'smart border' or a 'national cyberspace fence', providing a dynamic layer of protection around critical infrastructure. The defence-in-depth approach seeks to limit potential entry points for cyber threats, prevent zero-day vulnerabilities and reduce opportunities for intrusion. This is achieved through a multi-layered system of defences, including firewalls, antivirus software, real-time intrusion detection systems and cryptographic protocols. By leveraging AI, these tools can adapt and respond in real time, enhancing threat detection, malware protection and network security.

AI-powered patching and threat-hunting operations enable a more proactive approach to cyber security. This capability allows for disruption of enemy operations, such as the takedown of botnets and malware removal, before they achieve their objectives. By increasing defensive responses (including their speed, accuracy and certainty), AI bolsters the resilience of cyber infrastructure deterrence. AI-driven systems reinforce integrated deterrence strategies by demonstrating the capability to conduct retaliatory network strikes and defence operations, compelling adversaries to adjust their calculus and reconsider large-scale cyber attacks.[42]

Finally, by automating content verification and detection, AI enhances the efficiency and reliability of counterdisinformation operations. This is achieved through flagging of disinformation, hate speech recognition, detection of synthetic contents and blocking of fake news, thereby safeguarding the integrity of information environments, a capability that is especially critical in the context of hybrid warfare.[43]

AI, like cyber technologies, has long been associated with unfulfilled promises of world-changing capabilities. In this context, the UK Cyber Security Centre (2018) cautions against 'hyperbole about the capabilities of cyber [state] actors', noting that the vast majority of people are much more likely to fall victim to cyber crime than become affected by cyber war.[44] Similarly, it is essential to recognise that AI is not a weapon itself but a general purpose enabling technology with multi-domain applications. It serves as a force multiplier across military and cyber domains by enhancing precision, automation and operational speed and amplifying the effect of offensive and defensive cyber operations.

While conventional firepower remains the primary threat to soldiers on the battlefield, the rise of AI-enabled cyber warfare has already started to reshape the risk landscape. AI drives offensive and defensive cyber operations towards greater effectiveness, autonomy and adaptability, resulting in faster, more precise and more complex cyber operations that increasingly reduce reliance on human decision-making. Notably, AI-powered hacking is no longer a distant scenario but an emerging reality.[45] This shift is further reflected in the rise of LAWS in warfare, in which cyber operations played a pivotal supporting role in areas such as data integration, command and control, safeguarding communication networks and protection against cyber attacks. And as it deepens military capabilities, the AI–cyber nexus raises concerns regarding automated escalation, operational unpredictability and overreliance on AI-driven decision-making, presenting new risks and a spectrum of ethical, operational and regulation dilemmas for military planners, policymakers and international organisations.

The war in Ukraine as a theatre of AI-enhanced cyber operations

The ongoing conflict between Russia and Ukraine,[46] the largest of the digital age, offers potentially unique insights into the role of emergent technologies in modern warfare. Both Russia and Ukraine have engaged in the conflict armed with advanced cyber capabilities,[47] and the integration of AI has allowed some analysis to describe the war as a 'living laboratory' for AI-enabled warfare,[48] potentially marking the onset of an AI-driven RMA. While the presence of AI in warfare is evident, including autonomous vehicles, swarm munitions, precision targeting, command and control systems and geospatial intelligence, this perspective requires caution, particularly regarding cyber warfare, in which identifying evidence of AI-enhanced cyber operations remains a significant challenge, making any assessment reliant on data released by state agencies, private consultancies and non-governmental organisations (NGOs).

Nevertheless, the emerging AI–cyber nexus is evident in both offensive and defensive cyber operations, particularly in disinformation campaigns, enhanced spear-phishing attacks, deepfakes and autonomous threat detection and mitigation. Examples of the latter come from the improvements in individual actors' cyber defence architecture. For example,

Microsoft, through its support to Ukraine, reported that its Defender tool, powered by AI algorithms, successfully detected, classified and blocked Russia's Iridium unit wiper malware aimed at a shipping company in Lviv. This was achieved without any existing signatures or any human intervention.[49]

These advancements have been achieved in the context of Russia's persistent cyber aggression against Ukraine. Since 2014, Russia has perpetrated a series of cyber attacks against Ukraine, positioning the country as a potential 'ground zero' for the evolution of cyber warfare. Russian hacker groups have systematically targeted critical infrastructure, including government agencies, railways, the banking and financial sectors, power stations and the electric grid, causing widespread power outages. Nuclear facilities, hospitals, pharmaceutical companies, shipping enterprises and oil refineries have also been subjected to these operations. Concurrently, Russia has employed disinformation campaigns and electoral interference, leveraging so-called 'active measures', a term rooted in Russian intelligence parlance. The scope of Russia's attacks extended to Ukraine's entire internet infrastructure, compromising an estimated 80 per cent of its computer networks,[50] reflecting their unprecedented scale and sophistication. Distributed denial of service (DDoS) attacks have emerged as the predominant form of cyber attack, significantly affecting national critical infrastructures. Data from the CyberPeace Institute indicates that between July and September 2023, DDoS attacks accounted for 89 per cent of detected cyber incidents.[51]

These attacks are not isolated events, but, rather, form a larger framework of Russian information warfare. In this context, computer network operations carried out by Russia are not confined to wartime, nor are they considered a distinct function or domain. Instead, they are integral components of the broader concept of information warfare, which blurs the boundaries of cyber activities and other forms of information operations, viewing such delineations as artificial. In Russian doctrine, cyber space is subsumed within the larger information space, encompassing both technical systems, such as computers, and the cognitive domain. Consequently, activities such as DDoS attacks, hacking and state-sponsored broadcasting by outlets as Russia Today are all regarded as elements of a unified strategy, one that is conducted continuously,[52] eroding the line between peace and conflict.

Reflecting this strategy, although the large-scale military invasion officially began on February 24, 2022, the initial salvos occurred in cyber space, with cyber intrusions commencing weeks earlier. These attacks were designed not only to degrade Ukrainian morale but also to bolster Russia's capabilities and project an atmosphere of menace in advance of the military offensive. A notable example is Russia's disruption of the Viasat satellite communications network immediately before its tanks crossed the Ukrainian border. Russian hackers attacked Viasat's modems, rendering them inoperable.

In addition, disruptive cyber attacks caused widespread access blockages to telecommunications and internet services, further restricting the functionality of the banking system, official government websites and Ukrainian news outlets. Also, in February 2022, cyber experts discovered the circulation of destructive malware known as WhisperGate in Ukraine.[53] Later, in March, one of the most severe cyber attacks took place, targeting Ukraine's largest fixed-line telecommunications provider, Ukrtelecom. The latter suffered a connectivity collapse,[54] reducing its operation to just 13 per cent of prewar levels and causing nationwide disruptions. Another instance of Russia's numerous cyber attacks was revealed in 2023 when the Security Service of Ukraine (SBU) announced that Russian hackers infiltrated the systems of Kyivstar, a large Ukrainian telecom company, and had been operating undetected for months.[55]

A complex network of state and non-state actors underpins Russia's cyber war efforts. This includes a 'cyber brotherhood' of Russian-speaking threat actors primarily located in the Commonwealth of Independent States (CIS). A new trend of 'crowdsourced hacktivism' has also emerged, adding instability to the already volatile dark web ecosystem. Leaked documents, known as the 'Vulcan files', expose Russia's covert global cyber operations over several years. At the forefront is NTC Vulcan, a Moscow-based cyber security consultancy, whose engineers have collaborated with Russian intelligence agencies since at least 2016. They have developed highly invasive cyber systems, such as Scan-V, which identifies internet vulnerabilities; Amezit, designed for surveillance, internet control and disinformation campaigns via fake social media profiles; and Crystal-2V, which focuses on disrupting rail, air and sea infrastructure.[56]

Building on these tools, integrating AI into cyber warfare has significantly expanded such operations' scope and effectiveness. On both sides, the most prominent activities have focused on intelligence gathering and psychological warfare rather than outright destruction and disruption.[57] Russia's cyber offensive, in particular, has employed AI as a psychological warfare tool, aiming to destabilise populations through disinformation and

FIMI operations[58] as well as by employing methods to steal personal and financial data.

One of the largest disinformation operations, known as Doppelgänger,[59] began in February 2022 by a pro-Russian network notorious for spreading AI-generated anti-Ukrainian disinformation. Considered the largest and most persistently aggressive Russian-origin operation to date, the campaign has demonstrated the evolution of Russian TTPs as well as the use of AI to create scalable manipulative content for information warfare, targeting Ukrainian, the US and European audiences through fake government and news websites as well as social media accounts.[60] Another example is the operation dismantled by Facebook in September 2023. A small network of individuals operating in Russia and Ukraine disseminated disinformation via fabricated websites and false narratives, particularly regarding Ukraine's allegiance to the West and its national sovereignty. This network also created fake profiles of purported Kyiv residents across various platforms such as Facebook, Instagram, Twitter, YouTube and Telegram, as well as Russian platforms such as Odnoklassniki and VK, using AI-generated visuals through techniques such as deepfakes (GANs).[61] These are just two examples of AI use in FIMI operations, carried out by Russian and pro-Russian actors aimed to discredit Ukrainian leadership and disseminate anti-NATO and anti-Ukrainian narratives to audiences in the US, Europe and the Global South.[62]

Russian AI-powered cyber operations have not been confined to social media. For instance, during the initial stages of the conflict, an AI-generated deepfake video of President Zelensky declaring Ukraine's surrender to Russia was shared on Twitter and uploaded to a hacked Ukrainian news website.[63] This deepfake, of strategic significance, demonstrated Russia's active use of AI in psychological warfare, leveraging recent advancements in AI technology to destabilise the population.

Russia's disruptive cyber and information operations against Ukraine have proven far less impactful than anticipated. Ukraine demonstrated cyber resilience, both in its cyber defensive measures and AI-enhanced counteroffensive operations, in more general terms. For instance, to counter Russian propaganda denying significant troop casualties, Ukraine's Ministry of Internal Affairs launched a website called Poter.net, featuring a searchable database containing the names of dead Russian soldiers, identified using AI facial recognition and linking the results to open-source information from Russian social media,[64] allowing families to locate their relatives (72,012 Russian soldiers as of March 20, 2024).[65]

Ukrainian cyber initiatives, such as the IT Army of Ukraine (composed of four hundred thousand volunteers) or the CyberResistance,[66] bolstered by international hacktivist teams, have played a critical role in countering Russia's aggression. This has included cyber alliances, such as with the Belarusian Cyber Partisans, a hacker group claimed to have breached the internal systems of the Russian drone developer, obtaining intelligence that has directly supported Ukrainian military operations.[67] Ukrainian authorities have acknowledged that intelligence gathered from such cyber attacks has informed ground operations conducted by the armed forces.

The private sector has also been instrumental in fortifying Ukraine's cyber defences in a clear example of the WaaS model. US-based companies such as Palo Alto Networks, Palantir,

Microsoft, Google, Amazon and ESET have provided essential support, including cloud-based data storage solutions.[68] This cooperation has facilitated rapid insights into cyber resilience, offering valuable lessons for Ukraine and its Western allies.[69] Furthermore, Western cyber threat intelligence[70] has enhanced Ukraine's agility in anticipating adversary cyber moves with greater effectiveness.[71]

As the conflict reached its thousandth day in November 2024, drones have become a ubiquitous presence both on the front lines and in the areas that are no-go for humans. The Ukrainian first-person view (FPV) drones (UAVs) and Russian counterparts are now responsible for the majority of battlefield losses, surpassing artillery in their effectiveness.[72] This shift has led to what analysts describe as a 'furnace of software-defined warfare', exemplified by AI-guided drones achieving an especially high hit rate, 80 per cent higher than human-operated drones.[73] For example, the Ukrainian Saker Scout drones can autonomously identify and attack 64 types of Russian 'military objects'.[74] However, only 10 per cent of the drones in the conflict are currently AI-guided, and deep-strike drones with fully autonomous targeting systems are expected to be deployed in 2025 (capable of hunting, selecting and engaging targets).[75]

On the ground, AI-enabled autonomous ground vehicle systems are increasingly being used on the frontlines, supporting logistics, reconnaissance and strike operations, including landmine activation and deactivation. War risks have accelerated the adoption of such systems, which are becoming more automated through AI command-and-control software. At the outset of the conflict, few predicted that it would evolve into a 'war of robots'.[76] The rapid deployment of LAWS reflects an ongoing arms race for technological supremacy and for the advantages stemming from (drones') quantity. While the fundamental character of warfare remains unchanged, instances of AI integration with conventional weapons, as well as the emerging AI–cyber nexus, illustrate the evolution in military operations, echoing references to the Ukraine war as the 'living laboratory' of AI-enhanced warfare.

In parallel, the role of cyber warfare in conflict remains a contested subject. Quantifying cyber attacks and assessing their impact on military operations continues to pose significant challenges. While prewar predictions anticipated synchronised Russian military and cyber operations, these have failed to materialise in a decisive manner. Despite expectations of catastrophic, watershed cyber attacks on critical infrastructure and military or civilian targets, they have not occurred, highlighting the limitations of cyber attacks in achieving strategic military objectives, as they lack the capacity to compel an enemy to surrender or alter its warfighting behaviour.[77]

Both sides have employed AI in various applications, including facial recognition, intelligence gathering (e.g., lateral movements within networks to locate sensitive data and high-value assets), communication interception, encryption, electronic warfare, command-and-control systems for some AWS and as a strategic tool for operation analysis. AI has been used to enhance cyber defence capabilities, threat intelligence and the rapid deployment of protective software to cloud services and computer networks. According to a Microsoft report,[78] Ukraine's use of AI has significantly improved its ability to detect and respond to cyber attacks. AI has also been a tool for producing deepfakes and countering disinformation campaigns.[79]

Finally, it is evident that Russia's poor war planning extended into the cyber domain. Russian attacks on routers, firewalls and email servers, while disruptive, have done little to advance Moscow's strategic objectives. The use of Detect AI, a Russian platform to detect fake content, has been a significant challenge. Moreover, Russia's much-publicised 'battlefield AI' has failed to deliver decisive outcomes on the battlefield, suggesting that the country's capabilities have been overstated and Putin's 'cyber heartland' rhetoric is hollow.

Although the Russia–Ukraine war, including its drone and cyber dimensions, has not become a true AI war, maybe the conflict marks the beginning of an AI-driven RMA. This revolution may diverge from previous RMAs as a growing wave of AI military innovations emerges, driven by actors competing for technological supremacy.

Conclusion

The integration of AI into warfare represents a transformative evolution, progressing from the Gulf War's initial glimpses into cyber assisted operations to the current deployment of autonomous systems. These technologies promise to preserve lives, reduce human risk and prioritise precision and automation over traditional attributes like individual heroism and chance. The war in Ukraine exemplifies this trajectory, demonstrating AI's capacity to enable precise targeting, enhance situational awareness and accelerate decision-making. While these developments reflect the shift from human-controlled to partially autonomous systems, they emphasise AI as a force multiplier, complementing rather than replacing human involvement.

In the cyber domain, the race for technological superiority has reshaped modern conflict, ushering in the algorithmic warfare era. AI has facilitated the development of sophisticated offensive and defensive capabilities, including advanced cyber attack tools, self-replicating malware that adapts to routine network activity and identifies high-value targets, adaptive spear-phishing and deepfake-driven disinformation campaigns. On the defensive side, AI has bolstered automated threat detection, anomaly identification and rapid response. However, this technological arms race also encapsulates the 'capability–vulnerability paradox', wherein advancements not only empower but also introduce exploitable weaknesses.

The AI–cyber nexus further raises critical questions about the future of conflict in cyber space. While there is hope that AI-enhanced cyber operations might resolve disputes and preempt traditional wars by confining hostilities to the digital realm, there is also the looming threat of fully autonomous, AI-driven 'flash wars', in which self-replicating cyber weapons unleash indiscriminate attacks that destabilise global security and erode human oversight.

The Ukraine war provides examples of AI-driven cyber offensive and defensive operations. Especially Russia's persistent cyber aggression has deployed AI-driven disinformation campaigns such as Doppelgänger, in addition to leveraging deepfakes to destabilise political environments and undermine trust. Conversely, Ukraine has countered these threats with tools, including AI algorithms that autonomously detected and blocked Russian wiper malware or employing AI-powered facial recognition as a tool of disinformation warfare.

The war in Ukraine highlights the importance of cyber resilience and strategic cooperation, which enabled Ukraine to sustain key state functions amidst relentless digital assaults, eventually ensuring national sovereignty and security. However, beyond technical capabilities, the rapid evolution of AI in warfare underscores the necessity of a human-centred approach to its governance. Autonomous drones and malware, often offering unparalleled precision and speed, raise ethical and operational concerns, as seen by their inability to interpret human gestures like surrender. Moreover, AI-enhanced disinformation campaigns and FIMI, such as Doppelgänger, involving deepfakes and social media manipulation, amplify threats to cognitive security and integrity,[80] exploiting human vulnerabilities to distort perceptions of reality and polarise societies. Combined with cyber attacks targeting critical infrastructure, such as hospitals and financial systems, these developments jeopardise multiple dimensions of human security – personal, community, economic,[81] health and political,[82] reinforcing the urgent need for frameworks that safeguard cognitive integrity, human rights and societal stability.[83]

Despite these challenges, international regulatory efforts remain fragmented. Recognition from bodies such as the United Nations Development Programme,[84] which identified cyber attacks and AI technology tools as a new threat that could undermine and erode human security, and initiatives, such as the EU's AI Act and the Global Digital Compact,[85] signal progress, yet the absence of comprehensive governance frameworks leaves gaps in addressing the ethical, normative and legal dilemmas posed by AI's rapid proliferation, demanding urgent action to ensure governance frameworks that balance innovation with the protection of fundamental rights and global security.

The Ukraine war serves as both a cautionary tale and a call to action. It highlights AI's potential to enhance both offensive and defensive strategies but also underscores the critical need for a new analytical mindset and robust international cooperation. To mitigate risks, safeguard human security and address the ethical complexities of AI in warfare, a comprehensive, human-centred approach to AI governance is imperative. In an era of rapidly advancing technology, ensuring stability and security requires not only innovation but also a commitment to the principles that underpin human rights, human security and societal well-being.

Notes

1 Arquilla and Ronfeldt claim that cyber war 'refers to conducting, and preparing to conduct, military operations according to information-related principles. It means disrupting if not destroying the information and communications systems, broadly defined to include even military culture, on which an adversary relies in order to "know" itself: who it is, where it is, what it can do when, why it is fighting, which threats to counter first' (30). John Arquilla and David Ronfeldt, 'Cyberwar is coming', *Comparative Strategy* 12:2 (1993), 141–165. https://doi.org/10.1080/01495939308402915
2 Manuel De Landa, *War in the Age of Intelligence Machines* (New York: Zone Books, 1991).
3 Fred Kaplan, *Dark Territory: The Secret History of Cyber War* (New York: Simon & Schuster, 2016).
4 We are assuming the following categorisation of the war/military domains: land, sea, air, outer space, cyber space and cognitive.
5 Can Kasapoğlu and Barış Kırdemir, *Wars Of None: Artificial Intelligence And The Future Of Conflict* (Istanbul: Centre for Economics

and Foreign Policy Studies, 2019). http://www.jstor.org/stable/resrep21050 (accessed 5 February 2026); Can Kasapoğlu and Barış Kırdemir, 'Artificial intelligence and the future of conflict' in Tomás Valášek (ed.), *New Perspectives on Shared Security: NATO's Next 70 Years* (Brussels: Carnegie Europe, 2019) 35–39. https://carnegieeurope.eu/2019/11/28/artificial-intelligence-and-future-of-conflict-pub-80421 (accessed 28 November 2019).

6 Kai-Fu Lee, *AI Superpowers: China, Silicon Valley, and the New World Order* (Boston, MA: Harper Business, 2018).

7 Matthias Schulze and Mika Kerttunen, 'Cyber operations in Russia's war against Ukraine. Uses, limitations, and lessons learned so far', *SWP Comment* March (2023), 1–8. https://doi.org/10.18449/2023C23

8 Christopher Whyte, 'Problems of poison: New paradigms and "agreed" competition in the era of AI-enabled cyber operations', *2020 12th International Conference on Cyber Conflict (CyCon)* 1300 (2020), 215–232. https://doi.org/10.23919/CyCon49761.2020.9131717; James Johnson, 'Artificial intelligence and future warfare: Implications for international security', *Defense & Security Analysis* 35:2 (2019), 147–169. https://doi.org/10.1080/14751798.2019.1600800; James Johnson, 'The AI–cyber nexus: Implications for military escalation, deterrence and strategic stability', *Journal of Cyber Policy* 4:3 (2019), 442–460. https://doi.org/10.1080/23738871.2019.1701693; James Johnson, 'A threat to strategic stability', *Strategic Studies Quarterly* 14:1 (2020), 16–39. https://www.jstor.org/stable/26891882 (accessed 5 February 2026); James Johnson, *Artificial Intelligence and the Future of Warfare: The USA, China, and Strategic Stability* (Manchester: Manchester University Press, 2021); James Johnson, 'Strategic stability: A perfect storm of nuclear risk?' in James Johnson (ed.), *AI and the Bomb: Nuclear Strategy and Risk in the Digital Age* (Oxford: Oxford Academic online edn, 2023), 37–71. https://doi.org/10.1093/oso/9780192858184.003.0002; Michael C. Horowitz, 'Artificial intelligence, international competition, and the balance of power', *Texas National Security Review* 1:3 (2018), 36–57. http://hdl.handle.net/2152/65638 (accessed 5 February 2026); Benjamin M. Jensen, Christopher Whyte and Scott Cuomo, 'Algorithms at war: The promise, peril, and limits of artificial intelligence', *International Studies Review* 22:3 (2020), 526–550. https://doi.org/10.1093/isr/viz025; Ingvild Bode, Hendrik Huelss, Anna Nadibaidze, Guangyu Qiao-Franco and Tom Watts, 'Algorithmic

warfare: Taking stock of a research programme', *Global Society* 38:1 (2024), 1–23. https://doi.org/10.1080/13600826.2023.2263473; Martin C. Libicki, 'Correlations between cyberspace attacks and kinetic attacks', *2020 12th International Conference on Cyber Conflict (CyCon)* 1300 (2020), 199–213. https://api.semanticscholar.org/CorpusID:220367274 (accessed 5 February 2026); Nori Katagiri, 'Artificial intelligence and cross-domain warfare: Balance of power and unintended escalation', *Global Society* 38:1 (2024), 34–48. https://doi.org/10.1080/13600826.2023.2248179; Kirsi Helkala, James Cook, George Lucas, Frank Pasquale, Gregory Reichberg and Henrik Syse, 'AI in cyber operations: Ethical and legal considerations for end-users' in Tuomo Sipola, Tero Kokkonen and Mila Karjalainen (eds), *Artificial Intelligence and Cybersecurity: Theory and Applications* (Cham: Springer, 2023) 185–206. https://www.prio.org/publications/13384 (accessed 5 February 2026); Mariarosaria Taddeo, David McNeish, Alexander Blanchard and Elizabeth Edgar, 'Ethical principles for artificial intelligence in the defence domain', in Fabio Cristiano, Dennis Broeders, François Delerue, Frédérick Douzet and Aude Géry (eds), *Artificial Intelligence and International Conflict in Cyberspace* (London: Routledge, 2023), 159–185. https://doi.org/10.4324/9781003284093; Mariarosaria Taddeo, 'Three ethical challenges of applications of artificial intelligence in cybersecurity', *Minds and Machines* 29:2 (2019), 187–191. https://doi.org/10.1007/s11023-019-09504-8; Lucas Kello, 'Cyber legalism: Why it fails and what to do about it', *Journal of Cybersecurity* 7:1 (2021), tyab014. https://doi.org/10.1093/cybsec/tyab014; Jensen Whyte and Andrew C. Dwyer, 'The unknowable conflict: Tracing AI, recognition, and the death of the (human) loop', in Fabio Cristiano, Dennis Broeders, François Delerue, Frédérick Douzet and Aude Géry (eds), *Artificial Intelligence and International Conflict in Cyberspace* (London: Routledge, 2024), 19–46; Lance Y. Hunter, Craig D. Albert, Josh Rutland, Kristen Topping and Christopher Hennigan, 'Artificial intelligence and information warfare in major power states: How the US, China, and Russia are using artificial intelligence in their information warfare and influence operations', *Defense & Security Analysis* 40:2 (2024), 235–269. https://doi.org/10.1080/14751798.2024.2321736; Anthony King, 'Digital targeting: Artificial intelligence, data, and military intelligence', *Journal of Global Security Studies* 9:2 (2024), ogae009. https://doi.org/10.1093/jogss/ogae009

9 Thomas Reinhold and Christian Reuter, 'Cyber weapons and artificial intelligence: Impact, influence and the challenges for arms control' in Thomas Reinhold and Niklas Schörnig (eds), *Armament, Arms Control and Artificial Intelligence: The Janus-Faced Nature of Machine Learning in the Military Realm* (Cham: Springer International Publishing, 2022), 145–158.

10 Cameran Ashraf, 'Defining cyberwar: Towards a definitional framework', *Defense & Security Analysis* 37:3 (2021), 274–294. https://doi.org/10.1080/14751798.2021.1959141

11 Paul Scharre, 'Debunking the AI arms race theory', *Texas National Security Review* 4:3 (2021), 121–132. http://dx.doi.org/10.26153/tsw/13985

12 Peter Apps, 'Commentary: Are China, Russia winning the AI arms race?', *Reuters* (2019). https://www.reuters.com/article/us-apps-ai-commentary/commentary-are-china-russia-winning-the-ai-arms-race-idUSKCN1P91NM/ (accessed 5 February 2026).

13 Mohammad Eslami and Alena Vysotskaya Guedes Vieira (eds), *The Arms Race in the Middle East: Contemporary Security Dynamics* (Cham: Springer International Publishing, 2023).

14 Tim Hwang and Alex Pascal, 'Artificial intelligence isn't an arms race', *Foreign Policy* (2019). https://foreignpolicy.com/2019/12/11/artificial-intelligence-ai-not-arms-race-china-united-states/ (accessed 5 February 2026); Scharre, 'Debunking the AI arms race theory'.

15 Mohammad Eslami and Alena Vysotskaya Guedes Vieira, 'Introducing the arms race in the Middle East in the twenty first century: A "powder keg" in the digital era?', in Mohammad Eslami and Alena Vysotskaya Guedes Vieira (eds), *The Arms Race in the Middle East: Contemporary Security Dynamics* (Cham: Springer International Publishing, 2023), 3–13.

16 Raluca Csernatoni, 'Beyond the hype: The EU and the AI global "arms race"', *Carnegie Europe* (2019). https://carnegieendowment.org/posts/2019/08/beyond-the-hype-the-eu-and-the-ai-global-arms-race?lang=en (accessed 5 February 2026); Mohammad Eslami, Nasim Sadat Mosavi and Muhammed Can, 'Sino–Iranian cooperation in artificial intelligence: A potential countering against the US hegemony', in Paulo Duarte, Francisco Leandro and Enrique Galán (eds), *The Palgrave Handbook of Globalization with Chinese Characteristics: The Case of the Belt and Road Initiative* (Singapore:

Springer Nature Singapore, 2023), 543–559; Hwang and Pascal, 'Artificial intelligence isn't an arms race'.

17 Kai-Fu Lee, *AI Superpowers*.

18 Radina Gigova, 'Who Vladimir Putin thinks will rule the world', *CNN News* (2017). https://edition.cnn.com/2017/09/01/world/putin-artificial-intelligence-will-rule-world/index.html (accessed 5 February 2026). This is in addition to the increasing importance of the cyber dimensions of strategic partnerships. Maria Papageorgiou and Mohammad Eslami, 'Strategic partnerships and the promotion of bilateralism: The case of Sino-Russian relationship', in Yichao Li, Francisco Leandro, Jorge Tavares da Silva and Carlos Rodrigues (eds), *The Palgrave Handbook on China–Europe–Africa Relations* (Singapore: Palgrave Macmillan, 2024). https://doi.org/10.1007/978-981-97-5640-7_6

19 H. J. Mackinder, 'The geographical pivot of history', *The Geographical Journal* 23:4 (1904), 421–437. https://doi.org/10.2307/1775498

20 We propose the conceptualisation of cyber capabilities in a tripartite framework, including human expertise, knowledge/intelligence and infrastructure. Human expertise involves professionals' specialised knowledge and skills, such as ethical hackers, cryptographers and software developers, essential for crafting and executing effective cyber strategies. Knowledge/intelligence focuses on acquiring and analysing information regarding potential vulnerabilities, malware signatures, threat actor behaviours and network traffic patterns, which are vital for enhancing threat detection, risk assessment and system optimisation. Infrastructure includes advanced technological tools, such as firewalls, security information and event management (SIEM) systems and intrusion detection/prevention systems (IDS/IPS) for real-time threat monitoring, while also relying on high-performance computing (HPC) resources, which support brute-force testing, vulnerability scanning, deep-packet inspection and large-scale simulations.

21 Before the surge of AI enthusiasm, a body of investigative journalism highlighted concerns about a looming cyber arms race, framing it as a trajectory towards catastrophic global consequences; Chris Miller, *Chip War: The Quest to Dominate the World's Most Critical Technology* (New York: Simon & Schuster, 2022); Nicole Perlroth, *This is How They Tell Me the World Ends: The Cyberweapons Arms Race* (London: Bloomsbury Publishing, 2021); David E. Sanger, *The Perfect*

Weapon: War, Sabotage and Fear in the Cyber Age (Melbourne: Scribe, 2018); Adam Segal, *Hacked World Order: How Nations Fight, Trade, Manoeuvre, and Manipulate in the Digital Age* (New York: PublicAffairs, 2016); Edward Moore Geist, 'It's already too late to stop the AI arms race – we must manage it instead', *Bulletin of the Atomic Scientists* 72:5 (2016), 318–321. https://doi.org/10.1080/00963402.2016.1216672; Michael T. Klare, 'AI arms race gains speed', *Arms Control Today* 49:2 (2019), 35. https://www.jstor.org/stable/26633411 (accessed 5 February 2026).

22 Mohammad Eslami, Alena Vieira, Arshin Adib-Moghaddam, Lauro Borges, Maria Papageorgiou, Fabio Cristiano, Ibrahim Al-Marashi, Tom Sauer and Christian Kaunert, 'The geopolitics of AI-driven arms races', *Geopolitics* (2025), 1–43.

23 Ingvild Bode and Hendrik Huelss, *Autonomous Weapons Systems and International Norms* (Montreal: McGill-Queen's University Press, 2019); Nick Bostrom, *Superintelligence: Paths, Dangers, Strategies* (Oxford: Oxford University Press, 2014).

24 The Bletchley Declaration by Countries Attending the AI Safety Summit, November 1–2, 2023. https://www.gov.uk/government/publications/ai-safety-summit-2023-the-bletchley-declaration/the-bletchley-declaration-by-countries-attending-the-ai-safety-summit-1-2-november-2023 (accessed 6 February 2026).

25 China endorsed the declaration, which contained the statement: 'We appreciate the global community's endeavours thus far to collaborate on AI to advance inclusive economic growth, sustainable development, and innovation, to safeguard human rights and basic freedoms, and to cultivate public trust and confidence in AI systems to fully unlock their potential'. *The Guardian*, 'UK, US, EU and China sign declaration of AI's "catastrophic danger"' (2023). https://www.theguardian.com/technology/2023/nov/01/uk-us-eu-and-china-sign-declaration-of-ais-catastrophic-danger?utm_source=substack&utm_medium=email (accessed 5 February 2026).

26 *Reuters*, 'G7 industry ministers agree to cooperate on AI, supply chains, presidency says' (2024). https://www.reuters.com/world/g7-agreed-align-rules-ai-italian-presidency-says-2024-03-14/?utm_source=substack&utm_medium=email (accessed 5 February 2026).

27 UN document A/78/L.49 'Seizing the opportunities of safe, secure and trustworthy artificial intelligence systems for sustainable development', 11 March 2024. https://undocs.org/Home/Mobile

?FinalSymbol=A%2F78%2FL.49&Language=E&DeviceType=Desktop&LangRequested=False (accessed 5 February 2026).

28 Chase Cunningham, *Cyber Warfare – Truth, Tactics and Strategies* (Birmingham: Packt Publishing Ltd, 2020).

29 John Arquilla, *Bitskrieg: The New Challenge of Cyberwafare* (Cambridge: John Wiley & Sons, 2021).

30 Joe Burton and Simona R. Soare, 'Understanding the strategic implications of the weaponization of Artificial Intelligence', *2019 11th International Conference on Cyber Conflict (CyCon), NATO Cooperative Cyber Defence Centre of Excellence* (2019), 1–17. https://doi.org/10.23919/CYCON.2019.8756866

31 Donyae Johnson, Katie Kline and Marco Salvo, 'How artificial intelligence and quantum computing are evolving cyber warfare', *IWP – Institute of World Politics* (2019). https://www.iwp.edu/cyber-intelligence-initiative/2019/03/27/how-artificial-intelligence-and-quantum-computing-are-evolving-cyber-warfare/ (accessed 5 February 2026); Ronald J. Deibert and Louis W. Pauly, 'Mutual entanglement and complex sovereignty in cyberspace', in Didier Bigo, Engin Isin and Evelyn Ruppert (eds), *Data Politics: Worlds, Subjects, Rights* (London: Routledge, 2019), 81–99.

32 Matthias Schulze and Mika Kerttunen, 'Cyber operations in Russia's war against Ukraine: Uses, limitations, and lessons learned so far' (No. 23/2023), SWP Comment.

33 Raphael Satter, 'Microsoft says it caught hackers from China, Russia and Iran using its AI tools', *Reuters* (2024). https://www.reuters.com/technology/cybersecurity/microsoft-says-it-caught-hackers-china-russia-iran-using-its-ai-tools-2024-02-14/ (accessed 5 February 2026).

34 Kasapoğlu and Kırdemir, 'Wars of none'; Louise Amoore and Rita Raley, 'Securing with algorithms: Knowledge, decision, sovereignty', *Security Dialogue* 48:1 (2016), 3–10. https://doi.org/10.1177/0967010616680753; Lucy Suchman, 'Algorithmic warfare and the reinvention of accuracy', *Critical Studies on Security* 8:2 (2020), 175–187. https://doi.org/10.1080/21624887.2020.1760587; Lucas Kello, *The Virtual Weapon and International Order* (New Haven, CT: Yale University Press, 2017). https://doi.org/10.2307/j.ctt1trkjd1.18; Kello, 'Cyber legalism'.

35 Kasapoğlu and Kırdemir, 'Wars of none', 'Artificial intelligence and the future of conflict'; Amoore and Raley, 'Securing with

algorithms'; Suchman, 'Algorithmic warfare and the reinvention of accuracy'; Kello, *The Virtual Weapon and International Order*; Kello, 'Cyber legalism'.

36 As Waltzman argues, 'cognitive security' is one of the new multi-sectoral fields in which actors engage in 'a continual arms race to influence – and protect from influence large groups of people online' (7). Rand Waltzman, *The Weaponization of Information: The Need for Cognitive Security* (Santa Monica, CA: RAND Corporation, 2017). https://doi.org/10.7249/CT473

37 Muhammad Mudassar Yamin, Ullah Mohib, Ullah Habib and Basel Katt, 'Weaponized AI for cyber attacks', *Journal of Information Security and Applications* 57:102722 (2021). https://doi.org/10.1016/j.jisa.2020.102722

38 Burton and Soare, *Emerging Technologies and International Security*.

39 Nicole Kobi, 'To cripple AI, hackers are turning data against Iiself', *WIRED* (2018). https://www.wired.com/story/artificial-intelligence-hacking-machine-learning-adversarial/ (accessed 5 February 2026).

40 Jacquelyn Schneider, 'Digitally-enabled warfare: The capability-vulnerability paradox' (2016). https://www.cnas.org/publications/reports/digitally-enabled-warfare-the-capability-vulnerability-paradox (accessed 5 February 2026).

41 Johnson, 'Artificial intelligence and future warfare'; Katagiri, 'Artificial intelligence and cross-domain warfare'; San Murugesan, 'The AI-cybersecurity nexus: The good and the evil', *IT Professional* 24:5 (2022), 4–8. https://doi.org/10.1109/MITP.2022.3205529

42 Johnson, 'Artificial intelligence and future warfare'; Johnson, 'The AI-cyber nexus'; Gregory C. Allen and Taniel Chan, 'Artificial intelligence and national security', *Bulletin of the Atomic Scientists* 74:2 (2018), 123–130. https://thebulletin.org/2018/02/artificial-intelligence-and-national-security/ (accessed 5 February 2026); Gregory M. Reichberg, Henrik Syse, Kirsi Helkala, James Cook, George R. Lucas Jr. and Frank Pasquale, 'AI in cyber operations: Ethical and legal considerations for end-users', in Tuomo Sipola, Tero Kokkonen and Mika Karjalainen (eds), *Artificial Intelligence and Cybersecurity: Theory and Applications* (Cham: Springer, 2023), 185–206.

43 The AI-cyber nexus will facilitate the convergence and application of emergent technologies in warfare such as AR/VR 3D printing, that could help in training and simulating operations and used in wargaming.

44 Ilan Levy, *Active Cyber Defence: One Year On* (London: National Cyber Security Centre, 2018). https://www.ncsc.gov.uk/files/ACD%20-%20one%20year%20on_0.pdf (accessed 5 February 2026).

45 Csernatoni, 'Beyond the hype'; Scharre, 'Debunking the AI arms race theory'; Horowitz, 'Artificial intelligence, international competition, and the balance of power'; Johnson, 'Artificial intelligence and future warfare'; Johnson, 'The AI-cyber nexus'.

46 Jim Masters, 'Russia invades Ukraine: Kinetic warfare and cyber-attack timeline', *MSSPs Alert* (2024). https://www.msspalert.com/news/ukraine-russia-cyberattack-timeline-updates-amid-russia-invasion (accessed 5 February 2026).

47 Marcus Willett, 'The cyber dimension of the Russia–Ukraine war', *Survival* 64:5 (2022), 7–26. https://doi.org/10.1080/00396338.2022.2126193

48 Robin Fontes and Jorrit Kamminga, 'Ukraine a living lab for AI warfare', *National Defense* (2023). https://www.nationaldefensemagazine.org/articles/2023/3/24/ukraine-a-living-lab-for-ai-warfare (accessed 5 February 2026).

49 Brad Smith, 'Defending Ukraine: Early lessons from the cyber war', *Microsoft* (2022). https://blogs.microsoft.com/on-the-issues/2022/06/22/defending-ukraine-early-lessons-from-the-cyber-war/ (accessed 5 February 2026).

50 Perlroth, *This is How They Tell Me the World Ends.*

51 *Cyber Peace Institute*, 'Cyber Dimensions of the Armed Conflict in Ukraine Quarterly Analysis Report July to September 2023'. https://cyberconflicts.cyberpeaceinstitute.org/report (accessed 5 February 2026).

52 Kier Giles, *Handbook of Russian Information Warfare* (Rome: NATO Defense College, 2016), 7–8.

53 Max Hunder, Jonathan Landay and Stefaniia Bern, 'Ukraine's top mobile operator hit by biggest cyberattack of war', *Reuters* (2023). https://www.reuters.com/technology/cybersecurity/ukraines-biggest-mobile-operator-suffers-massive-hacker-attack-statement-2023-12-12/ (accessed 5 February 2026).

54 Thomas Brewster, 'Most severe cyberattack since Russian invasion crashes Ukraine internet provider', *Forbes* (2022). https://www.forbes.com/sites/thomasbrewster/2022/03/28/huge-cyberattack-on-ukrtelecom-biggest-since-russian-invasion-crashes-ukraine-telecom/ (accessed 5 February 2026).

55 Tom Balmforth, 'Exclusive: Russian hackers were inside Ukraine telecoms giant for months', *Reuters* (2024). https://www.reuters.com/world/europe/russian-hackers-were-inside-ukraine-telecoms-giant-months-cyber-spy-chief-2024-01-04/ (accessed 5 February 2026).

56 Nikolai Antoniadis, Sophia Baumann and Christo Buschek et al., '"The Vulcan Files": A look inside Putin's secret plans for cyber-warfare', *Spiegel International* (2023). https://www.spiegel.de/international/world/the-vulkan-files-a-look-inside-putin-s-secret-plans-for-cyber-warfare-a-4324e76f-cb20-4312-96c8-1101c5655236 (accessed 5 February 2026).

57 *The Economist*, 'Lessons from Russia's cyber-war in Ukraine' (2022). https://www.economist.com/science-and-technology/2022/11/30/lessons-from-russias-cyber-war-in-ukraine (accessed 5 February 2026).

58 An archive of Russian FIMI operations regarding the war in Ukraine can be found here: https://www.stopfake.org/en/main/ (accessed 5 February 2026).

59 Ravie Lakshmanan, 'Russia's AI-powered disinformation operation targeting Ukraine, U.S., and Germany', *The Hacker News* (2024). https://thehackernews.com/2023/12/russias-ai-powered-disinformation.html (accessed 5 February 2026); Thomas Rid, 'The Lies Russia Tells Itself', *Foreign Affairs* (2024). https://www.foreignaffairs.com/united-states/lies-russia-tells-itself (accessed 5 February 2026).

60 Inskit Group, 'Obfuscation and AI content in the Russian influence network "Doppelgänger" signals evolving tactics', *Recorded Future Insikt Group* (2023). https://www.recordedfuture.com/research/russian-influence-network-doppelgangers-ai-content-tactics (accessed 5 February 2026).

61 Margarita Konaev, *Tomorrow's Technology in Today's War: The Use of AI and Autonomous Technologies in the War in Ukraine and Implications for Strategic Stability* (Washington, DC: Center for Naval Analyses, 2023). https://www.cna.org/reports/2023/10/ai-and-autonomous-technologies-in-the-war-in-ukraine (accessed 5 February 2026).

62 Smith, 'Defending Ukraine'.

63 Jane Wakefield, 'Deepfake presidents used in Russia–Ukraine war', *BBC Technology* (2022). https://www.bbc.com/news/technology-60780142 (accessed 5 February 2026).

64 Robyn Dixon, 'Ukraine turns to Clearview AI to identify dead Russian soldiers and notify their families', *Time* (2023). https://time.com/6334176/ukraine-clearview-ai-russia (accessed 5 February 2026).

65 AI was also used to identify (198) Ukrainian children abducted from Ukraine to Russia. Ukraine's current efforts are geared towards using AI to establish a competitive edge vis-a-vis Russia. Vitaliy Goncharuk, 'Survivel of smartest? Defense AI in Ukraine', *Defense AI* (2024). https://defenseai.eu/wp-content/uploads/2024/02/daio_study2422_survival_of_the_smartest_vitaliy_goncharuk.pdf (accessed 5 February 2026).

66 *Time*, 'How tech giants turned Ukraine into an AI war lab' (2024). https://time.com/6691662/ai-ukraine-war-palantir/ (accessed 5 February 2026).

67 David Kirichenko, 'Belarus cyber partisans prepare for uprising', *Center for European Policy Analysis (CEPA)* (2024). https://cepa.org/article/belarus-cyber-partisans-prepare-for-uprising/ (accessed 5 February 2026).

68 Sam Bendett, 'Roles and implications of AI in the Russian-Ukrainian conflict', *Russia Matters* (2023). https://www.russiamatters.org/analysis/roles-and-implications-ai-russian-ukrainian-conflict (accessed 5 February 2026).

69 *Microsoft*, 'How technology helped Ukraine resist during wartime' (2023). https://news.microsoft.com/en-cee/2023/01/20/how-technology-helped-ukraine-resist-during-wartime/ (accessed 5 February 2026).

70 Cate Burgan, 'Lessons from Ukraine: NSA cyber chief lauds industry intel', *MeriTalk* (2022). https://www.meritalk.com/articles/lessons-from-ukraine-nsa-cyber-chief-lauds-industry-intel/ (accessed 5 February 2026).

71 Schulze and Kerttunen, 'Cyber operations in Russia's war against Ukraine'.

72 Mohammad Eslami and Lauro Borges, *The Drones Race and International Security* (Cham: Springer International Publishing, 2025).

73 Artem, 'FPV interceptions of Russian UAVs: A new era of aerial combat' (2024). https://tochnyi.info/2024/11/fpv-interceptors-2024/ (accessed 5 February 2026).

74 *Defense Express*, 'Ukrainian forces get an AI-powered saker scout drone, and its algorithms can solve an important problem' (2023).

https://en.defence-ua.com/weapon_and_tech/ukrainian_forces_get_an_ai_powered_saker_scout_drone_and_its_algorithms_can_solve_an_important_problem-7842.html (accessed 5 February 2026).

75 *The Economist*, 'How Ukraine Uses Cheap AI – Guided Drones to Deadly Effect against Russia' (2024). https://www.economist.com/europe/2024/12/02/how-ukraine-uses-cheap-ai-guided-drones-to-deadly-effect-against-russia (accessed 2 February 2025).

76 Max Hunder, '"War of robots": How 1,000 days of Russia's invasion of Ukraine spurred an automation boom' (2024). https://www.reuters.com/world/europe/how-1000-days-conflict-fuelled-robot-wars-between-russia-ukraine-2024-11-18/ (accessed 5 February 2026).

77 Robin Fontes and Jorrit Kamminga, 'Ukraine a living lab for AI warfare', *The Economist* (2024). https://www.economist.com/europe/2024/12/02/how-ukraine-uses-cheap-ai-guided-drones-to-deadly-effect-against-russia (accessed 5 February 2026).

78 Smith, 'Defending Ukraine'.

79 Olena Churanova, 'Russian AI-generated propaganda to pose more problems for Ukraine', *Euractiv* (2022). https://www.euractiv.com/section/global-europe/news/russian-ai-generated-propaganda-to-pose-more-problems-for-ukraine (accessed 5 February 2026).

80 Janne Hakala and Jazlyn Melnychuk, *Russia's Strategy in Cyberspace* (Riga: NATO Strategic Communications, 2021). https://stratcomcoe.org/cuploads/pfiles/Nato-Cyber-Report_11-06-2021-4f4ce.pdf (accessed 5 February 2026).

81 Economic security is associated with sustaining a decent standard of living with access to essential resources, income and economic opportunities, while health security is associated with the access to healthcare services and secure health infrastructure: Commission on Human Security, *Human Security Now* (Washington, DC: Communications Development Inc., 2003). https://digitallibrary.un.org/record/503749/files/Humansecuritynow.pdf (accessed 5 February 2026).

82 Arshin Adib-Moghaddam (ed.), *Is Artificial Intelligence Racist? The Ethics of AI and the Future of Humanity* (London: Bloomsbury Publishing, 2023).

83 Human security comprises seven dimensions of daily life areas, namely the economic, food, health, environmental, personal, community and political. Personal security: physical safety and

protection against violence, crime and human rights abuses. Community security: fostering a safe and inclusive community and protection against ethnic tensions and violent conflicts. Political security: protection of human rights, democratic governance and the rule of law. Commission on Human Security, *Human Security Now: Commission on Human Security* (Washington, DC: Communications Development Inc., 2003). https://digitallibrary.un.org/record/503749?v=pdf (accessed 5 February 2026).

84 United Nations Development Programme (UNDP), *New Threats to Human Security in the Anthropocene: Demanding Greater Solidarity* (New York: UNDP, 2022). https://hs.hdr.undp.org/part-2.html (accessed 5 February 2026).

85 Hendrik Huelss, 'Norms are what machines make of them: Autonomous weapons systems and the normative implications of human-machine interactions', *International Political Sociology* 14:2 (2020), 111–128. https://doi.org/10.1093/ips/olz023

3

Information apocalypse: merging AI and quantum in psychological operations

Muhammed Can and Helin Yontar

Introduction

The significance of technology for humanity has evolved considerably over the past decade, especially with the advent of emerging technologies that have introduced tools simplifying the daily lives of societies. In the same vein, from the eolithic era to the present, technologies that have been integral to daily human life have either undergone significant evolution or have become obsolete. For instance, the adoption of bronze and iron not only had social and political ramifications but also led to the creation of new specialisations and the discovery of new explorations.[1] This, in turn, enabled humankind to develop new tools and vehicles, marking a pivotal moment in technological advancement. In principle, the technological experience of humankind today mirrors that of the eolithic ages, characterised by a constant evolution and the production of new types of outputs facilitated by emerging technologies. Therefore, few would challenge the assertion that emerging technologies are profoundly transforming every facet of what is considered normal, from the daily lives of societies to international trade and military operations. This evolution has been anticipated, to a degree, in light of the exponential growth in data, advancements in computing power and the realisation of sophisticated algorithms.[2] Indeed, the consequences of this transformation have far-reaching effects on global politics, including the shaping of election campaigns through artificial intelligence-based (AI) tools and the utilisation of large language models (LLMs) in the online information ecosystem, such as social media. These AI technologies provide more precise and nimble solutions than any human could possibly achieve, profoundly shifting the landscape of digital communication and the political strategies of state and non-state actors that could be seen in almost decade-old global strategies to tame AI development.[3] Simultaneously, the proliferation of emerging technologies, especially AI, strengthens individuals' capacity to generate more content, thereby enhancing their output and, to some extent, accelerating their productivity. In his influential work, Mustafa Suleyman contends that the swift dissemination of emerging technologies, categorised as general purpose technologies (GPTs), is an inevitable result of the dramatic decrease in development costs. Indeed, this trend not only transforms potential users into what he terms 'homo technologicus' but also renders traditional policies aimed at curbing their exponential proliferation ineffective, ultimately challenging existing regulatory frameworks and societal norms.[4]

Yet, as these technologies diffuse rapidly through various application programming interfaces (APIs), new threats are emerging, especially within information ecosystems. These include the widespread dissemination of disinformation, more potent influence campaigns and AI-based social engineering attacks, which are increasingly becoming integral components of contemporary psychological operations (PsyOps).[5] Similar to AI, quantum computing holds significant promise as a transformative force in the way the internet functions. However, its development is characterised by complex processes, and the widespread adoption and practical application of these technologies have yet to be realised.[6] Should quantum computing become more accessible for general use, thereby attaining the status of a GPT, it could have significant implications for global politics and security, despite arguments to the contrary.[7] This is partly due to the evolving encryption standards in internet communication, which will, indeed, lay the groundwork for new quantum-based algorithms.[8] Simultaneously, the progression of quantum computing is set to bolster the capabilities of threat actors, encompassing both state and state-backed criminal groups such as advanced persistent threats (APTs).[9] This suggests that advancements in AI and quantum computing are likely to escalate the ongoing technological competition among states, particularly within the information ecosystem, due to the rapid diffusion and generation of vast amounts of information.[10]

In this context, this chapter aims to explore the following question: how might advancements in AI and quantum computing shift the information ecosystem, particularly in the context of PsyOps carried out by both state and non-state actors? To address the question posed, we first examine the recent surge in information generation or, more specifically, the production of AI-based information within the digital realm. We then argue that the widespread adoption of quantum computing could significantly escalate the frequency and sophistication of disinformation campaigns. Subsequently, we explore how AI-based tools, including LLMs and other machine learning (ML) models, could be exploited by threat actors in PsyOps and disinformation campaigns, which, at the end of the day, is likely to accelerate the escalation of the digital arms race in the foreseeable future.[11]

Dawn of AI-based information ecosystems

In recent years, countries have found themselves grappling with a host of multi-faceted challenges, including but not limited to cyber assaults, the dissemination of misinformation, disinformation, political and social upheaval and the exploitation of internal tensions. These have a critical impact on the realm of information operations, a tool extensively used by all types of entities, to shape public opinion, eroding trust in media and institutions, casting doubt on political figures, creating problems on societal divisions and ultimately influencing over the decision-making processes of the electorate.

These challenges arise as a result of an expanding digital landscape, fuelled by the rapid integration of cutting-edge technologies. AI, as one of them, has advanced quickly, leading to the creation of LLM products such as ChatGPT and BARD. These models are very big and learn from a lot of data to generate complex text, including essays, stories and even computer code as well as images, sounds and many more. This blurs the line between human and machine; writing and creating images and music; raising new questions and ethical issues that need careful thought.[12] The fast progress of these models has raised concerns about how they might be misused.

Their ability to generate output that looks like it was created by a human has implications in many areas.

While the propagation of online misinformation is not a new phenomenon, the swift evolution of information technologies, particularly the widespread utilisation of AI, has revolutionised the creation and dissemination of information, including disinformation.

Despite the numerous advantages of AI-driven systems, they also introduce numerous ethical dilemmas to human rights and democratic processes. Concerns voiced by experts include algorithmic bias leading to discriminatory outcomes, such as racial or gender biases, personalised content potentially fostering informational tunnel vision (referred to as the filter bubble), infringements upon user privacy, susceptibility to user manipulation and unauthorised manipulation of video and audio content.

Simultaneously, while evaluating AI technology, it is imperative to acknowledge the root of the problems. An example of that is the built-in biases ingrained within human nature. Human judgement and decision-making processes are susceptible to various cognitive, perceptual and motivational biases. Researchers such as Hilke Shellman, the author of *The Algorithm*, conduct valuable research on AI use in hiring and AI bias. However, while acknowledging the presence of bias in the judgement of others, they often overlook their own biases.[13] Apart from the general inclination towards self-enhancement, two primary factors contribute to this phenomenon known as the 'bias blind spot'.

First, individuals tend to rely heavily on introspective evidence when evaluating their biases, despite biases often operating unconsciously. Second, there is a prevalent belief among individuals that their perceptions directly mirror reality, leading them to perceive those who hold different views as biased. This tendency to deny personal bias while recognising bias in others underscores a significant deficiency in self-awareness, with far-reaching implications for interpersonal and intergroup conflicts.[14] Understanding the distinction is vital, especially in cases regarding disinformation and misinformation. AI's impact is significant due to its ability to amplify information at an unprecedented scale, serving as a catalyst rather than the root cause of the problem.

While recognising the dual nature of AI applications, it is significant to explore the potential of AI in the online misinformation and disinformation context while also looking into the constraints and risks of AI usage techniques. Looking at various solutions and potential advancements in AI could help mitigate the threat of disinformation fuelled by AI technology, thereby contributing to the ongoing discourse surrounding the intersection of technology, democracy and information integrity.

Risks and opportunities of AI usage in information ecosystems

The use of AI in information systems poses significant risks that require meticulous oversight. One major concern among the public is that AI can perpetuate biases present in the data it learns from, increasing the likelihood of unfair outcomes such as discriminatory decision-making or unequal treatment based on sensitive attributes such as race, gender or socioeconomic status. There is also the risk of AI inadvertently spreading inaccurate or misleading information if it fails to verify facts properly. Another issue is the potential for AI to rapidly generate and disseminate low-quality or deceptive content, eroding trust in information sources. Ethical considerations arise regarding how AI selects content for users, including concerns about privacy and fairness.

It is noteworthy that the majority of the issues leading to these risks remain deeply embedded within human activity. This technology can also assist in improving how we handle information and address areas in which human biases may already be present. To go a bit deeper into this topic, it is important to note that access to information is vital for building inclusive knowledge societies. It is possible to argue that the imperative of preserving cultural and linguistic diversity can be a strategic measure for ensuring the sustained realisation of favourable outcomes.[15]

According to the latest estimates, 328.77 million terabytes of data are created each day.[16] It is very important to use AI to turn this amount of data into valuable information. However, there is a digital divide due to unequal socioeconomic conditions limiting communication, particularly in rural or economically disadvantaged areas, where access to high-speed internet and technological devices may be limited or non-existent. Disparities in education and digital literacy further compound the problem, as individuals who lack the necessary skills and knowledge may struggle to make use of available technologies effectively. Access to information is not only a crucial analytical framework but can also have a significant influence on the decision-making processes of people.

Keeping people uninformed, especially in underprivileged communities, can serve as a means of control. Modern digital technology, with its capability to store and process vast amounts of data quickly, holds the potential to bridge this gap and provide universal access to information, particularly during crises.

Understanding how we approach data, either as information or infrastructure or, as mentioned above, a control mechanism is key. Data might help to grasp issues such as poverty, hunger and education, aiding in sustainable development planning that should pave the way for promoting a fair opportunity society. While social systems have different mechanisms to process this data and provide information to their members, AI has changed how information is created and shared to create easier access and relevant information for everyone.[17] Nevertheless, AI is not always used in creating easier and better access to information at all times; it can also become a strong tool in deceiving people's perception of events.

The twisting of truth has been a recurring issue throughout history. Take *damnatio memoriae*, for example, in which people were deliberately erased from historical records – something that started back in Ancient Egypt. But now, with the rapid advancements in information and communication technologies, producing misleading information has become almost effortless, as it can take seconds to create. The misinformation can spread like wildfire, thanks to its easy dissemination through various channels, including the use of AI techniques.

Before going any deeper into this topic, it is possible to argue that our perception and understanding of the term are the same. Disinformation, as commonly understood, refers to false, inaccurate or misleading information shared with the intent to deceive the recipient. An example of this can be the use of deepfakes and robocalls (i.e., telemarketing, scams, political calls, healthcare scams, utility scams, phishing attempts and debt collection efforts). This is distinguished from misinformation, which is false or misleading information shared unintentionally, such as a forwarded WhatsApp message suggesting that drinking warm water with lemon juice can cure cancer. The rise of new digital technology and social media has significantly increased the creation and spread of both mis- and disinformation. However, it is primarily disinformation that has been identified as a significant threat by European Union (EU) institutions, prompting legislative and technical interventions. The focus on this aspect comes from the manipulative nature of disinformation and the urgent requirement to safeguard fundamental rights and freedoms, particularly the freedom of expression and information. However, tackling this challenge is quite complex.

Numerous initiatives worldwide are actively working to combat disinformation. According to recent data from the Duke Reporters' Lab, there are currently 437 fact-checking projects operating across more than 60 countries.[18] Historically, fact-checking has heavily relied on manual verification methods, with human intervention being the primary means to ascertain the accuracy of information. However, with the exponential growth of disinformation, manual fact-checking is increasingly seen as inadequate and inefficient in evaluating the vast volume of information circulating online. Consequently, there has been a growing interest in automating the process of online fact-checking, with initial proposals for AI-assisted fact-checking emerging approximately a decade ago. Interest in this area further surged following significant events such as the election of US President Donald Trump, underscoring the urgency and importance of developing AI-powered solutions for fact-checking.[19]

Various organisations, including the EU, African Union (AU), Federal Trade Commission (FTC), United Nations (UN) AI Advisory Body and the State Council in China, among others, have undertaken efforts concerning AI regulation. Meanwhile, companies are developing AI technologies to facilitate both textual and visual content generation. Since the Turing test was introduced in 1950, there has been significant debate about distinguishing between human and machine conversational partners. LLMs such as GPT-3, GPT-4, LamDA, PaLM, Gopher and others have demonstrated the ability to generate language that significantly resembles human speech, especially in limited conversational contexts. Today, chatbots are capable of performing tasks such as ordering food or providing advice in fields such as medicine and law. However, existing regulations primarily focus on disclosing the commercial use of chatbots to customers, without mandating a technical means to differentiate between machine-generated and human-generated language.

Digital watermarking has been proposed as a solution to the problem of copyright protection of multimedia documents in networked environments throughout the years. This suggestion, in the past, made it possible to tightly associate a code (called a watermark) to an image allowing the identification of the data creator, owner and many others.[20] The overall goal here has been to protect the intellectual property of the personal output. A similar logic is being implemented, as a system is being tested out by tech companies and organisations today, and there is an effort in creating tools that can identify both AI-created images and text.

This necessity stems from the inherently asemantic nature of LLMs and the potential for humans to ascribe emotional and cognitive attributes to machines, which could easily lead to manipulation, the spread of misinformation or emotional distress. Establishing this differentiation between human-created and AI-created output calls for subtle yet easily identifiable markers denoting the machine's origin. One suggested approach involves implementing a code based on equidistant letter sequences. While such codes are absent in human-written texts, their inclusion in machine-generated content could serve ethical purposes effectively. Another important issue revolves around the responsibility for information ownership. Recently, companies such as *The New York Times* have filed lawsuits against tech companies behind some of the most advanced AI technologies, such as OpenAI.[21] In the case of *The New York Times*, the company argues that OpenAI's ChatGPT is generating outputs based on *The New York Times* articles and giving outputs that leverage the credibility of *The New York Times*, but the accuracy of this information cannot be verified. This situation jeopardises the integrity of the news outlet and its commitment to delivering accurate news. It is crucial to emphasise the importance of maintaining the following distinction. Content authored by AI lacks the credibility and accountability associated with human-created content in most cases, as human-created content has a clear responsibility and the copyright.

Humans are responsible for their writing and possess semantic understanding; when published news reports turn out to be wrong, it is possible to go back to the journalist to ask for further information and clarification regarding how the news was produced and distributed. However, LLMs lack such comprehension and operate solely on statistical patterns.

Consequently, an article produced by AI in a newspaper or an essay generated by a student using language-generation software may lack the critical thinking skills, reliability and authenticity expected from human-created content.[22]

What is particularly intriguing, at this point, is the shift in focus from solely safeguarding intellectual property rights to a broader concern about preventing the widespread dissemination of false information and assigning responsibility to the sources of information. While proposing solutions such as adding watermarks to AI-generated images or developing tools to distinguish between human and AI output, it remains uncertain if these measures alone will effectively address the issue of false information spread.

The field of journalism serves as a prime arena for exploring how human-created content and social media are the scene at which this is taking place as AI-created content becomes more relevant. Scholars from Universidad de Santiago de Compostela researched the impact of AI on journalism and the news production process,[23] acknowledging the limitations of its interpretative approach, aimed at navigating a dynamic environment impacted by AI. They argue that the future holds an expansive array of possibilities not only confined to communication or journalism but extending to broader social transformations. These encompass capabilities such as emotion recognition for relationship management, micro-segmentation of audiences for tailored product design/delivery, on-demand creation of personalised products and instant access to multilingual content, customisable with various voices or presenter prototypes. Regarding news production, automation is expected to predominantly impact structured, data-driven, thematic coverage rather than local events. The algorithm's role will primarily involve replicating repetitive tasks, underscoring the need for journalists to focus on strategic implementation while delegating routine operations to machines. The aim here is increased participation from journalists in shaping agendas, highlighting their intellectual input.

Moreover, in the current information ecosystem, it is vital to keep humans at the forefront of decision-making. It is of high importance to understand that humans should retain control over when, where and how AI technology is used. Collaboration among individuals requires deliberate determination of the appropriate contexts for integrating AI into our processes.

Focusing solely on replacing journalists with AI and automating journalism completely could lead to unintended consequences. Instead, it is important to explore how AI can complement and enhance journalists' abilities. This shift in perspective will shape the future of AI in journalism, ensuring it aligns with our intentions and values. Similar to the ethical obligations borne by journalists for the content they disseminate, individuals hold a significant responsibility in shaping the trajectory of our collective future. The integration of AI is progressively pervasive across diverse sectors and industries.

Crucial role of culture in AI-driven information ecosystems

Culture plays a vital role in shaping people's interaction with information, especially in environments influenced by AI. Recognising this, any human-centric initiative should consider cultural sensitivity. When technological advancements clash with cultural norms, they often fail to achieve the goal of expanding people's choices. The words 'Culture eats strategy for breakfast' are attributed to Peter Duckner,[24] who highlights the paramount significance of culture over strategic planning. In scholarly discussions, it highlights the crucial importance of cultural awareness in successfully navigating organisational contexts.[25] Cultural awareness is essential, particularly in the digital information landscape, which now has a huge effect on various aspects of human lives. The cultural composition of digital spaces not only influences their impact but can also limit their audience, leading to unequal information distribution.

Acknowledging the significance of cultural representation in digital technology helps people consider its influence on digital spaces and their audience better. This does not highlight the need for fair access and representation enough, especially for minority groups facing barriers in accessing and understanding information due to their cultural backgrounds. To address this, integrating cultural considerations into global information systems has been proposed to increase worldwide access to information and services, accommodating cultural variations in categorisation, classification and idea presentation.[26]

Today, as it was in the past, cultural factors significantly shape how we interact with information, particularly in AI-influenced contexts. Recognising the importance of cultural representation in digital technology underscores the urgent need for equitable access and representation, particularly for minority groups facing obstacles in accessing and understanding information due to their cultural backgrounds. Addressing this challenge requires integrating cultural considerations into global information systems, aiming to enhance worldwide access to information and services by acknowledging and accommodating cultural disparities in idea presentation.

To effectively integrate cultural sensitivity into AI-driven information environments, it is essential to value cultural diversity and inclusivity. This involves embedding cultural awareness into the design, development and deployment of AI technologies to ensure they cater to diverse cultural communities' needs and preferences. Cultivating cultural understanding among AI developers and practitioners can mitigate bias and can result in promoting greater trust and acceptance among culturally diverse populations. Embracing cultural sensitivity in AI technology development can also nurture a more inclusive and equitable information ecosystem, enabling individuals from all cultural backgrounds to access and engage with information according to their cultural contexts and preferences.

In the realm of AI-powered information ecosystems, the quest for inclusivity and accessibility is deeply entwined with the battle against misinformation and disinformation. Culturally, backgrounds sculpt people's understanding of the world, shaping how we perceive and interpret information. Unfortunately, this susceptibility to influence becomes a vulnerability in the face of deliberate misinformation campaigns. These campaigns exploit cultural nuances and beliefs, manipulating audiences and creating doubt and confusion. Consider, for example, the phenomena of filter bubbles and echo chambers perpetuated by AI algorithms as discussed earlier. These invisible digital enclaves insulate users, bringing them all together within a comfortable echo chamber of familiar ideas and perspectives that misinformation finds a breeding ground to flourish in, shielded from scrutiny and dissent. Without exposure to diverse viewpoints, our cultural biases are reinforced and misinformation gains a stronghold in our digital consciousness.

Language plays an even more important role in this narrative. For AI systems tasked with combating falsehoods, this presents a formidable challenge. Cultural nuances and language-specific contexts add layers of complexity, making the identification and interpretation of misinformation an incredibly difficult task. As misinformation spreads across diverse cultural and linguistic landscapes, the need for robust language models and translation algorithms becomes more evident. Even if these challenges are there, there is also an opportunity for progress by embracing cultural sensitivity and prioritising inclusivity. This decision pertains to human agency, necessitating deliberate consideration and subsequent action. AI technologies can also become powerful allies in the fight against misinformation. Imagine AI systems that actively seek out diverse perspectives, challenging cultural biases and fostering critical engagement. In this vision, inclusive AI technologies serve as beacons of hope in our digital landscape. They empower individuals to navigate complex cultural terrains with confidence, equipping them with the tools to distinguish fact from fiction. By integrating cultural awareness into every aspect of AI development, humans prepare the needed environment for a resilient information ecosystem thriving on diversity, transparency and trust.

Quantum computing and future implications of common usage

Before delving into specifics, it is imperative to clarify what quantum computing entails and why its development is significant for the structure of the internet. Quantum computing is a scientific discipline within computer science that encompasses elements of information theory, quantum mechanics and computer science.[27] However, what distinguishes quantum computing from classical computing is its approach to data manipulation and storage. In classical computing, data processing is conducted in binary form, in which computations rely on electrical impulses representing either a 1 or a 0. Having said that, quantum computing utilises quantum bits, or qubits, that enable quantum computers to leverage the principle of superposition, which allows qubits to exist in both binary states simultaneously, vastly increasing their computational power and efficiency compared to their classical equivalents.[28] In other words, how qubits operate can be exemplified using a prominent thought experiment known as Schrödinger's cat (equation), which refers to an entity that can exist in different places at the same time.[29] This capability, indeed, ushers the advent of a new era in which traditional cryptography, as we currently understand it, may become obsolete. Yet it is imperative to note that there remains a necessity to integrate classical cryptographic solutions with quantum cryptography. Similarly, as with every emerging technology, discussions related to quantum computing and its theoretical underpinnings are often fraught with hyperbolic predictions, particularly when it comes to national security implications of quantum computing, which this chapter does not address. In his article, Smith holds the view that:

> It is uncertain whether quantum technologies will live up to these high expectations. If they fall short, they will not be alone.

> We interpret new and emerging technologies on the basis of collective expectations about imagined futures, including our dreams and nightmares. These expectations are often unmet following hyperbole or hype.[30]

In the context of comparing contemporary cryptography with quantum cryptography, the Global Risk Institute finds that quantum computers have the potential to decrypt communications encrypted with Rivest-Shamir-Adleman (RSA-4096) in just three days – a feat that is impossible with classical computing.[31] Indeed, this does not necessarily imply that all encryption methods are vulnerable to quantum computing. Rather, the US National Institute of Standards and Technology recommends various encryption standards that are deemed to be quantum-resistant, including CRYSTALS-Kyber, CRYSTALS-Dilithium, Falcon and SPHINCS+.[32]

Having a quantum-resistant algorithm is a critical point for the future of internet communication, as many cyber attacks stem from disrupting communication, particularly through on-path attacks or man-in-the-middle (MITM) attacks. Furthermore, according to the Open Web Application Security Project's (OWASP) periodic assessment, which is considered a reference point for cyber security professionals, cryptographic failure is the second-most common cause of data exfiltration and network compromise among the top ten causes.[33] This reality, indeed, underscores the critical importance of quantum encryption, not only for private corporations but also for state actors due partly to vulnerable nature of encryption standards. Herman and Friedson share a similar perspective on the risks posed by quantum computation to national security, as follows:

> The danger lies in the sheer enormity of critical information that is now protected by such asymmetric encryption, including bank and credit card information, email communications, military networks and weapons systems, self-driving cars, the power grid, AI, and more. While asymmetric encryption is effective at thwarting today's hackers armed with classical computers, quantum computers will be able to hack into these systems and disrupt their operation and/or steal protected data.[34]

This does not suggest, however, that quantum computing will evolve into an omnipotent entity capable of solving all of humanity's challenges. Instead, it may represent a threat to national security, especially as it becomes more widespread, particularly during the transitional period. This period will necessitate significant changes to the internet's infrastructure, from fibre-optic cables to routers, servers and protocols currently in use. In other words, quantum computing will bring both benefits and risks in the transition period in terms of internet communication. Rosch-Grace and Straub argue that 'The combination of these benefits and risks may lead to a proliferation scenario where there is a cyclic accelerated increase in the number of quantum computers and the level of national utilization driven by the fear of an adversary possessing superior quantum computing capabilities'.[35] This argument suggests that if quantum computing becomes more prevalent, transitioning from classical encryption and internet infrastructure to the quantum computing era will present a challenging and hypothetically unwarranted situation for both state actors and private companies, even with governance mechanisms in place.

Therefore, it is highly likely that an escalated environment in which actors (particularly state-backed cyber-criminal groups) wage constant cyber attacks by leveraging quantum computing will be witnessed.[36] Furthermore, this development could inevitably prompt a new arms race among major powers, analogous to the ongoing competition in other technological domains, such as AI.[37] In essence, it can be argued that the race for quantum supremacy, especially between the US and China, may have already begun.[38] While it is highly possible that countries with the capability to develop quantum computing will achieve their objectives (both long and short term) in the race for quantum supremacy, it remains unclear to what extent they will utilise their quantum capabilities in hybrid warfare and PsyOps, particularly within the information ecosystem. Nonetheless, one salient point remains: should quantum computing be appropriately integrated into current machine learning systems? The amount of time required for data processing could substantially decrease, which, at the end of the day, means that advancements in quantum computing might enable AI systems to become more efficient and agile compared to the AI systems in use today.[39] Therefore, as mentioned before, although quantum computing has not yet become widely common or transformed into a general-purpose technology, it is possible to grasp the ways in which it might transform in the future of PsyOps when combined with AI. At this point, social engineering attacks, a prominent component of cyber security that could be extensively utilised in PsyOps, may be considered an appropriate case study, as they have increasingly come to rely on AI-based tools and will definitely be impacted by the diffusion of the quantum computing.[40]

AI-based psychological operations and changing cyber space dynamics

Social engineering attacks are not a new phenomenon in cyber space; rather, they have been consistently employed by various actors (both state and non-state actors) to manipulate, deceive and trick their victims based on victim's hypothetical trust perception and vulnerability to psychological pressure. The range of these attacks spans from physical security to network security.[41] More importantly, almost 90 per cent of cyber attacks involve human error, typically originating from cognitive biases or misperceptions.[42] Renowned white hat cyber security specialist Kevin Mitnick describes this reality in his seminal work by pointing out 'Security is too often merely an illusion, an illusion sometimes made even worse when gullibility, naïveté, or ignorance come into play [...] In the end, social engineering attacks can succeed when people are [...] simply ignorant about good security practices'.[43]

The widespread adoption of generative AI, especially LLMs and its availability to people from all walks of life, make social engineering attacks more scalable, robust and convincing. Even more concerning is the existence of malicious plugins in LLMs, such as 'wormgpt', which could potentially transform an ordinary individual into a sophisticated hacker.[44] Yet, it is imperative to note that these types of models still suffer from technical flaws. In the same vein, this does not negate the reality that the advent of generative AI has led a new phase in the online information ecosystem, which is likely to result in an increase not only in disinformation campaigns but also in social engineering attacks in the coming years.[45] Indeed, automating a social engineering attack is not a new phenomenon; instead 'research has shown that social engineering is easy to automate in many cases and can therefore be performed on a large scale'.[46]

Before delving into how social engineering attacks could be influenced by AI-based tools, it is significant to first introduce the overview of these types of attacks and main motivations behind them. Myers and Jernigan classify main goals of social engineering attacks as reconnaissance, credential harvesting, identity fraud, monetary theft and influence campaigns.[47] Indeed, these attacks specifically target the vulnerabilities of victims by triggering manipulative emotions or creating perceptions such as authority, intimidation, scarcity, trust, urgency, familiarity/liking and many others.[48] As can be seen, actors who opt for social engineering attacks have a diverse spectrum of motivations. These attacks include, most commonly, phishing, spear-phishing, whaling and vishing.

First, phishing typically involves unsolicited emails through which attackers aim to harvest or acquire a victim's credentials related to various platforms such as social media or banking, personally identifiable information (PII), personal health information (PHI) and many more. This can be accomplished by delivering a malicious payload that might include a uniform resource locator (URL) or macros embedded in PDFs or Word documents. Second, spear-phishing distinguishes itself from a general phishing attack by the specificity of the target, while also typically involving a reconnaissance phase, during which attackers gather information about their victim. Contrary to phishing campaigns that send emails en masse, spear-phishing is more targeted, aiming at a smaller, more specific group of individuals. Third, whaling is a subtype of phishing attacks that specifically targets high-value individuals, such as executives (e.g., chief executive officer, chief financial officer, chief information security officer) of the targeted organisation or corporate entity. Fourth, smishing, another subtype of phishing attacks, leverages short message services (SMS) targeting cell phones of the victims. Fifth, vishing, which could be used as a sequence of phishing emails, in what is called telephone-oriented attack delivery (TOAD), involves direct phone calls or voice over IP (VoIP) communications, in which the attacker impersonates someone who might seem legitimate, aiming to exploit the victim's cognitive vulnerabilities. Finally, pretexting attacks comprise different techniques (such as vishing, phishing or smishing) that aim to create plausible scenarios (pretext) to convince a victim to act upon a desired action.[49]

Indeed, there are various social engineering attacks, including dumpster diving, tailgating, watering hole attacks and many others. Nevertheless, these attacks are less relevant to PsyOps and are likely to be less affected by advancements in AI compared to phishing attacks and their variants, partly due to the physical requirements of these attacks. For instance, dumpster diving refers to a reconnaissance activity that involves examining the victim's trash bins, while tailgating involves physically following the victim to bypass entry restrictions into specific buildings. Thus, these types of attacks cannot be automated and are considered to be the most resistant to AI integration. That being said, as the usage of LLMs continues to increase, the scale and robustness of phishing attacks are also on the rise. For instance, advancements in voice spoofing/cloning technology could enable an attacker to precisely mimic someone familiar to the victim, making it easier to convince them to carry out tasks that align with the attacker's goals.[50] Furthermore, it was common for attackers to make grammatical mistakes or engage in typo squatting in their phishing emails, which can now be considered less of an issue thanks to LLMs. These models are capable of generating near-perfect content in various languages, significantly reducing the telltale signs of phishing attempts.[51] Beyond phishing attacks, a recent study has shown that LLM agents can autonomously hack websites, offering a glimpse into the future landscape of AI-based psychological operations.[52] Even more concerning are studies demonstrating that AI can be utilised for deceptive behaviours, potentially serving as a future reference for deception operations in strategic, tactical and operational levels. Furthermore, these studies have shown that it is possible to manipulate AI training datasets through various techniques, such as data poisoning or creating silent backdoors in the models, without the awareness of the model's owner or developer. This fact highlights critical vulnerabilities within AI systems that could be leveraged for malicious purposes, emphasising the necessity for strict security protocols, such as input validation, in the development and deployment of AI. Moreover, growing concern has prompted major technology companies in recent years to establish teams dedicated to AI red teaming, which reveals that these initiatives extend beyond addressing mere AI safety issues, focusing on proactively identifying and mitigating potential security threats before they can be exploited by attackers.[53]

Conclusion

The convergence of AI is fundamentally altering the landscape of information generation, analysis and dissemination. Upon thorough examination of these subjects, it becomes evident that the stakes are high, and the ramifications are profound. From the emergence of AI-driven information ecosystems to the associated risks and benefits, and from the pivotal influence of cultural factors to the imperative of human agency, the discourse surrounding AI technology, democracy and information integrity is complex and requires an evaluation from diverse perspectives. The widespread adoption of AI technologies has revolutionised the processes of information creation and distribution, consequently reshaping the dynamics of public discourse and decision-making. Nevertheless, within this era of technological advancement, ethical dilemmas and risks loom prominently, encompassing issues such as algorithmic bias, privacy infringements and the propagation of misinformation. Grappling with these intricacies necessitates an acknowledgement of the inherent biases ingrained within human nature alongside a recognition of the pressing need for responsible AI development and deployment.

Prioritising inclusivity, cultural awareness and human empowerment must remain central in this discussion. By infusing AI technologies with an appreciation for diverse cultural perspectives and fostering collaborative interactions between humans and machines, it can be possible to mitigate bias, cultivate trust and foster a more equitable information landscape.

The long evolution of technology from the eolithic era to the present day underlies the significant impact of technological evolution on human society, international trade, wars and invention of new technologies. With that being said, today, emerging technologies, particularly AI and quantum computing, are reshaping the information ecosystem and redefining the norms of international order (to some extent), productivity and global security. The rapid diffusion of these technologies, through various means such as new APIs and plug-ins, offers unprecedented opportunities for innovation, but they also simultaneously introduce significant threats, markedly in the realm of PsyOps and disinformation campaigns.

The potential for quantum computing to become a general-purpose technology could further complicate the future of internet communication through ramifications for encryption standards and the capabilities of both state and non-state actors.

This chapter has explored the ambivalent nature of technological progress, stressing the ways in which the proliferation of AI and the expectations related to quantum computing's evolution might profoundly impact the information ecosystem. Through examining the surge in AI-based information production (thanks to generative AI) and the potential for quantum computing to enhance the frequency and sophistication of disinformation campaigns, we indicate the urgency of addressing these developments, particularly in the security realm. Furthermore, we argue that the evolution of AI and quantum computing not only accelerates the digital arms race among countries (particularly between the US and China) but also challenges existing regulatory frameworks and societal norms, necessitating a revision of strategies to harness the benefits of these technologies while reducing their risks. As we stand on the cusp of significant technological shifts, it is imperative to foster a balanced approach that embraces innovation and safeguards against the multi-faceted threats posed to digital and societal areas, including the security and daily lives of people.

Notes

1 Ian McNeil, *An Encyclopedia of the History of Technology* (London: Routledge & CRC Press, 1996). https://www.routledge.com/An-Encyclopedia-of-the-History-of-Technology/McNeil/p/book/9780415147927 (accessed 5 February 2026).

2 Paul Scharre, *Four Battlegrounds: Power in the Age of Artificial Intelligence* (New York: W. W. Norton, 2024); Melanie Mitchell, *Artificial Intelligence: A Guide for Thinking Humans* (London: Pelican, 2020).

3 Muhammed Can and Halid Kaplan, 'Transatlantic partnership on artificial intelligence: Realities, perceptions and future implications', *Global Affairs* 6:4–5 (2020), 537–557. https://doi.org/10.1080/23340460.2020.1854049

4 Mustafa Suleyman, *The Coming Wave* (New York: Random House USA, 2023).

5 Evgeny A. Mikheev and Timofey A. Nestik (2019) 'The use of artificial intelligence technologies in information and psychological warfare', *The European Proceedings of Social and Behavioural Sciences.* https://doi.org/10.15405/epsbs.2019.07.53

6 Jon Lindsay, *Quantum Computing and Classical Politics: The Ambiguity of Advant* (London: Taylor & Francis, 2022). https://www.taylorfrancis.com/chapters/oa-edit/10.4324/9781003110224-7/quantum-computing-classical-politics-jon-lindsay (accessed 5 February 2026).

7 Jon Lindsay, 'Why quantum computing will not destabilize international security: The political logic of cryptology', *SSRN* (2018). https://papers.ssrn.com/sol3/papers.cfm?abstract_id=3205507 (accessed 5 February 2026); Frank Smith, 'Quantum technology hype and national security', *SSRN* (2020). https://papers.ssrn.com/sol3/papers.cfm?abstract_id=3707056 (accessed 5 February 2026).

8 *NIST*, 'NIST releases first 3 finalized post-quantum encryption standards' (2024). https://www.nist.gov/news-events/news/2024/08/nist-releases-first-3-finalized-post-quantum-encryption-standards (accessed 5 February 2026).

9 Faruk Hossain, Md Jobair, Sharaban Tahora, Masrura Tasnim, Hossain Shahriar and Nazmus Sakib, 'A review of quantum cybersecurity: threats, risks and opportunities' *2022 1st International Conference on AI in Cybersecurity (ICAIC)* (2022). https://doi.org/10.1109/icaic53980.2022.9896970

10 Michael C. Horowitz, 'Artificial intelligence, international competition, and the balance of power', *Texas National Security Review* 1:3 (2018), 37–57. https://doi.org/10.15781/T2639KP49

11 Scott Monteith, Tasha Glenn, John R. Geddes, Peter C. Whybrow, Eric Achtyes and Michael Bauer, 'Artificial intelligence and increasing misinformation', *The British Journal of Psychiatry* 224:2 (2024), 33–35. https://doi.org/10.1192/bjp.2023.136; Mohammad Eslami and Alena Vysotskaya Guedes Vieira, 'Introducing the arms race in the Middle East in the twenty first century: A "powder keg" in the digital era?' in Mohammad Eslami and Alena Vysotskaya Guedes Vieira (eds), *The Arms Race in the Middle East: Contemporary Security Dynamics* (Cham: Springer International Publishing, 2023), 3–13; Mohammad Eslami, Nasim Sadat Mosavi and Muhammed Can, 'Sino–Iranian cooperation in artificial intelligence: A potential countering against the US hegemony', in Paulo Duarte, Francisco Leandro and Enrique Galán (eds), *The Palgrave Handbook of Globalization with Chinese Characteristics: The Case of the Belt and Road Initiative* (Singapore: Springer Nature Singapore, 2023), 543–559; Mohammad Eslami and Alena Vysotskaya Guedes Vieira (eds), *The Arms Race in the Middle East: Contemporary Security Dynamics* (Cham: Springer International Publishing, 2023).

12 Khaled Hayawi, Shadman Shahriar and Sree S. Mathew, 'The imitation game: detecting human and AI-generated texts in the era of ChatGPT and BARD', *ArXiv* (2023). https://arxiv.org/abs/2307.12166 (accessed 5 February 2026).

13 Hilke Schellmann, *The Algorithm: How AI Decides Who Gets Hired, Monitored, Promoted, and Fired and Why We Need to Fight Back Now* (New York: Hachette Books, 2024).

14 Emily Pronin, 'Perception and misperception of bias in human judgment', *Trends in Cognitive Sciences* 11:1 (2007), 37–43. https://doi.org/10.1016/j.tics.2006.11.001

15 Maria Papageorgiou, Muhammed Can and Alena Vysotskaya Guedes Vieira, 'China as a threat and balancing behavior in the realm of emerging technologies', *Chinese Political Science Review* 9:4 (2024), 441–482. https://doi.org/10.1007/s41111-024-00248-0
16 Petroc Taylor, 'Data growth worldwide 2010–2025', *Statista* (2023). https://www.statista.com/statistics/871513/worldwide-data-created/ (accessed 27 May 2024).
17 Jandhyala Prabhakar Rao and Rambhatla Siva Prasad, 'Tangible and intangible impact of AI usage: AI for information accessibility', *The International Review of Information Ethics* 29 (2021). https://doi.org/10.29173/irie423
18 Duke Reporters' Lab, 'Duke Lab Gives fact-checkers, researchers new tools to thwart misinformation' (2023). https://reporterslab.org/2023/12/15/duke-lab-gives-fact-checkers-researchers-new-tools-to-thwart-misinformation/ (accessed 5 February 2026).
19 Katarina Kertysova, 'How AI changes the way disinformation is produced, disseminated, and can be countered', *Security and Human Rights* 29:1–4 (2018). https://doi.org/10.1163/18750230-02901005
20 Rui Zhang Liu and Tian Nan Tan, 'Watermarking for digital images', *ICSP '98: Fourth International Conference on Signal Processing* 2 (1998), 944–947. https://doi.org/10.1109/ICOSP.1998.770768
21 Michael M. Grynbaum and Ryan Mac, 'The Times sues OpenAI and Microsoft over AI use of copyrighted work', *The New York Times* (2023). https://www.nytimes.com/2023/12/27/business/media/new-york-times-open-ai-microsoft-lawsuit.html (accessed 5 February 2026).
22 Ariel Grinbaum and Leonidas Adomaitis, 'The ethical need for watermarks in machine-generated language', *ArXiv* (2022). https://doi.org/10.48550/arXiv.2209.03118
23 Juan Manuel Tuñez-López, Carlos Fieiras Ceide and Manuel Vaz-Álvarez 'Impact of artificial intelligence on journalism: Transformations in the company, products, contents and professional profile', *Communication & Society* 34:1 (2021), 177–193. https://doi.org/10.15581/003.34.1.177-193
24 Carolyn Whitzman, '"Culture eats strategy for breakfast": The powers and limitations of urban design education', *Journal of Urban Design* 21 (2016), 574–576. https://doi.org/10.1080/13574809.2016.1206825
25 Harry C. Triandis, 'Cultural intelligence in organizations', *Group & Organization Management* 31 (2006), 20–26. https://doi.org/10.1177/1059601105275262

26 Huan Chen, Sylvia Chan-Olmsted and My Thai, 'Culture sensitivity and information access: A qualitative study among ethnic groups', *NSUWorks* (2023). https://nsuworks.nova.edu/tqr/vol28/iss8/16/ (accessed 5 February 2026).

27 Eleanor Rieffel and Wolfgang Polak, *Quantum Computing a Gentle Introduction* (Cambridge, MA: The MIT Press, 2014).

28 Robert S. Sutor, *Dancing with Qubits: How Quantum Computing Works and How It Can Change The World* (Birmingham: Packt Publishing Ltd., 2019).

29 Wei-Bo Gao, Chao-Yang Lu, Xing-Can Yao, Ping Xu, Otfried Gühne, Alexander Goebel, Yu-Ao Chen, Cheng-Zhi Peng, Zeng-Bing Chen and Jian-Wei Pan, 'Experimental demonstration of a hyper-entangled ten-qubit Schrödinger cat state', *Nature Physics* 6:5 (2010), 331–335. https://doi.org/10.1038/nphys1603

30 Frank L. Smith, 'Quantum technology hype and national security', *Security Dialogue* 51:5 (2020), 499–516. https://doi.org/10.1177/0967010620904922

31 Vlad Gheorghiu and Michele Mosca, 'GRI quantum risk assessment report – Part 1', *Global Risk Institute* (2021). https://globalriskinstitute.org/publications/resource-estimation-framework-quantum-attacks-cryptographic-functions/ (accessed 5 February 2026).

32 National Institute of Standards and Technology, 'Post-quantum cryptography: CSRC', *CSRC* (2024). https://csrc.nist.gov/projects/post-quantum-cryptography (accessed 5 February 2026).

33 Open Web Application Security Project, 'OWASP TO 10:2021.? OWASP Top 10:2021, 2024'. https://owasp.org/Top10/ (accessed 1 September 2024).

34 Arthur Herman and Idalia Friedson, *Quantum Computing: How to Address the National Security Risk* (Washington, DC: Hudson Institute, 2018). https://s3.amazonaws.com/media.hudson.org/files/publications/Quantum18FINAL3.pdf (accessed 5 February 2026).

35 Dominic Rosch-Grace and Jeremy Straub, 'Analysis of the likelihood of quantum computing proliferation', *Technology in Society* 68 (2022). https://doi.org/10.1016/j.techsoc.2022.101880

36 Artur Gruszczak and Sebastian Kaempf, *Routledge Handbook of the Future of Warfare* (Abingdon: Routledge, 2024).

37 Edward Moore Geist, 'It's already too late to stop the AI arms race – we must manage it instead', *Bulletin of the Atomic Scientists* 72:5 (2016), 318–321. https://doi.org/10.1080/00963402.2016.1216672

38 James Der Derian and Stuart Rollo, 'Quantum 3.0: What will it mean for war, peace, and world order?', *Global Perspectives* 5:1 (2024). https://doi.org/10.1525/gp.2024.93888
39 Vedran Dunjko and Hans J. Briegel, 'Machine learning and artificial intelligence in the quantum domain: A review of recent progress', *Reports on Progress in Physics* 81:7 (2018). https://doi.org/10.1088/1361-6633/aab406
40 Mohammad Eslami, Alena Vieira, Arshin Adib-Moghaddam, Lauro Borges, Maria Papageorgiou, Fabio Cristiano, Ibrahim Al-Marashi, Tom Sauer and Christian Kaunert, 'The geopolitics of AI-driven arms races', *Geopolitics* (2025), 1–43.
41 Fatima Salahdine and Naima Kaabouch, 'Social engineering attacks: A survey', *Future Internet* 11:4 (2019), 89. https://doi.org/10.3390/fi11040089
42 Sumeet Wadhwani, 'What is social engineering, success rate, motives, tools' *Spiceworks* (2023). https://www.spiceworks.com/it-security/cyber-risk-management/articles/social-engineering-still-rampant/#:~:text=is%20widely%20undercounted.-,Hackers%20leverage%20social%20engineering%20in%20as%20much%20as%2090%25%20of,fear%2C%20or%20oblige%20to%20orders (accessed 5 February 2026).
43 Kevin D. Mitnick and William L. Simon, *The Art of Deception: Controlling the Human Element of Security* (New York: Wiley, 2003), 4.
44 Ravie Lakshmanan, 'WormGPT: New AI tool allows cybercriminals to launch sophisticated cyber attacks', *The Hacker News* (2023). https://thehackernews.com/2023/07/wormgpt-new-ai-tool-allows.html (accessed 5 February 2026).
45 Ashwin Krishnan, 'Generative AI is making phishing attacks more dangerous: Techtarget', *TechTarget* (2023). https://www.techtarget.com/searchsecurity/tip/Generative-AI-is-making-phishing-attacks-more-dangerous (accessed 5 February 2026).
46 Katharina Krombholz, Heidelinde Hobel, Markus Huber and Edgar Weippl, 'Advanced social engineering attacks', *Journal of Information Security and Applications* 22 (2015), 113–122. https://doi.org/10.1016/j.jisa.2014.09.005
47 Mike Meyers and Scott Jernigan. *CompTIA Security + Certification Guide* (3rd edn) (New York: McGraw Hill, 2021).
48 Meyers and Jernigan, *CompTIA Security*.
49 Meyers and Jernigan, *CompTIA Security*.

50 Jesse William McGraw, 'New social engineering threat: AI voice cloning', *cybernews.com* (2024). https://cybernews.com/editorial/ai-voice-cloning (accessed 5 February 2026).
51 Bob Violino, 'AI tools such as ChatGPT are generating a mammoth increase in malicious phishing emails', *CNBC* (2023). https://www.cnbc.com/2023/11/28/ai-like-chatgpt-is-creating-huge-increase-in-malicious-phishing-email.html (accessed 5 February 2026).
52 Richard Fang, Rohan Bindu, Akul Gupta, Qiusi Zhan and Dainel Kang, 'LLM agents can autonomously hack websites', *ArXiv* (2024). https://arxiv.org/html/2402.06664v1 (accessed 5 February 2026).
53 David Cohen, 'Examining malicious hugging face ML models with silent backdoor', *JFrog* (2024). https://jfrog.com/blog/data-scientists-targeted-by-malicious-hugging-face-ml-models-with-silent-backdoor/ (accessed 5 February 2026); Peter S. Park, Simon Goldstein, Aidan O'Gara, Michael Chen and Dan Hendrycks, 'AI deception: A survey of examples, risks, and potential solutions', *ArXiv* (2023). https://arxiv.org/abs/2308.14752 (accessed 5 February 2026).

4

Deepfakes in narrative warfare

Christopher Schwartz, Justin M. Pelletier, David I. Schwartz, Matthew Wright and Andrea Hickerson

Introduction

In March 2022, shortly after the invasion of Ukraine by the Russian Federation, a deepfake was released that depicted Ukrainian president Volodomyr Zelensky ordering his nation's forces to stand down.[1] Although the deepfake failed to dislocate Ukraine's armed forces, this incident, nonetheless, demonstrated the military potential of deepfakes. There is, thus, a need to reckon with deepfakes from the standpoint of military doctrine and not only in the short term. Whether and how today's geopolitical rivals deploy deepfakes as weapons will impact the trajectory of the global information environment. The danger is that the internet may become unrecognisable as such by the middle of this century.

Overview

Such a reckoning is best begun through philosophy, i.e., attaining a high-level theoretical grasp of (i) what deepfakes are; (ii) the kind of warfare they belong to, namely, narrative warfare; and (iii) the bedrock concepts and intuitions in the military traditions of today's three near-peer competitors: the Russian Federation, the People's Republic of China (PRC) and the United States of America (US).

With respect to (i) *deepfakes*, we propose that these are a category of content produced via artificial intelligence (AI) for the purpose of either simulating, manipulating or fictionalising objective reality. The term 'deepfake', thus, traverses very different relationships to fidelity: sometimes the content is motivated by good-faith intentions to represent subjective realities or express fictions and fantasies – such as in therapeutic applications[2] or protecting privacy in doctor–patient communication[3] – and other times they are motivated by bad-faith intentions to deceive about objective realities. Hence, the world has seen deepfakes that simulate real identities, places and situations, or manufacture entirely unreal or non-real ones, for reasons ranging from satire to illustration; the world has also seen deepfakes that manipulate real identities, places and situations for reasons ranging from revenge to narrative warfare. More bedevilling still, deepfakes motivated by good-faith intentions can end up being redeployed for bad-faith purposes.

The mercurial nature of deepfakes makes them well suited for (ii) *narrative warfare*, which is multi-vectoral, strategic communication that aims to shape perceptions and influence/manipulate the behaviour of a target audience in support of the 'narrator's military objectives. We hold to the distinction that while all stories are narratives, not all narratives are stories.[4] Stories and narratives are two ways of presenting ideatic content to an audience; a story is typically linear, with a beginning, middle and end, all constrained to a single medium, while a narrative may unfold across mediums via a variety of delivery agents and not necessarily in a linear fashion. Crucially, the narrator is attempting to direct the attention of the target audience and create conditions that increase their receptivity and persuadability. Achieving this goal requires undertaking the very ambitious task of attacking and influencing/manipulating their information environment, as opposed to just 'telling a story', i.e., communicating in such a fashion that abides by the rules and structures of the information environment as is.

As for (iii) exploring how military doctrine might reckon with deepfake-augmented narrative warfare,[5] we apply ways of war analysis to postulate and explore the philosophical standpoints of the three great powers with respect to *military deception*, i.e., 'actions executed to deliberately mislead adversary military, paramilitary, or violent extremist organization [sic] decision-makers, thereby causing the adversary to take specific actions (or inactions) that will contribute to the accomplishment of the friendly mission'.[6] Ways of war is an interpretive method for military history that seeks to distil a given nation's historical battlefield experiences into an understanding of how that nation is likely to seek to wage war. Put simply, nations have philosophical traditions and practices, or 'ways of war', that express how they think about warfare.

The stakes

Underlying our arguments in this chapter is the deeper realisation that war is increasingly being waged across an information environment that has multi-faceted physical, cyber and psycho-social dimensions. Not only this, but these dimensions are growing both more internally complex and interconnected with each other. Hence, the imminent future of war will be infrastructural, digital and mental, and in important respects, these elements will be blurred together, making it a challenge for both adversaries and defenders to formulate clear lines of attack and defence.

Of course, war has always been waged across an information environment, and deceiving the opponent is a perennial stratagem. Over two millennia ago, Sun Tzu remarked, 'All warfare is based on deception'.[7] Deepfake-augmented narrative warfare represents a dangerous ratcheting-up of that perennial truth.[8] The world has already seen the damage malicious narratives can do via conspiracy theories, which have been plaguing public discourse and stoking political violence globally. Yet, the accelerating proliferation of conspiracy theories may only be a harbinger of darker times to come if certain choices are made to weaponise deepfakes.

Deepfakes are the atomic bombs of narrative warfare. The shadow they can cast over the informational battlespace inspires – and requires – a bold question: what might the internet end up looking like by the middle of this century? We envision two diametrically opposed scenarios: it either (i) becomes a *dark forest* or (ii) embraces *classical liberalism.*

Our inspiration for the dark forest scenario is the science fiction novel of the same name by Chinese novelist Cixin Liu (Liu Cixin).[9] This scenario envisions a world of disconnected, mutually hostile national intranets, in which nations or regional entities retreat behind firewalls – and perhaps even altogether sever their telecommunications from the rest of the world

– in an effort to secure control over their domestic information ecosystems. The classically liberal scenario, by contrast, envisions a universal internet that facilitates global digital integration, transparency and the free exchange of ideas.

As scholars, we use these scenarios as evaluative tools, not predictive models. However, we also recognise that, for Russia, China and the US, these scenarios are strategic choices. Indeed, Moscow and Beijing seem to have already chosen to pursue the dark forest. The real question, then, is what Washington will choose. Will the US also embrace deception wholesale like its rivals? Will it also strive to partition the internet into separate national or regional intranets? Or will it innovate a form of deepfake-augmented narrative warfare that is consistent with its professed democratic values? And not only that, can a democratic form of deepfake-augmented narrative warfare be used, if perhaps somewhat paradoxically, to help bring about a universal internet?

Before proceeding, we should be transparent about our own position on these questions. For starters, we are rooted in the American context, so we will be writing largely from that standpoint. We believe that the democratic ideals enshrined in the US Constitution are ultimately more constructive for global prosperity than the ideals of Washington's competitors in Moscow and Beijing. Consequently, we also believe that the classically liberal scenario is the better strategic choice. The dark forest may seem to offer nations control and safety in the short term, but by suppressing dialogue and mutual understanding, it risks fostering distrust and hostility, creating a brittle and dangerous environment. Conversely, the classically liberal scenario acknowledges insecurity in the short term – through openness and vulnerability to influence – but frames it as a pathway to long-term global peace.

As for the specifics of establishing a universal internet, the idea arouses a slew of practical and ethical questions. We will outline some of those questions further below, but it is suffice to say that we do not have answers, even provisional ones. Still, we find the idea to be a provocative one in a constructive way.

Procedure

We will proceed as follows. First, we will elaborate our philosophical definitions of deepfakes and narrative warfare. We will then conduct our ways of war analysis with the goal of formulating what deepfake-augmented narrative warfare may end up looking like for each of the three rival nations. Special attention will be paid to the US, for whom we will outline ideas for what democratically appropriate uses of weaponised deepfakes might look like. Finally, we will close by discussing the dark forest and classically liberal scenarios.

Deepfakes and narrative warfare

We define deepfakes and narrative warfare as follows:

Deepfakes are a category of content produced via AI and chiefly characterised by either the simulation, manipulation or fictionalisation of real identities, places or situations.

Narrative warfare is a form of strategic communication characterised by multi-vectorality and weaponisation, i.e., the narrator aims to shape perceptions and influence the

> behaviour of a targeted audience in support of military objectives by attacking and manipulating the audience's information environment.

In addition to these notes, two small points of clarification. First, deepfakes can be textual as well as audiovisual, e.g., the output from chatbots such as OpenAI's ChatGPT and Anthropic's Claude. Second, narrative warfare is not solely the domain of national-level actors, i.e., governments; it can be waged by any number of sub- and non-national actors, e.g., corporations, terrorist organisations, activist movements and the like. Our discussion will focus on national-level actors because we believe this class of actors potentially wields the most destructive power in narrative conflict.

Deepfakes

When defining deepfakes, it is important to be mindful of the various intellectual tensions surrounding them. One tension arises from the divergent ways in which forensics specialists and the general public approach the phenomenon. Forensics specialists will tend to designate a piece of content as a deepfake according to its method of creation,[10] while the public will tend to focus on assessing whether the depiction is 'fake'. Another tension arises from the varying intentions behind, and perceptions of, a given deepfake, i.e., from its creator, its propagators and its audience(s).[11] Finally, law enforcement, national security and the military will tend to focus on the potential misuses of deepfakes, a focus that can collide with democratic concerns over ensuring technological innovation and free speech.

Although the notion of fakeness is emotionally charged and ambiguous, we think the general public is, nonetheless, on the right track. The term 'fake' connotes a concern for fidelity, and this does, indeed, strike us as the key issue for defining deepfakes. The heart of the matter is this: sometimes a deepfake represents someone's view of reality, sometimes it represents an outright fiction or fantasy and sometimes it deceives about shared reality. For example, it is a rainy day outside the office, but your colleague makes a deepfake depicting it as a sunny day. Their motivation could be either to express their own happy mood, to make themselves feel better or to trick someone into going outside without an umbrella.

Philosophically, what this means is that deepfakes are a breed of simulation, even when what they are simulating is not empirically factual. Contrary to the idea often heard in online discourse that deepfakes are inherently 'bad' because they are 'inauthentic', the danger they actually pose is when they become *dissimulative*, by which we mean when they are being used to deceive about objective reality. And importantly, a deepfake can become dissimulative on purpose or by accident at any point in its life cycle.

To grasp these subtleties, take for example a married couple who desire a child and make a deepfake of themselves holding a baby. The reality depicted in this deepfake is their *inner* world; it would be unfair, even cruel, to describe the image as 'fake' solely because it does not correspond with the couple's outer world. At the same time, the empirical fact remains that they do not yet have a baby. This gap between their subjective and objective realities introduces an epistemological hazard, for a relative may see the deepfake on one of their social media profiles and mistakenly believe that they have finally become parents.

Or consider an activist who makes a deepfake depicting a politician accepting a bribe. The activist may be perfectly aware that there have never been any accusations of corruption raised against the politician, but they believe strongly that this person is part of a conspiracy attempting to systematically undermine their community. Soon, the deepfake is being amplified by social media influencers and accounts influenced or controlled by a rival nation in order to undermine the politician.

All that being said, the insights of forensics do have philosophical relevance, for the technology that makes deepfakes possible and the techniques used to create them help to delineate them from other content categories. For starters, the term 'deepfake' originally emerged in 2017 as the username of a Reddit user who specialised in using AI to create non-consensual pornography of Hollywood actresses. The prefix 'deep' connoted 'deep learning', a form of AI based on artificial neural networks.

The term 'deepfake' connotes both a verb and a noun, i.e., the act of creating a deepfake ('that person was deepfaked') and the deepfake itself ('that is a deepfake'). While slightly ambiguous, using 'deepfake' in these ways is not inaccurate.

Techniques of deepfake creation

To also be clear about an important point, deepfakes are not just *any* content created via AI tools. When such tools are used to edit and enhance a photo or video, the result is not a deepfake per se. Deepfakes should be understood as also being the products of very specific uses of AI: (a) swapping, (b) puppeteering and (c) generation.

Swapping entails applying an element of one piece of media onto another, as in face-swapping, which occurs when one person's face is applied on top of the face of another.

Puppeteering, sometimes also called 'puppet-mastering', entails manipulating a piece of media from within, such that, e.g., the face itself is artificially made to say or do things that it does not in the original source material.

Generation entails creating an entire piece of media from scratch, as in text-to-image or text-to-video generation. For example, if a user writes the prompt, 'A smiling face', and a smiling face is created – perhaps either of someone who does not exist or of someone real, if the user specifies it and that person's face is in the training data.

This leads to another important issue about deepfakes, which is that they are usually distinguished from 'cheapfakes', which are manipulations of media produced without using AI. For example, manipulating photos with Photoshop used to be a common cheapfake technique – although the current software version now has AI built into it. Indeed, because AI is increasingly being integrated into consumer software, as with Photoshop, it is possible that the notion of cheapfakes could vanish. Alternatively, it may be that the term 'cheapfake' will eventually designate *consumer-grade* deepfakes, i.e., produced via AI tools that the average person or small enterprise can financially afford.

Finally, the term 'generation' may be confusing because, in media reports, it has been used to connote the general act of creating a deepfake, including swapping and puppeteering. When in the context of specific techniques, it may help to think of 'generation' as *conjuring*, e.g., the user writes the prompt, 'The Eiffel Tower is burning', and video footage of the catastrophe appears on the computer screen as if from thin air. Thinking of deepfakes as conjured captures the experience many people have had when using 'generative AI', as well as clarifies why the term 'generative AI' is sometimes used synonymously with 'deepfake'.

Narrative warfare

How exactly should 'narrative warfare' be defined? Let us start with the concept of 'narrative' itself, the origins of which is well-established. We find it in the concept of 'strategic narrative', which, per Amjad Mehmood Bhatti and Nasir Mehmood, has historically been central to US geostrategy since the Monroe Doctrine's assertion of Washington's hemispheric dominance. Strategic narratives serve multiple purposes, such as justifying policies, mobilising popular support and shaping perceptions.[12] In this sense, narrative warfare can be seen as a more focused and operationalised evolution of strategic narrative, tailored to the specific demands of modern information and influence campaigns.

The term 'narrative warfare' itself, as a distinct phrase, is of uncertain historical origin. In the American context, its conceptual roots can likely be traced to the 2001 RAND study by military theorists John Arquilla and David Ronfeldt, and a 2006 book, *The Transformation of Strategic Affairs*, by Lawrence Freedman.[13] By 2010, the US Joint Forces Command was discussing how to win 'the battle of the narrative', which is, to our knowledge, the first explicit linkage of narrative to the concept of warfare.[14] In 2011, the Defense Advanced Research Project Agency (DARPA) began soliciting the research community for research into 'narratives',[15] and interest in narrative warfare, as well as other narrative-related topics such as narrative intelligence, has been gaining steam ever since.

At present, the US military appears to situate narrative warfare as a subset of information warfare, a broader framework encompassing activities aimed at gaining competitive advantages through the use and manipulation of information. Information warfare operates across various levels, from tactical to strategic, and involves technical, psychological, offensive and defensive dimensions. Offensive actions include disrupting or degrading an adversary's information systems, while defensive actions focus on safeguarding one's own information infrastructure.

This does not seem accurate to us, as narrative warfare has different strategic objectives. Information warfare seeks to disrupt, degrade or destroy adversaries' information systems, while narrative warfare focuses on guiding an audience's ideas, emotions and actions toward the narrator's goals. This distinction suggests that narrative warfare has more potential to operate constructively, through improving an adversary's information environment, for example, to promote narratives aligned with democratic ideals. By contrast, information warfare operates destructively; insofar that it can act constructively, it would be to facilitate something like constructive narrative warfare, e.g., by manipulating the target information space.

A related difference between the two kinds of warfare is that information warfare seeks to in some sense scramble the target audience's frameworks of meaning, while narrative warfare emphasises persuasion, often through storytelling.[16] In other words, information warfare seeks to *confuse* a target country's populace about what is and is not true, while narrative warfare seeks to *convince* them that something is true, e.g., that the narrator's country is benevolent. Indeed, narrative warfare might not involve harming the target's information ecosystem at all, but actually improving it. Consider Radio Free Europe/Radio Liberty (RFE/RL),[17] which promoted narratives of freedom and democracy through accurate reporting, countering censorship and disinformation in ways that enhanced information integrity.

All that being said, there is another way in which it can be argued that narrative warfare is a subset of information warfare, and that is on the issue of defence. While narrative warfare emphasises persuasion and influence, its effectiveness will also depend on defending against competing narratives. This means safeguarding the credibility of one's own narratives while countering adversarial disinformation – an essential component that brings narrative warfare into closer alignment with the broader goals of information warfare.

An example of narrative attack

Let us bracket the question of whether narrative warfare is distinct from, or a variant of, information warfare and, instead, focus on an example of a narrative attack. In such an attack, the objective of the attacker – the 'narrator' – is to direct the attention of the audience while creating conditions that increase their receptivity to whatever it is their attention is being guided. Note that the audience can be anyone, whether a rival nation's general public or ruling elite, its intelligence services and military forces, private sector and so on.

To achieve their objective, the narrator must gain insight into the spatial, temporal, linguistic, cultural, political, psychological and technological contingencies of their intended campaign. Regardless of the choice, a paramount consideration will be to maintain secrecy. Like cyber warfare, narrative warfare is shadowy and deceptive, for it is imperative that the audience believes in the authenticity of the narrative. Also like cyber warfare, narrative warfare typically takes the form of exploits and penetration testing: what are the fragile points in existing cultural and social dynamics? Are there any biases that can be leveraged or grievances that can be aroused, and if so, which demographics are subject to them? What is the political economy of the media ecosystem? Are there any actors within that ecosystem who might have their own susceptibilities or incentives to disseminate the content on the narrator's behalf or technological backdoors that can be used to slip the content into feeds?

To illustrate, consider the 2023 narrative attack against the Russian Federation, which used a multi-modal deepfake.[18] Russian television and radio stations were hacked and used to broadcast a video and voice deepfake of Russian President Vladimir Putin announcing a formal declaration of war against Ukraine, and with it, martial law and a full-scale mobilisation. There were also rumours on Telegram (a messaging service popular in the former Soviet Union) of conscription orders being handed out to men of military age in the city of Belgorod, which is near the Ukrainian border.[19]

Clearly, the narrator had insight into the cyber security of the Russian telecommunications infrastructure, and they combined this with an understanding of the Russian government's reluctance to upgrade the label on their armed intervention in Ukraine from a 'special military operation' to full-fledged war and commit to a mass conscription.[20] The likely goal of the attack was to strike at the social contract between the government and the population, which relies on an unspoken transaction in which the Russian people remain depoliticised as long as the authorities do not demand much of them.[21]

This narrative attack was impressive, for it involved a combination of narrative and cyber elements, and if the rumours about fake conscription orders in Belgorod were true, human assets on the ground as well. Yet, if the narrator's goal was, indeed, to strike at the fragility of the Russian social contract, they failed. While authorities were livid, the deepfake was met with overwhelming indifference from everyday people. As of this writing, no studies have been done to ascertain why the audience reacted this way, but given the social contract, we suspect they found the deepfake prima facie unbelievable. The narrator may have overestimated their credulity.

We should also note that Russian authorities have since taken steps to inoculate their population against future deepfakes of their leadership, frequently warning the public about the danger.[22] Memorably, in what could have very well been a staged event, Putin was asked a question by a deepfake of himself during a live news conference. The Russian president defiantly denounced not only the epistemological inauthenticity of the deepfake but also its moral illegitimacy, declaring, 'I see you may resemble me and speak with my voice. But I have thought about it and decided that only one person must be like me and speak with my voice, and that will be me'.[23]

The ways of war

Ways of war is an interpretive method for military history that seeks to distil a given nation's historical battlefield experiences into an understanding of how that nation is likely to seek to achieve political ends through military means. It examines cultural traditions that inform contemporary nation-states. Our ways of war analysis is intended to identify historically persistent differences between the Russian, Chinese and American culture that may portend how their respective nation-states will approach deepfake-augmented narrative warfare.

Because deception is a crucial element to narrative warfare, and deepfakes have an immense potential to deceive audiences, we will focus on how these nations have conceptualised deception and deployed it on the battlefield and institutionalised it in military doctrine. We have discerned the following patterns:

> Russian and Chinese doctrines conceive the information environment as a thing to tightly control, both for offensive and defensive purposes. Deception is elemental to this pursuit, although it is conceptualised in a more aggressive manner in the Russian way of war, and more fluidly in its Chinese counterpart.
>
> By contrast, the American way of war emphasises using deception to achieve decisive victory. Beyond this, though, deception has a difficult relationship with the democratic principles professed in the US Constitution.

Before diving in, we should also note that each nation's cultural and political traditions will shape not only its strengths but also its vulnerabilities to deepfake-augmented narrative warfare. These vulnerabilities will be key to understanding how each system might defend against or exploit deepfakes in conflict. Russian and Chinese strategies also tend to emphasise tight control over the information environment to protect state narratives, while American strategy tends to rely on public trust, free discourse and decentralised media systems. There are clear pros and cons to both approaches. Tight control over information may reduce the number of avenues of narrative attack but may also mean the population is, so to speak, less 'inoculated' due to their overall lack of exposure.[24] The reverse may be the case for the more open American approach: adversaries have many more avenues of narrative attack, but because the population is more exposed, they also become more resilient.

It is not a given, however, that inoculation would be the inevitable or even likely outcome of the American strategy. Possibly just as likely is disengagement or an extended state of confusion. Consider, for example, the phenomenon known as the 'liar's dividend'.[25] When a population confronts the possibility that information can be falsified, they also become more susceptible to unmerited denials of reality. For example, a public figure can decry legitimate evidence of themselves engaging in unethical or criminal behaviour as 'fake', thereby triggering public uncertainty about whether or not the evidence has been falsified. The liar's dividend can be a useful means by which to escape accountability, but if done enough times, or at a large enough scale, it could become the default state of mental affairs. In other words, people will learn to assume that every image, video, audio and text they encounter online is a deepfake.

The Russian way of war

The Russian way of war, on the whole, is characterised by a focus on mass mobilisation, large ground forces and the use of combined arms tactics to grind down an enemy through attrition. The focus is on achieving incremental tactical and operational objectives.[26] Deception is seen as a key means by which to achieve these objectives. Indeed, deception is so deeply ingrained in Russian military thought that it even has a specialised term: *maskirovka* (маскировка).[27] This term connotes wearing masks in layers and, crucially, wielding those masks as weapons for offensive and defensive purposes. That the Russian way of war actually has an explicitly martial concept of deception probably goes a long way to explain why Russia has been extremely proactive at both information and narrative warfare in recent decades.[28]

The Battle of Borodino (1812), which was fought during Napoleon Bonaparte's invasion of the Russian Empire,[29] exemplifies the Russian pursuit of attrition. The Russian commander, General Mikhail Kutuzov, recognised that his army was outnumbered and outgunned by the French, which meant that direct confrontation would likely result in defeat. Kutuzov adopted a strategy of delaying tactics, using his infantry and artillery to hold the French advance while his cavalry attacked from the flanks and rear. This enabled Kutuzov to wear down the French army over a period of several days, inflicting heavy casualties, breaking the momentum of Bonaparte's advance and, ultimately, forcing him to withdraw. More than a century later, attrition would again be central to the Soviet defence of Stalingrad (1942–43), as the city's defenders sought to gradually exhaust the German advance.[30]

Deception enters the equation through the Russian military doctrine's emphasis on the importance of morale and psychological factors in warfare. Russian military strategists believe that maintaining the morale and fighting spirit of troops is critical to achieving victory, and, concomitantly, they place a high value on the ability to demoralise and break the will of the opponent. For example, during the defence of Stalingrad, the Soviet Union successfully deployed loudspeakers to broadcast propaganda and messages from German prisoners of war who had been convinced to switch sides, thereby boosting the morale of their own troops while weakening that of the Germans.[31]

Although actual Russian doctrinal documents are difficult to obtain outside of the Kremlin,[32] Russian military thought relating to narrative warfare seems more evolved than its American rival. It is striking that a narrative often heard in Russian circles is that the collapse of the Soviet Union was itself due to narrative defeat, i.e., the Soviets' failure at managing the narrative about the benefits of communism. Moscow appears determined to rectify this perceived failure. We see this determination in the concept of *information confrontation* (*informatsionnoe protivoborstvo*, информационное противоборство),[33] which connotes (a) the struggle between states over the information environment, both global and national; and (b) the deployment of technical, physical and psychological means to conduct narrative warfare.[34] Put simply, information confrontation seeks to use physical or cyber means to achieve psychological effects, and vice versa, to use psychological means to achieve physical effects.

Information confrontation is not always called such. For example, it is often spoken of in the Western press as 'hybrid warfare', while Russian and non-Russian scholars will also speak of 'information struggle', and more confusingly, 'information warfare'.[35] Nonetheless, 'information confrontation' is generally the preferred term, as it better describes activities that span the entire continuum of war and peace as well as expresses the sense that such activities are occurring primarily below the threshold of explicit armed conflict.[36]

Information confrontation is often considered a key part of the 'Gerasimov Doctrine', attributed to the Chief of the General Staff of the Russian Armed Forces Valery Gerasimov.[37] However, it is not per se original to Gerasimov, for it really emerges from a deeper cultural current. The Russian military has long sought to 'aggravate existing divisions' in an opponent in order 'to degrade cohesion, create confusion (and fear), assert a Russian worldview, sow doubt regarding what is true and inflict considerable psychological effects to intimidate and frustrate decision-making processes'.[38]

It is also worth noting that Russian military organisations have a longstanding history of engagement with scholarly research that includes formal modelling of information flows and control schema. These models extend to operations research, wherein they are used to create probabilistic mappings for desired outcomes and managed decisions as well as to research into achieving *reflexive control*, i.e., the practice of getting one's opponent to voluntarily make a choice that actually benefits oneself.[39] In our view, what such research philosophically represents is a maturation of *maskirovka*.

Moscow is already widely suspected of waging deepfake-augmented narrative warfare in its ongoing armed conflict with Kyiv. According to the Microsoft Threat Analysis Center,[40] it is highly likely that they have weaponised deepfakes to turn popular opinion in the US against supporting Ukraine and against Vice President Kamala Harris.

The Chinese way of war

The Chinese way of war today is characterised by a focus on asymmetric warfare, information warfare and the use of cyber- and space-based capabilities to achieve 'death by a thousand cuts'.[41] These strategies have deeper roots in long-standing principles of flexibility, adaptability and indirect approaches that, in turn, trace their origins to a canon of seven military classics: the *Art of War*, penned by the aforementioned Sun Tzu, and six texts written during the Warring States through Tang Dynasty periods, viz., Taigong, Sima, Wuzi, Wei Liaozi, Huang Shigong and the dialogue between Emperor Taizong and General Li Jing.[42] These texts incorporate *wu wei* (無爲), or 'non-action', a concept originally from Taoism that, in the millennia since, has come to be emblematic of the Chinese way of war.

Wu wei as a martial concept connotes the pursuit of effortless victories – 'effortless' in the sense of using the minimal amount of effort necessary for attaining optimal battlefield results. The goal is to permit events in the battlespace to unfold naturally, rather than aggressively forcing a preferred outcome. A stunning example of this is the retreat of the Jin Dynasty from the Central Plains in 316 AD. When the Jin faced the threat of invasion by the Xiongnu-led Zhao state, instead of choosing to defend their cities at great cost, they implemented a strategic retreat.[43] The Jin's non-action enabled them to preserve their regime's core and prolong their dynasty's survival. Indeed, the retreat not only conserved vital resources and manpower but also provided the Jin with a strategic position to later consolidate and plan further resistance.

Deception is a central, even inherent feature of martial *wu wei*. Chinese military history is littered with examples of what may be described as 'effortless deception', with a distinct tendency to prey on the opponent's desire for decisive outcomes.[44] Examples include the Battle of Red Cliffs (208–09 AD), the Qing Dynasty's initial response to the Taiping Rebellion (1850–64), the Chinese Communist Party (CCP)'s manoeuvres during the Chinese Civil War (1927–49) and the overlapping Second Sino-Japanese War (1937–45).

The Battle of Red Cliffs: Taking place during the late Han Dynasty, this battle vividly exemplified the principle of *wu wei*.[45] Facing the mighty navy of Cao Cao, the allied forces of Sun Quan and Liu Bei were significantly outnumbered. Instead of engaging in a direct and possibly disastrous confrontation, the allies adopted a strategy of minimal direct action. Utilising the natural environment to their advantage, they spread false information and lured Cao Cao's forces into a trap. The allied commander, Zhou Yu, then used subtle manoeuvres to position their much smaller navy advantageously against the overextended fleet of Cao Cao. By setting Cao Cao's ships on fire, they caused chaos and inflicted heavy losses, leveraging the strategy of 'non-action' by letting the enemy's own vulnerabilities lead to their defeat rather than engaging in extensive combat.

The Taiping Rebellion: To deal with the rebels, the Qing Dynasty initially employed a strategy of *wu wei* in both political and military contexts.[46] Thus, rather than directly engaging the

Taiping forces, who were rapidly gaining control over large swathes of southern China, the Qing government initially chose to withhold direct military action, opting instead to see if the rebellion would exhaust itself. This period of non-action enabled the Qing leadership to avoid overstretching their resources, which were already engaged on multiple fronts. Although the Qing were eventually compelled to adopt a more active strategy when the rebellion gained too much momentum, this initial decision showcases non-action, deployed as a tactical pause to regather strength and reassess strategic priorities amidst internal turmoil.

The Chinese Civil War and the Second Sino–Japanese War: The CCP under Mao Zedong exemplified *wu wei* during the Japanese invasion of China when they engaged in a strategic retreat known as 'The Long March', as well as later during periods of the Second Sino-Japanese War.[47] Instead of confronting the Japanese forces head-on, the CCP employed guerrilla tactics, avoiding large-scale engagements and preserving their strength. This instance of non-action involved mobilising peasant support and strengthening their base in rural areas while the Kuomintang (KMT) forces bore the brunt of Japanese aggression. The CCP's strategy of minimal direct confrontation, focusing on survival and expansion of influence through grassroots support and indirect engagement, effectively allowed them to grow in power and ultimately prevail in the subsequent civil war against the KMT.

In each of these battles, the Chinese sought to input into the battlespace the right amount of resources; they were also willing to suffer tactical setbacks to achieve strategic goals.

It is also worth underlining the cunning involved in effortless deception, as over the centuries, a recurring Chinese stratagem has been to get both allies and opponents to overinvest their resources on Beijing's behalf. Chinese military philosophy even has an expression for it: to 'kill with a borrowed sword' (*jiedaosharen*, 借刀殺人).[48] Arguably, we are seeing this stratagem in the PRC's tacit alliance with Russia. Some observers have suggested that Beijing may view the ongoing armed conflict in Ukraine as a 'proxy war' with Washington.[49] Others suspect that Beijing is observing Moscow's fortunes to draw lessons for its own possible invasion of Taiwan.[50]

The PRC has also been actively extending martial *wu wei* into narrative warfare. For example, per the related principle of 'looting a burning house' (*chenhuodajie*, 趁火打劫), some observers suspect that Beijing has quietly opened an information front by using social media to divide American and Taiwanese voters.[51] If true, there is a doctrinal context for this 'looting'; in 2003, the CCP Central Committee and the Central Military Commission approved the *Three Warfares* as a guiding framework: psychological warfare, legal warfare and 'public opinion warfare'.[52]

With respect to deepfakes, while they can certainly traverse all three of these warfares, their natural home is as components of the third. We would, therefore, expect that Chinese deployments of deepfakes pursue a goal similar to what they are believed to seek via disinformation more generally: achieve *strategic distraction*, i.e., the liar's dividend at a grand scale, in which the opponent's general public, ruling elite and even military leadership are too confused to meaningfully counteract Beijing's objectives.[53]

The American way of war

The American way of war focuses on the use of technology to achieve decisive victory. This includes the development and use of advanced weapons systems and precision-guided munitions; large-scale offensive operations, such as amphibious assaults, airborne operations and dedicated expeditionary units capable of rapid deployment; and the use of naval and air assets to project power, as well as to rapidly deploy large numbers of troops and equipment to any part of the world.

Although other nations have an appetite for battlefield invention, the driving motive behind Americans' interest in technology is to achieve decisive victories reminiscent of Bonaparte's sweeping victory at Austerlitz.[54] Bonaparte routed the coalition arrayed against him and set the stage for his dominance over Europe for the next decade. He accomplished this through strategic employment of military deception, specifically the use of feints to overextend enemy formations.[55]

As evidenced in the battles at Yorktown (1781), Gettysburg (1863), Midway (1942), Normandy (1944), Inchon (1950) and Operation Desert Storm (1991), deception has played an increasingly important role in the 'Austerlizian' program of the American way of war. We will focus here on the four examples from the twentieth century:

Midway: Deception was a pivotal element in the American victory at Midway. Indeed, this battle is considered a textbook example of military intelligence and deception in warfare.[56] The American Navy, having broken Japanese naval codes, knew of Japan's plans to attack Midway

Island and used this information to set a trap. Additionally, American forces sent false radio messages indicating that Midway's water purification system had failed, which helped motivate the Japanese to proceed.

Normandy: The Normandy invasion is renowned for Operation Fortitude, one of the most successful deception campaigns in military history.[57] The Allies created a fictional First US Army Group, supposedly located in southeast England and preparing to attack Pas-de-Calais. This operation involved fake radio traffic, inflatable tanks and a phantom army commanded by General Patton. The deception kept significant German forces away from Normandy, contributing critically to the Allied success on D-Day.[58]

Inchon: In the Korean War, the Inchon landing involved deception to keep North Korean forces off balance and unaware of the real landing site.[59] General Douglas MacArthur's choice of Inchon as a landing site was in itself a form of deception, as the tidal conditions and fortified positions led many military planners to see it as an improbable location for an amphibious assault. The surprise of the Inchon landing was key to its success, allowing United Nations forces to rapidly recapture Seoul and cut North Korean supply lines.

Desert Storm: American forces utilised deception to secure a decisive victory against Iraqi forces.[60] The main element of deception was known as Operation Fortitude South, echoing Operation Fortitude. Fortitude South involved extensive use of false radio transmissions and the deployment of decoy forces, including inflatable tanks and empty tents arranged to mimic a full-scale military buildup. These decoys were positioned to suggest an impending assault on the

> Kuwaiti coast, which led the Iraqi military to concentrate their defences there. Meanwhile, the real coalition attack, spearheaded by American and allied troops, was launched in a sweeping 'left hook' strategy through the western desert of Iraq, far from the expected point of attack. This manoeuvre effectively bypassed the bulk of Iraqi defences, leading to minimal coalition casualties and hastening the end of ground combat operations.

In each of these battles, the use of deception ranged from straightforward concealment of movement to elaborate schemes involving fake armies and offensive counterintelligence. These techniques were integral to achieving tactical surprise and operational superiority, leading to decisive victories.

Turning now to narrative warfare, the US certainly has the technological capabilities to be a successful narrator, and it is easy to imagine how a well-timed and well-targeted deepfake could achieve decisive victory over an opponent, e.g., by confusing and distracting their military command. Moreover, Americans have already started to think about how narrative warfare could be integrated into their broader military doctrine. Inklings of this can be found in US Joint Doctrine Note 2-13,[61] the US Joint Concept for Operating in the Information Environment (JCOIE),[62] the US Army's Field Manual 3-13 Information Operations,[63] 'Operating in the Human Domain' by the US Special Operations Command (USSOCOM)[64] and US Joint Publication 3-13.4, which explicitly regards 'MILDEC', i.e., military deception.[65]

However, narrative warfare poses an ethical challenge to the American way of war in a way that it does not to its Russian and

Chinese counterparts, for it is not necessarily consistent with US Constitutional ideals of free speech and liberty of conscience. In other words, the question facing Americans is not whether they could wage narrative warfare but if they should and, if so, in which ways.

Our own answer to this question is that Americans should be willing and able to wage narrative warfare, but they do need to wage it in a way that is ethically consistent with their stated ideals. Towards that end, we now outline some proposals, including both offensive and defensive uses of deepfakes.

Offence

We propose that the following ideas for using deepfakes offensively in a manner that is consistent with US ideals and the American way of war:

Targeting deepfakes solely at the militaries of opposing nations, not civilian populations, e.g., infiltrating internal military communications systems with voice deepfakes of their commanders issuing fake orders or making negative remarks about the character of the rank and file.

Targeting civilian populations for deepfakes that actively promote democratic values, e.g., visualising for them what it would be like to have rule of law applied to corrupt officials or having genuine electoral control over their own governments.

Targeting hopes rather than fears, e.g., that it is possible for them to have prosperity and that material and emotional deprivations are not their nations' destinies but the result of understandable but misguided decisions.

We imagine that deployments of deepfakes in these and similar manners would be consistent with important moral principles, such as maintaining the distinction between regular versus irregular forces by targeting deepfakes at uniformed personnel and seeking to motivate rather than demoralise civilian populations, specifically to see it as being in their moral and material interest to turn against authoritarian regimes.

Defence

There are two distinct ways to think about defence in the context of deepfake-augmented narrative warfare: as a strategic posture and as a set of specific tactics. In terms of a strategic posture, a defensive US could seek to avoid direct narrative combat. One form this posture could take is narrative pacifism, i.e., a total renunciation of narrative warfare. This, though, seems unlikely and, depending on one's viewpoint, undesirable.

The more likely possibility is that if the US chooses a defensive strategic posture, it will engage in indirect narrative combat – as it were, it will defend itself by also going on the offence. There is a precedent for such an approach. As we noted earlier, the American government has long supported RFE/RL precisely on the dual premise that accurate and truthful journalism is an effective form of counterpropaganda and is itself a narrative, insofar that promoting such journalism evinces a worldview rooted in evidence, deliberation and anti-authoritarianism.[66]

As for purely defensive tactics, their development is already underway as of this writing. For example, DARPA is supporting research into automating content moderation to help protect the information environment from disinformation.[67] There is also ongoing research into techniques that could be used to inoculate audiences against influence operations.[68] For our part, we propose that the following ideas should also be considered:

Military training: deepfake simulations can prepare troops for encountering disinformation in real-world operations, enhancing cognitive resilience.
Public education: government agencies and nonprofits can use deepfake-based examples to educate citizens on recognising and mitigating disinformation.
Counterintelligence: the US could deploy deepfakes to dissimulate its own internal conditions, particularly its military conditions, so as to confuse their adversaries and reap the liar's dividend for itself.

Whatever course of action the US takes, it is inevitable and necessary for Washington to formulate some kind of doctrine to utilise and contend with deepfakes in narrative warfare. Whatever doctrine the American nation eventually formulates should express *disciplined initiative*, i.e., it must be sufficiently flexible to enable action in a variety of situations, consistent with the American way of war and sufficiently principled so as to not lose sight of just-war theoretical considerations.

The future

To close, one question remains: now that the tides of deepfake-augmented narrative warfare are rising, what might be the state of the global information environment by the middle of this century? At the outset of this chapter, we described deepfakes as the atomic bombs of narrative warfare. Thinking of them this way led us to pose the question of how the global information environment could evolve in the coming decades.

We have looked at real-life examples and trends in the historical development of the internet, and from these have extrapolated two polarised scenarios: the dark forest and classical liberalism. In brief, in the dark forest scenario, countries will retreat behind national or regional firewalls, resulting in a world of disconnected and mutually hostile national intranets. By contrast, in the classically liberal scenario, a universal internet in one form or another prevails, facilitating global digital integration and the free exchange and open debate of ideas.

The catch is that these scenarios are not just thought experiments, but actual strategic choices that are already being made right now, with very real trade-offs. In Russia and China, the choice towards the dark forest was already being made before deepfakes entered the terrain; in their wake, we expect Moscow and Beijing will double down. The wild card is the US. One would expect Washington to move in the direction of the classically liberal scenario, but it is also possible to see the US go down the same path of its adversaries.

What has already been happening

The seeds of the dark forest can already be seen in systems like the PRC's Great Firewall, which has evolved since 2006 into one of the most sophisticated mechanisms of information control in the world, and in legislation like Russia's 2019 'internet sovereignty' law.[69] With deepfake-augmented narrative warfare breaking out, the dark forest scenario offers very real safety for those within a sealed intranet – at least from external adversaries. The users of these intranets would likely remain vulnerable to their own governments deploying deepfakes for the purposes of maintaining domestic narrative control. Given the authoritarian nature of the Russian and Chinese governments, it strains credulity to believe that they have not already begun thinking how they could target deepfakes at their own citizenries.

Meanwhile, the classically liberal scenario would resemble the information environment that existed during the brief period between the collapse of the Soviet Union in late 1991 and the completion of the first phase of the PRC's 'Great Firewall' in 2006. We have in mind here not the more difficult elements of that period, such as the lack of content moderation and patchy infrastructure. Rather, we have in mind the spirit of possibility and openness that seemed to overall characterise digital culture at the time. Connectivity was generally seen as a virtue, not a vice; it was something to be championed, not feared. This has been the overall trajectory of the US since the 1990s.

On the question of deepfake-augmented narrative warfare, what the classically liberal scenario offers in terms of narrative security would probably depend on how one imagines its underlying infrastructure to work, whether there is much in the way of moderation, and if so, who acts as the moderators, according to which moderation rules and under which means of oversight. Generally, though, it seems reasonable to imagine that this scenario does not offer any robust narrative security to the users of the universal internet. The trade-off is that there would also be distinctly less narrative control, meaning that netizens would have greater capacity to choose narratives for themselves.

What could happen by mid-century

When treating these scenarios as strategic choices, immediately we must contend with a critique that can be raised against the classically liberal scenario and that is whether the very idea of a universal internet is illusory or naive. Per this logic, it would be illusory in the sense that there has never *been* a universal internet, even when it might have seemed like there was one. The internet has never actually been a single system; nor was every society integrated into it at the same time and rate; nor, even now, are they integrated into it equally. The idea of a universal internet would also be naive in the sense that we live in a world of competing powers and will continue to do so for the foreseeable future. For a universal internet to come into existence, then, it would not only need to be a single, unified and truly equitable system, but it might require some kind of planetary governance structure to establish and enforce. At the very least, the international community would need to be both more cooperative and more committed to democratic values than they have been – an indictment that, sadly, includes the US.

These are valid doubts, but it is also worthwhile to point out that the dark forest in its own right implies things about the international order that not only have yet to come to pass but are also unlikely to do so, at least anytime soon. For example, for the dark forest to take root, nation-states would need to become self-sufficient in ways that have, heretofore, been impossible, particularly with respect to key resources such as rare earths. As far as we can see, the only real solution to this problem would be for nation-states to forge larger region-states, which would be a radical step up from their current preference for trade and military alliances. Forging such region-states would be difficult to achieve politically, as nation-states are jealous of their sovereignty. It might also contravene the spirit of the dark forest, insofar that allies could expect to have access to each other's intranets as a way to build trust (and also make each other vulnerable to their own narrative meddling and subterfuge).

To repeat what we noted at the outset of this chapter, we ourselves think the classically liberal scenario is the best of the two choices, even if we do not have good answers to the many questions it raises. In the context of deepfake-augmented narrative warfare, we believe that the classically liberal scenario offers the most constructive approach for the world. Seeing as how Russia and China have already more or less made their choice, it is also the model most in line with professed American principles – that is to say, with the long-established US strategic narrative of democratic values. It is, therefore, the strategy that Washington should pursue.

Of course, the world has already been experiencing much in the way of narrative insecurity even without a dark forest or universal internet. We acknowledge this reality. Yet, history has shown that connectivity and openness have a self-correcting quality: over time, people tend to resist isolation and seek ways to balance security with freedom. Deepfake-augmented narrative warfare will lead to casualties, figuratively and literally, but we believe that it will be a price worth paying for a freer world.

Acknowledgement

This material is based upon work supported by the National Science Foundation under Award No. 2040209 and the US Department of Defense under Award No. W911NF-23-2-0036. Justin M. Pelletier would like to acknowledge the ongoing support he receives from the *Ordo Praedicatorum*.

Notes

1 Dan Evon, 'Bad deepfake of Zelenskyy shared on Ukraine news site in reported hack', *Snopes* (2022). https://www.snopes.com/news/2022/03/16/zelenskyy-deepfake-shared/ (accessed 5 February 2026).

2 Brenda K. Wiederhold, 'Can deepfakes improve therapy?', *Cyberpsychology, Behavior, and Social Networking* 24:3 (2021), 147–148. https://doi.org/10.1089/cyber.2021.29209.editorial

3 Hsuan-Chia Yang, Annisa Ristya Rahmanti, Chih-Wei Huang and Yu-Chuan Jack Li, 'How can research on artificial empathy be enhanced by applying deepfakes?', *Journal of Medical Internet Research* 24:3 (2022), e29506. https://doi.org/10.2196/29506

4 This is our distinction, which we acknowledge is reductive. For a detailed military discussion about many possible interpretations of 'narrative', see: Maj. Gittipong Paruchabutr, *Understanding and Communicating through Narratives* (Fort Leavenworth, KS: School of Advanced Military Studies, United States Army Command and General Staff College, 2012). https://apps.dtic.mil/sti/tr/pdf/ADA566587.pdf (accessed 5 February 2026).

5 We have coined this term to express both the particular idea of narrative warfare that specifically deploys deepfakes as well as the broader idea that narrative warfare will be different going forwards because of deepfakes.

6 Joint Chiefs of Staff, *Joint Publication 3-13.4: Military Deception* (2012). https://www.jcs.mil/Doctrine/Joint-Doctrine-Pubs/3-0-Operations-Series/ (accessed 5 February 2026).

7 Lionel Giles, *The Art of War, by Sun Tzu* (Project Gutenberg eBook, 2005. Originally published 1994), 24. https://www.utoledo.edu/rotc/pdfs/the_art_of_war.pdf (accessed 5 February 2026).

8 Mohammad Eslami, Alena Vieira, Arshin Adib-Moghaddam, Lauro Borges, Maria Papageorgiou, Fabio Cristiano, Ibrahim Al-Marashi, Tom Sauer and Christian Kaunert, 'The geopolitics of AI-driven arms races', *Geopolitics* (2025), 1–43.

9 Cixin Liu, *The Dark Forest* (New York: Tor Books, 2016).

10 Yisroel Mirsky and Wenke Lee, 'The creation and detection of deepfakes: A survey', *ACM Computing Surveys (CSUR)* 54:1 (2021), 1–41; Luisa Verdoliva, 'Media forensics and deepfakes: An overview', *IEEE Journal of Selected Topics in Signal Processing* 14:5 (2020), 910–932; Ruben Tolosana, Ruben Vera-Rodriguez, Julian Fierrez, Aythami Morales and Javier Ortega-Garcia, 'Deepfakes and beyond: A survey of face manipulation and fake detection', *Information Fusion* 64 (2020), 910–932. https://doi.org/10.1016/j.inffus.2020.06.014

11 Note that a deepfake's creator and propagator(s) are often not the same people, and its audience may change as it migrates through and across platforms.

12 Ahmed Bhatti and Mehmood Nessir, 'American strategic narrative – A success story or an archetypal rhetoric', *Routledge Open Research* 3:23 (2024). https://doi.org/10.12688/routledgeopenres.18100.1. Note that strategic narratives also reveal vulnerabilities, particularly what Bhatti and Mehmood call the 'narrative-policy gap', in which a government's actions contradict their stated values, undermining credibility.

13 Paruchabutr, *Understanding and Communicating through Narratives*, 7–12.

14 Paruchabutr, Understanding and Communicating through Narratives.

15 Paruchabutr, Understanding and Communicating through Narratives.

16 Jan K. Hanska, 'Storytelling or non-kinetic weaponry? Strategic communication from a narratological perspective', *Journal of Information Warfare* 14:1 (2015), 24–38. https://www.jstor.org/stable/26487516 (accessed 5 February 2026).

17 Radio Free Europe/Radio Liberty, https://about.rferl.org/ (accessed 5 February 2026).

18 Paul Sonne, 'Fake Putin speech calling for martial law aired in Russia', *The New York Times* (2023). https://www.nytimes.com

/2023/06/05/world/europe/putin-deep-fake-speech-hackers.html (accessed 5 February 2026).

19 These rumours were encountered on Telegram by author Christopher Schwartz.

20 Isabel van Brugen, 'Why is Vladimir Putin stalling?' *Newsweek* (2023). https://www.newsweek.com/why-vladimir-putin-stalling-russia-mass-full-scale-second-wave-mobilization-1821366 (accessed 5 February 2026).

21 Volodymyr Ishchenko and Oleg Zhuravlev, 'Imperialist ideology or depoliticization? Why Russian citizens support the invasion of Ukraine', *HAU: Journal of Ethnographic Theory* 12:3 (2022), 668–676. https://doi.org/10.1086/723802

22 *TASS*, 'Kremlin sounds alarm on deepfakes following fraudulent call using Putin's voice' (2024). https://tass.com/politics/1766895 (accessed 5 February 2026).

23 Jenni Reid, 'Putin quizzed by apparent AI version of himself during live phone-in', *CNBC* (2023). https://www.cnbc.com/2023/12/14/putin-confronted-by-apparent-ai-version-of-himself-during-live-phone-in.html (accessed 5 February 2026).

24 Q.v., Jon Roozenbeek and Sander van der Linden, *Inoculation Theory and Misinformation* (Riga: NATO Strategic Communications Centre of Excellence, 2021). https://stratcomcoe.org/publications/download/Inoculation-theory-and-Misinformation-FINAL-digital-ISBN-ebbe8.pdf (accessed 5 February 2026).

25 Q.v., Bobby Chesney and Danielle Citron, 'Deep fakes: a looming challenge for privacy, democracy, and national security', *California Law Review*, 107 (2019). https://www.californialawreview.org/print/deep-fakes-a-looming-challenge-for-privacy-democracy-and-national-security (accessed 5 February 2026).

26 Daniel Treisman, *The Return: Russia's Journey from Gorbachev to Medvedev* (New York: Simon and Schuster, 2012); James F. Dunnigan, *How to Make War: A Comprehensive Guide to Modern Warfare* (Swindon: BCA, 1982).

27 Jon Latimer, *Deception in War: The Art of the Bluff, the Value of Deceit, and the Most Thrilling Episodes of Cunning in Military History from the Trojan Horse to the Gulf War* (New York: Abrams, 2003).

28 Alan Kelly and Christopher Paul, *Decoding Crimea: Pinpointing the Influence Strategies of Modern Information Warfare* (Riga: NATO Strategic Communications Centre of Excellence, 2020).

29 Dominic Lieven, *Russia Against Napoleon: The Battle for Europe, 1807 to 1814* (London: Penguin UK, 2009).

30 John Keegan, *The Second World War* (vol. 268) (New York: Random House, 1997).

31 William Craig, *Enemy at the Gates: The Battle for Stalingrad* (Old Saybrook, CT: Konecky Konecky, 2004).

32 Indeed, we interpret the paucity of publicly available doctrinal documents from the Russian military, as well as from the Chinese military, as exemplifying their desire to enforce state control over narratives.

33 Karen-Anna Eggen, 'Designing around NATO's deterrence: Russia's Nordic information confrontation strategy', *Journal of Strategic Studies* (2024), 1–25. https://doi.org/10.1080/01402390.2024.2332328

34 Michelle Grisé, Alyssa Demus, Yuliya Shokh, Marta Kepe, Jonathan W. Welburn and Khrystyna Holynska, *Rivalry in the Information Sphere: Russian Conceptions of Information Confrontation, Research Report RRA198-8* (Santa Monica, CA: RAND Corporation, 2022). https://www.rand.org/pubs/research_reports/RRA198-8.html (accessed 5 February 2026).

35 Ulrik Franke, *War by Non-military Means: Understanding Russian Information Warfare* (Stockholm: Russia Studies Programme, Swedish Defence Research Agency, 2015). https://www.foi.se/rest-api/report/FOI-R—4065—SE (accessed 2 February 2023).

36 Derived from Eggen 2024, who cites Joe Cheravitch, 'The Role of Russia's Military in Information Confrontation', *Center for Naval Analyses* (2021). https://www.cna.org/reports/2021/06/role-of-russian-military-in-information-confrontation (accessed 5 February 2026); and Katri Pynnöniemi, 'Information-psychological warfare in Russian security strategy' in Roger E. Kanet (ed.), *Routledge Handbook of Russian Security* (London: Routledge, 2019), 216; Larisa V. Vorontsova and Dmitriy Frolov, *Past and Present Information Confrontation* (*Istoriya i sovremennost' informatsionnogo protivoborstva*) (Moscow: Garyachaya linja, 2019), 77; and (2019). https://www.ndc.nato.int/general-gerasimov-on-the-vectors-of-the-development-of-military-strategy/ (accessed 5 February 2026).

37 Valery Gerasimov, 'The value of science is in the foresight', *Military Review* (January–February 2016), 23–29. https://www.armyupress.army.mil/portals/7/military-review/archives/english/militaryreview_20160228_art008.pdf (accessed 5 February 2026).

38 This quote is from Eggen 2024, who references Lesley Kucharski, 'Russian multi-domain strategy against NATO: Information confrontation and U.S. forward-deployed nuclear weapons in Europe', *Lawrence Livermore National Laboratory* (2019), 2. https://doi.org/10.2172/1635758. See also: Jānis Bērziņš, 'The theory and practice of new generation warfare: The case of Ukraine and Syria', *The Journal of Slavic Military Studies* 33:3 (2020), 355–380. https://doi.org/10.1080/13518046.2020.1824109

39 Dmitry A. Novikov and Alexander Chkhartishvili, *Reflexion and Control: Mathematical Models* (London: Routledge, 2014).

40 Brad Smith, 'Securing US elections from nation-state adversaries', *Microsoft On the Issues* (2024). https://blogs.microsoft.com/on-the-issues/2024/09/18/securing-us-elections-from-nation-state-adversaries/ (accessed 5 February 2026); Clint Watts, 'As the U.S. election nears, Russia, Iran and China step up influence efforts', *Microsoft On the Issues* (2024). https://blogs.microsoft.com/on-the-issues/2024/10/23/as-the-u-s-election-nears-russia-iran-and-china-step-up-influence-efforts/ (accessed 5 February 2026).

41 For further elaboration on this characterisation, see, for example, Peter W. Singer and Allan Friedman, *Cybersecurity and Cyberwar: What Everyone Needs to Know* (Oxford: Oxford University Press, 2014); Dennis J. Blasko, *The Chinese Army Today: Tradition and Transformation for the 21st Century* (New York: Routledge, 2013); Toshi Yoshihara, *Chinese Information Warfare: A Phantom Menace or Emerging Threat?* (Darby, PA: DIANE Publishing, 2001); Evgeniya Yu Katkova and Anna S. Yunyushkina, 'Chinese concepts and opportunities in information warfare: China–US rivalry in cyberspace', *RUDN Journal of World History* 14:2 (2022), 197–210.

42 Ralph D. Sawyer, *The Seven Military Classics of Ancient China* (New York: Basic Books, 2020).

43 Tan Koon San, *Dynastic China: An Elementary History* (Kuala Lumpur: The Other Press, 2014).

44 James Irving Matray, *The Reluctant Crusade: American Foreign Policy in Korea 1941–1950* (Charlottesville, VA: University of Virginia, 1977).

45 Major James G. Pangelinan, *From Red Cliffs to Chosin: The Chinese Way of War* (London: Pickle Partners Publishing, 2015).

46 King-To Yeung, *Suppressing Rebels, Managing Bureaucrats: State-Building during the Taiping Rebellion, 1850–1864* (New Brunswick, NJ: Rutgers The State University of New Jersey, School of Graduate Studies, 2007).

47 Jennifer Lynn Cucchisi, 'The causes and effects of the Chinese Civil War, 1927–1949', *Seton Hall University Dissertations and Theses* (2022). https://scholarship.shu.edu/dissertations/2361 (accessed 5 February 2026).

48 The Thirty-Six Stratagems serve as a playbook of ruses and deceptions for creating winning military outcomes. There are many translations available, for example, the work by Tr. Verstappen. http://wengu.tartarie.com/wg/wengu.php?no=-1&l=36ji (accessed 5 February 2026).

49 E.g., Michael Cunningham, 'How China really views the war in Ukraine', *The Heritage Foundation* (2023). https://www.heritage.org/global-politics/commentary/how-china-really-views-the-war-ukraine (accessed 5 February 2026); Seth Cropsey, 'A global proxy war: Ukraine is now the center of our Eurasian competition with Russia and China', *The Hill* (2023). https://thehill.com/opinion/international/3942099-a-global-proxy-war-ukraine-is-now-the-center-of-our-eurasian-competition-with-russia-and-china/ (accessed 5 February 2026).

50 Reid Standish, 'China invasion of Ukraine seen as test case for Taiwan designs', *Radio Free Europe/Radio Liberty* (2023). https://www.rferl.org/a/china-invasion-ukraine-test-case-taiwan-designs/32435629.html (accessed 5 February 2026).

51 Dan De Luce and Gary Grumbach, 'AI gives Russia, China new tools to sow division in the U.S., undermine America's image, intel agencies say', *NBC News* (2024). https://www.nbcnews.com/politics/national-security/china-russia-ai-divide-us-society-undermine-us-elections-power-rcna142880 (accessed 5 February 2026). See also Sze-Fung Lee, 'Deepfakes with Chinese characteristics: PRC influence operations in 2024', *Jamestown Foundation China Brief* 24:7 (2024). https://jamestown.org/program/deepfakes-with-chinese-characteristics-prc-influence-operations-in-2024/ (accessed 5 February 2026).

52 For further information about this framework, see Peter Mattis, 'China's three warfares: A perspective', *War on the Rocks* (2018). https://warontherocks.com/2018/01/chinas-three-warfares-perspective/ (accessed 5 February 2026); 'China: The Three Warfares', US Department of Defense (2013). https://www.esd.whs.mil/Portals/54/Documents/FOID/Reading%20Room/Litigation_Release/Litigation%20Release%20-%20China-%20The

%20Three%20Warfares%20%20201305.pdf (accessed 5 February 2026).

53 Gary King, Jennifer Pan and Margaret E. Roberts, 'How the Chinese government fabricates social media posts for strategic distraction, not engaged argument', *American Political Science Review* 111:3 (2017), 484–501. https://doi.org/10.1017/S0003055417000144

54 Russell F. Weigley, *The American Way of War: A History of United States Military Strategy and Policy* (Bloomington, IN: Indiana University Press, 1977).

55 Robert M. Citino, *Quest for Decisive Victory: From Stalemate to Blitzkrieg in Europe, 1899–1940* (Lawrence, KS: University Press of Kansas, 2002).

56 Frank J. Stech and Christopher Elsässer, 'Midway revisited: Detecting deception by analysis of competing hypotheses', *Military Operations Research* 12:1 (2007), 35–55. https://apps.dtic.mil/sti/tr/pdf/ADA428173.pdf (accessed 5 February 2026).

57 Latimer, *Deception in War*.

58 Donald C. Daniel and Katherine L. Herbig, 'Propositions on mlitary deception', *The Journal of Strategic Studies* 5:1 (1982), 155–177. https://doi.org/10.1080/01402398208437105

59 Michael I. Handel, 'Intelligence and deception', *The Journal of Strategic Studies* 5:1 (1982), 122–154. https://doi.org/10.1080/01402398208437104

60 Latimer, *Deception in War*.

61 Joint Chiefs of Staff, 'Joint Doctrine Note 2-13: Commander's Communication Synchronization' (2013), III-9. https://edocs.nps.edu/2014/March/jdn2_13.pdf (accessed 5 February 2026).

62 Paul J. Selva, *Joint Concept for Operating in the Information Environment* (Washington, DC: United States Joint Chiefs of Staff, 2018).

63 Department of the Army, *Field Manual No. 3-13: Information Operations* (Washington, DC: Headquarters, Department of the Army, 2016).

64 Heather S. Gregg, 'The human domain and influence operations in the 21st century', *Special Operations Journal* 2:2 (2016), 92–105. https://doi.org/10.1080/23296151.2016.1195602

65 JP 3-13.4 (2012).

66 From the RFE/RL website (https://about.rferl.org/about-rfe-rl/rfe-rl-101/ [accessed 5 February 2026]): 'RFE/RL's mission is to promote democratic values by providing accurate, uncensored news, and open debate in countries where a free press is threatened and disinformation is pervasive. RFE/RL reports the facts, undaunted by pressure'.

67 The research project we are referring to here is called 'Civil Sanctuary'. https://www.darpa.mil/program/civil-sanctuary (accessed 5 February 2026).

68 Q.v., Roozenbeek and van der Linden, 'Inoculation theory and misinformation'.

69 Gavin Wilde and Justin Sherman, 'Putin's internet plan: Dependency with a veneer of sovereignty', Brookings Institute (2022). https://www.brookings.edu/articles/putins-internet-plan-dependency-with-a-veneer-of-sovereignty/ (accessed 5 February 2026).

5

AI and nuclear arms race: the next level?

Mohammad Eslami, Ibrahim Al-Marashi, Lauro Borges and Alessandra Russo

Introduction

International arms control efforts have failed to prevent nuclear proliferation entering the 2020s,[1] as nuclear-armed countries have modernised their arsenals, several non-nuclear-armed countries have increased their enrichment capacities and are very close to weaponisation,[2] and non-nuclear states have pursued nuclear programs in cooperation with nuclear powers.[3] All three of these efforts will be enhanced with advances in artificial intelligence (AI). Concurrently, the weaponisation of AI will enhance nuclear capabilities in several ways, such as improving targeting accuracy of tactical nuclear bombs, shortening response times and even enabling autonomous decision-making in critical scenarios. Advanced command and control systems utilising AI algorithms could help reduce human error, providing quicker and more reliable responses to potential threats.[4] However, from a normative perspective, it is essential to strike a balance between autonomy and human oversight to avoid dangerous scenarios in which the human role in decision-making diminishes.[5]

With enhanced capabilities, AI-enhanced nuclear weapons might compel other nations, particularly adversaries, to seek similar autonomous capabilities.[6] This chapter aims to explain how and to what extent AI-assisted systems can affect the world's nuclear security and whether the most recent AI advancements can lead to an escalation of the nuclear arms race,[7] primarily focusing on four roles of AI in the nuclear domain: production, targeting, testing and safeguarding, which, in turn, affect strategic decision-making, autonomous weapons systems and enhanced target recognition capabilities.[8] Understanding these risks are crucial for scientists, policymakers and society at large, enabling the design of effective governance frameworks to mitigate the negative consequences of AI in this domain as well as examine the peaceful uses of AI nuclear technologies.[9] A significant body of literature has explored the intersection of nuclear security, proliferation and AI and its potential effect and impact on international security and stability. However, given the growing complexities and challenges in international arms control efforts that have ensued entering the 2020s, this chapter offers an update on the literature from the past decade, encompassing recent advancements in AI technology and nuclear proliferation.

This chapter is structured as follows: first, we describe the contemporary strategic and international context behind today's nuclear arms race; second, we offer a brief history of the convergence between AI and the nuclear domain; then, we describe the links between AI and nuclear proliferation; subsequently, we analyse how the connection between AI and nuclear technology affects international security; and finally we offer our concluding remarks.

An AI-enhanced nuclear arms race in the contemporary era: myth or reality?

The historical inflection point for this chapter is not the Trinity test or the atomic bomb being deployed over Japan in 1945. Instead, it is the development of acoustic homing torpedoes during the Second World War, which represented one of the earliest examples of automated targeting systems, in which weapons selected targets based on sensor inputs without direct human intervention. This laid the groundwork for further exploration of AI in the scientific community, leading to advancements in mathematical and logical problem-solving as well as the development of early AI models such as expert systems and rule-based reasoning.[10] In the 1960s, the US Department of Defense's Advanced Research Projects Agency (DARPA) provided the bulk of American AI funding. The Pentagon bankrolled AI research on the assumption that intelligent machines would complement human soldiers in Cold War combat. AI technologies were also applied to nuclear industries, primarily to assist in research on nuclear energy and reactor design. For example, AI-based methods were employed to simulate and optimise nuclear reactions in reactors through automation of various systems. The 1970s marked the emergence of expert systems, an AI subfield that focused on capturing and utilising the knowledge of human experts. Expert systems were employed in the nuclear industry to aid in reactor diagnostics, safety analysis and decision-making processes. These systems utilised rule-based reasoning to diagnose faults, provide recommendations and enhance overall operational efficiency.[11] By the early 2000s, AI technologies were integrated into the nuclear industry to improve operational monitoring and maintenance practices. Predictive maintenance systems enhanced equipment monitoring and fault prediction, reducing downtime and improving safety.[12] Machine learning algorithms were developed to study historical data and identify patterns to provide advanced warnings for potential equipment failures.[13] Today, giving full autonomy to AI-based applications in the face of nuclear risks has several proponents. However, the reliability of AI-based applications is still under question.[14]

The advances of AI converge with the increase in nuclear proliferation in the twenty-first century. Only a few months after taking presidential office, on April 5, 2009, Barack Obama prioritised nuclear disarmament in a speech in Prague, committing America to a nuclear-free world.[15] Obama's arms control achievements included nuclear negotiations with Iran[16] and North Korea[17] and decreasing the number of nuclear warheads in the world, mainly between the US and Russia with the 'New Start', which was part of a foreign policy that sought a reset with Moscow in the aftermath of its 2008 invasion of Georgia.[18] Although Obama acknowledged that he might not see that day in his lifetime, it seemed, at the time, that the world's powers were moving towards reducing their nuclear arsenals and counting less and less on nuclear weapons as a deterrent. However, security dynamics in the aftermath of Russia's annexation of Crimea in 2014 affected the global nuclear balance.[19] Then, China announced its plan to expand the number of its nuclear warheads to achieve parity with the US.[20] Concerns over American isolationism under Trump administration led to the possibility of European nuclear proliferation, albeit only France and Britain are equipped with nuclear weapons, with less than 5 per cent of the world's nuclear warheads.[21] Nuclear disarmament is no longer a global priority, representing a return to the tensions of the Cold War era and nuclear arms races.[22]

It is worth noting that the contemporary nuclear arms race is not limited to the nine countries with nuclear arsenals. The new nuclear arms race will most likely take place among those countries that have peaceful nuclear programs and are capable of uranium enrichment mainly in East Asia and Europe. This is not to mention that there are several countries that do not have any active nuclear reactors and have the aspiration of going nuclear (such as Saudi Arabia,[23] Türkiye[24] and Algeria[25]). The most recent technological advancements in the fields of computer science and AI would make the acquisition of nuclear bombs faster, easier and more cost-efficient. James Johnson, an expert on the intersection of nuclear weapons, AI and and strategic affairs, writes:

> Algorithms that underlie complex autonomous systems today are too unpredictable, vulnerable (to cyber attacks), unexplainable (the 'black-box' problem), brittle, and myopic to be used unsupervised in safety-critical domains. For now, there is a broad consensus amongst nuclear experts and nuclear-armed states that, even if the technology permitted, AI decision-making that directly impacts nuclear command-and-control functions (i.e., missile-launch decisions), should not be pre-delegated to AIs. Whether this fragile consensus can withstand mounting first-mover advantage temptations in a multipolar nuclear order is less certain. Whether human commanders – predisposed to anthropomorphise subjects, cognitive offloading, and automation bias – can avoid the temptation to view AI as a panacea for the cognitive fallibilities of human decision-making is also unclear.[26]

Johnson highlights AI limitations and underscores how predelegating decision-making to AI systems in the safety-critical domain of nuclear command-and-control functions is highly dangerous due to AI algorithms issues of unpredictability and vulnerability. While caution in integrating AI into nuclear operations is paramount, evolving technological capabilities and geopolitical dynamics might push actors to pursue an advantage on competitors by employing greater autonomy in nuclear command-and-control, ushering in a AI-nuclear arms race.

Going into the future, AI and information technology will affect the nuclear domain.[27] While nuclear-armed states have adopted AI technology into the nuclear sectors, there is still no evidence of which country would grant autonomy to its AI-based nuclear bombs, akin to the dystopian scenario in the *Terminator* movie series franchise. One view is that AI-based technologies are capable of performing tasks that could destabilise the nuclear balance or undermine nuclear deterrence, while another school argues that AI is unlikely to have an impact on nuclear command and control and will remain limited to the automation of nuclear cycles, not the autonomy of nuclear warheads.

The existing literature in the field of AI and the nuclear realm falls into three schools. The first asserts that AI-assisted applications are not capable of revolutionising the nuclear industry and, therefore, are not dangerous technologies opposed to the second group. To Rickli, the weaponisation of AI does not necessarily represent a challenge for nuclear deterrence. Algorithm-based systems in military decision-making functions such as 'AI advisers' – which can assess a nuclear threat and plan the best response in the shortest time available – will have an enormous impact on conflict escalation management.[28] Combined with current developments in missile technologies and hypersonic missiles, they could create a system that drastically reduces the already short decision-making time to respond to a nuclear attack.[29] The potential impacts of AI on nuclear risk is twofold. AI can increase mutual vulnerability against nuclear weapons. AI can result in the production of faster, smarter, more accurate and more versatile warheads, leading to an uncontrolled nuclear arms race. AI can also encourage 'technologically disadvantaged states' to develop their nuclear arsenal in the face of the new symmetric and asymmetric military technologies of their adversaries. In addition, AI is capable of assisting non-state actors and even terrorist[30] groups to develop nuclear bombs.[31]

This second school of scholars also believes that AI should be excluded from any aspect of nuclear war and systems related to nuclear industries,[32] as it could, for example, cause an arms race and strategic instability. Nuclear deterrence requires a security policy that allows authorised operators to detect threats needing a nuclear response and launch a nuclear response and never allow unauthorised personnel to launch nuclear weapons. While in computer systems, there are always some malfunctions, the mentioned laws are likely to be violated by AI-supported nuclear systems. The existence of these vulnerabilities and lack of trust in AI-based applications should make nuclear-armed states reconsider the integration of AI into their nuclear programs.

The third school acknowledges the former two have valid points, as AI-based technologies can have stabilising and destabilising impacts as well.[33] AI could increase stability by reducing the likelihood of human error and biases while also supporting the compliance and verification of arms control regimes.[34] This group of scholars claims that the integration of AI in nuclear programs reduces risk and prevents computing errors and predicts system malfunctions and disorder.[35]

AI integration into the nuclear industry: from automation to autonomy

As mentioned earlier, AI plays a role in the nuclear industry in terms of production, targeting, testing and safeguarding.

Production

In the production cycle, AI can increase nuclear material production by making their production more efficient, optimising output and reducing costs of developing nuclear weapons. Research conducted by the Arms Control Negotiation Academy (ACONA) demonstrates that AI can be used in all critical stages of nuclear material production, including mining and milling, conversion, enrichment, fuel fabrication, electricity generation, spent fuel storage and reprocessing. It is in the three sensitive stages of nuclear material production, enrichment and reprocessing that AI can play the most influential role, through anomaly detection, automated optimisation and automated discovery.[36]

Targeting

In the targeting domain, AI can create a semiautonomous nuclear weapon system, augmenting intelligence, surveillance and reconnaissance; automated target recognition and terminal guidance; and delivery and defence systems used against nuclear attacks.[37] In the military application of AI, targeting is part of the decision-support system, with or without direct participation in a nuclear launch. It is likely that by 2040, AI could help humans with the decision-making process. Such an advance would reduce human error by providing more transparency, preventing the risk of miscalculation. However, there are still concerns about the potential possibility of hacking, poisoning its training data or manipulating its inputs by an AI-capable adversary.[38]

Along these lines, AI could handle delivery and defence systems used against nuclear attacks.[39] AI's role in targeting is not limited to decision-support. By the end of the 2020s, AI could enhance intelligence, surveillance and reconnaissance (ISR) of stealth aircraft and submarines and tracking mobile intercontinental ballistic missiles; automated target recognition and terminal guidance; as well as autonomous nuclear-weapon systems.[40]

Ultimately, the integration of AI into the nuclear chain of command and its subsequent proliferation would lead to a paradigm shift in deterrence strategies and strategic decision-making.[41] This shift brings forth vulnerabilities in nuclear deterrence: AI-enabled capabilities pose a host of novel challenges, the most critical being the automation of strategic decision-making processes, which introduces risks of escalation due to the unpredictability of AI systems. While experimental wargaming suggests that human involvement in decision-making can mitigate escalation,[42] scenarios in which decisions are mainly made by AI proved to exacerbate escalation by rendering de-escalation processes more opaque and challenging and might even hinder conflict termination efforts. The inherent difficulty in interpreting signals from adversaries in deterrence is further exacerbated by the challenge of distinguishing between human and AI decisions and intentions. This underscores the importance of understanding the dynamics of human–machine interaction for managing escalation risks in AI-enhanced conflicts. Another wargame conducted by RAND Corporation has highlighted how the mix of human and AI agents in different roles can have an impact on the escalatory dynamics between both sides in a crisis.[43] The differences in how the two sides configure their human versus machine decision-making could escalate tensions during a crisis that transcend classic notions of deterrence. The acceleration of decision-making processes facilitated by AI increases the likelihood of inadvertent escalation during crises, even with human involvement in decision-making, as miscalculation escalation could ensue.[44] This dilemma is further exacerbated by the black-box problem, as AI operators are aware of the systems' inputs and outputs but cannot observe the process by which the former is converted into the latter. This problem makes it challenging for AI operators, as well as those on the opposing side, to comprehend the heuristics and trace the decision-making processes of these systems, making de-escalatory communication and transparency that much more challenging.[45]

The transformations that AI would entail highlights the need for 'meaningful human control' in all automated nuclear processes. Meaningful human control is a complex and evolving concept that was first conceived of in relation to weaponised conventional lethal autonomy but that was also applied to the application of AI in the nuclear realm. It entails preserving human judgement and input in the deployment of autonomous systems of every kind, aiming to ensure compliance with the law of armed conflict.[46] To exercise meaningful human control, human operators should have a functional understanding of how the targeting system operates, sufficient situational understanding, the capacity to scrutinise machine targeting decision-making and the possibility to abort the application of lethal force.[47] Survey experiments in the realm of crisis management have found that national security experts are generally less confident in and hesitant to act on AI-provided information; however, they tend to advocate similar or even more aggressive retaliatory measures against attacks by AI-enabled systems compared to human-directed attacks.[48] Differing perceptions heavily influence decision-makers' confidence levels and willingness to use lethal force during interstate crises and might cause harsher retaliatory measures in the case that the enemy has employed AI systems to conduct an attack.

This analysis, however, does not take into account one critical issue in the achievement of meaningful control and judgement over AI systems: 'automation bias'. This kind of bias was first studied in the field of civil aviation, relating to the automation in navigation in civil aviation, which highlighted how pilots tended to uncritically overrely on the outputs given by systems, especially in time-sensitive and information-heavy situations, resulting in cognitive overload.[49] Nuclear deterrence and brinkmanship are inherently intense, time-sensitive and cognitively demanding situations; achieving complete immunity from automation bias may be impossible, as the natural reaction of the human brain to offload cognitive tasks when overstimulated intensifies under frantic circumstances.[50] This bias in strategic nuclear and crisis decision-making is a significant issue, especially in light of a recent study that demonstrated that off-the-shelf large language models resulted in unpredictable and escalatory behaviour in simulated wargames. The study highlights the necessity for extreme caution when integrating AI models and systems in sensitive military and foreign-policy decision-making contexts.[51] The study reports that 'models tend to develop arms-race dynamics, leading to greater conflict' and that GPT-3.5, GPT-4-base and Llama models are prone to use courses of action involving nuclear strikes in some scenarios.[52] Automation bias-driven decision-making, coupled with unpredictable and escalation-prone AI systems, could spell disaster for brinkmanship management and needs proper and careful ex ante system testing and assessment.

Testing

Testing is another domain in which AI can play a significant role. While nuclear tests have decreased remarkably during the past years, new nuclear weapons are tested by nuclear aspirants.[53] AI-based technologies and their advances in the simulation of nuclear detonations have led to a decrease in nuclear tests, as 'AI allows deducing tests based on seismic information, measurement of radionuclides and developing predictions, even fed with incomplete data or estimates'.[54] Simulating nuclear detonations using AI-assisted applications allows researchers to accurately predict and analyse the behaviour of nuclear weapons under various conditions, providing insights into the physics and dynamics of a nuclear explosion, helping scientists understand the consequences of these devastating events.

Additionally, AI can be used for testing single equipment pieces, such as gas centrifuges, molecular pumps and solvent extractors. It can be used to detect anomalies in tasks such as automatic centrifuge rotor state recognition; constructing a digital representation or simulation of the chemical separations component to determine anomalies, failures and trends; and identifying better design alternatives for determining pH level and chemical structures of dissolved nuclear fuel, among others. The computing power of AI can accelerate the testing phase of each component, resulting in a much faster process for acquiring nuclear weapons. However, monitoring and regulation of these tasks is paramount in order to achieve effective testing and avoid overreliance and production errors that might lead to unreliable and faulty infrastructure and critical, dangerous malfunctions.

Safeguarding

In terms of safeguarding, according to the International Atomic Energy Agency (IAEA), AI would enhance remote analysis through multi- and hyperspectral imagery, radar imaging, three-dimensional reconstructions of objects, high-frequency image collection and automated detections of changes.[55] The UN body uses satellite imagery to monitor nuclear facilities and sites in support of its safeguarding activities, and AI has become a reliable tool for image processing and data analysis over the past decade.[56] The Vienna Center for Disarmament and Non-Proliferation (VCDNP) also analyses how AI could increase efficiency in the analysis of large amounts of information for the IAEA, leveraging AI to categorise data, detect changes and process natural language through its collaborative analysis platform.[57] AI can also improve measures and protocols implemented to prevent the misuse, diversion or unauthorised access to nuclear materials and facilities, and detect technical disorders in the enrichment and production process through its collaborative analysis platform, therefore, lowering the dangers associated with the development of nuclear warheads.[58]

AI and a high-tech nuclear arms race: implications for international security

In light of the impact of AI in nuclear production, targeting, testing and safeguarding, the question remains as to which countries are more likely to lead the race in their nuclear capabilities with AI technology. Currently, the United States has the top AI companies in the world, but China's Alibaba has been significantly expanding its market presence in the field.[59] Still, creating new innovation and staying ahead in it is not sufficient; it is also necessary to diffuse its application throughout one's own economy. There can be a wide disparity between innovation and diffusion. China, for example, lags behind the US in the diffusion of innovative technologies.[60] The ability of other economies to catch up and keep up with the United States and China in AI technology will set the pace of its diffusion.

Furthermore, integrating AI into the nuclear industry for military purposes in the targeting domain presents unique challenges. Up to the 1930s, cutting-edge military technology – including warships and aircraft – consisted primarily of hardware structures and controls that were integrated into a relatively uniform design and production process. During and after the Second World War, weapons systems acquired new electronics and propulsion systems – such as the jet engine – that required the inputs from a variety of disciplines related to hardware and software.[61] As complexity increased, catching up in cutting-edge military technology through emulation became harder. Today, leadership in the development and production of military technology rests on tacit knowledge and collective knowhow, both of which are a function of the organisational experience of companies and the collective efforts of designers, engineers, managers and specialised workers with different backgrounds and expertise.[62] These complex systems rest on a trial-and-error approach through which companies, scientists, experts and governments learn the most cost-effective practices and trajectories to produce breakthrough and incremental civilian and military–technological innovation.[63] In simpler words, whereas it took less than a decade for Germany to catch up with Britain in naval power before World War I, building warships that outperformed the British Dreadnought, it took China two decades to build a fifth-generation stealth aircraft with an adequate, stealth-enhancing, domestically manufactured engine.[64] Fifth-generation aircraft are marked by a complex set of features that include advanced sensors and algorithms that fuse multiple data inputs, automatically process those inputs into decision-related quality information and display that information to the pilot; stealth; and data-link connectivity.[65] The development of these software and hardware technologies requires an advanced aerospace industrial base, which entails accumulating hands-on experience at each level of the design, development and production stage – from the engineers working on the aircraft design and features to the specialised workers applying stealth coating.[66] This inhibits the diffusion and imitation of such cutting-edge military technology because it demands that countries make heavy investments in the development of their own defence-industrial foundations and capabilities.[67] Taking that into account, it is reasonable to expect that the diffusion of AI and its impact on nuclear industries and military technology will not be equally distributed worldwide, as they are expected to vary across countries and regions, with the technological prominence currently pointing toward the US and China. As building an AI industry and applying this technology into the military domain will take cumulative tacit knowledge and organisational experience, fuelled by trial and error, the countries with access to extensive funding and expertise are more likely to thrive in the AI-era nuclear arms race.

The weaponisation of AI for targeting and recognition capabilities will erode mutual assured destruction (MAD) between nuclear-armed adversaries. MAD rests on the premise that a nuclear attack on another nuclear power is too costly because the ensuing retaliation would ensure the destruction of the state that initiated the first nuclear strike. This theory is partially driven by confidence that the targeted state's nuclear arsenal would survive a first strike. However, in the past few decades, improvements in precision guidance technology and the subsequent reduction of circular error probable (CEP)[68] of conventional and nuclear-armed ballistic missiles and bombs have significantly increased the accuracy of nuclear delivery systems.[69] This means that, today, even lower yield strikes on the nuclear arsenal of an opponent can inflict irreversible military damage while avoiding a large number of civilian casualties. The incorporation of AI into targeting and recognition technologies will augment the precision-targeting and information-sharing capabilities of weapons systems, allowing them to autonomously share ISR data among one another to confuse or evade enemy defences and increase precision striking.[70] Therefore, countries that possess better AI-driven targeting capabilities are likely to have the upper hand in a new arms race. They will be able to more easily eliminate the nuclear forces of an opponent with a first strike due to the superiority of their AI-powered targeting technology and, as a result, reduce the leverage of weaker, technologically backwards nuclear powers relative to stronger nuclear powers,[71] thereby increasing the power disparity in the international system. Taking these factors into consideration, it is evident that AI has the potential to significantly impact the dynamics of the contemporary nuclear arms race on various levels.

The first level: nuclear-armed states

The initial level pertains to the nine states that have already procured and are seeking to optimise their existing nuclear arsenals using AI-assisted programs.[72] The current high-tech nuclear arms race includes the enduring competition between the United States and Russia, coupled with China's ambitious pursuit of a substantial and technologically advanced nuclear arsenal.[73]

Moreover, AI might aid of France and the United Kingdom, as they reduce their dependence on America's nuclear arsenals.[74]

The conflict between India and Pakistan, and India and China, has led to a nuclear arms race between three states that border each other, with tensions over disputed borders in Kashmir and Ladakh, respectively.[75] Additionally, North Korea[76] and Israel[77] are not parties to the Nuclear Non-Proliferation Treaty (NPT) and will also enhance their nuclear capabilities through AI, which will further reduce the financial costs associated with the development and maintenance of their arsenal.[78]

The second level: peaceful nuclear states

The second level involves states with peaceful nuclear programs with the potential for obtaining nuclear arms. The peaceful use of nuclear programs by certain nations has long been a source of scrutiny and apprehension among international actors.[79] While these programs are ostensibly designed for civilian purposes, generating energy or advancing scientific research, the ease at which they can transition to military applications raises concerns regarding the intentions and trustworthiness of states involved. AI provides the potential to accelerate the process of going 'nuclear', to cross the threshold of weaponisation,[80] especially for those countries that already possess enrichment technologies. Such a situation encompasses a wide array of regions across the globe, including Europe, East Asia, the Middle East[81] and Latin America.[82]

The decision to transition from peaceful nuclear programs in response to perceived threats is a reactive approach, which underscores the role of the security dilemma, wherein one state's pursuit of self-defence through nuclear capabilities can inadvertently trigger similar responses from rival states, resulting in an escalating cycle of armament. As a result, the delicate balance of power and stability within the regions mentioned is inevitably disrupted, potentially leading to heightened tensions and an increased risk of conflict.

Europe, as a region with a history of power struggles and geopolitical rivalries, presents a case of particular interest. Countries within the European Union maintain diverse nuclear postures, some relying on external security guarantees, while others possess independent nuclear capabilities. The possibility of peaceful European nuclear programs becoming militarised adds a layer of complexity to the security dynamics within the region, especially in countries such as Germany, the Netherlands, Poland, Belgium, Romania, Sweden and, most importantly, Ukraine, which is in direct military conflict with a nuclear power.[83] It poses questions regarding the effectiveness of existing non-proliferation efforts and arms control agreements as well as the potential implications for stability and cooperation among European nations in light of the most recent advancements of AI and other emerging technologies.[84]

Similarly, East and South Asia, characterised by long-standing regional disputes and rivalries, has witnessed an expansion of nuclear programs in recent times. The potential militarisation of these programs by countries such as Indonesia,[85] Japan[86] and South Korea[87] presents unique challenges due to the complex web of alliances and historical animosities prevalent in the region. The inclusion of East Asia within the scope of the emerging arms race heightens concerns regarding regional security, exacerbating the existing tensions over territorial disputes, historical grievances and the competition for influence.

The Middle East, a politically volatile region with numerous security dilemmas, is an area where the expansion of peaceful nuclear programs into military dimensions could take place following the most recent advancements of Iran,[88] the United Arab Emirates (UAE) and Egypt in the field of AI. The historical context of the region, marked by deep-rooted rivalries, religious divides and ongoing conflicts, amplifies the risks associated with the potential nuclear arms race. Given the already precarious security situation in the Middle East,[89] any further escalation arising from the militarisation of nuclear capabilities would likely exacerbate tensions, undermine trust and hinder diplomatic efforts for conflict resolution.

In Latin America, the emergence of new nuclear powers or the transition of existing peaceful nuclear programs, including Brazil, Argentina (as a country that went nuclear once) and Mexico,[90] into military applications could disrupt the region's history of relative nuclear stability. A shift in the region's nuclear landscape would have implications for regional security arrangements as well as potentially engendering a ripple effect throughout the broader international nuclear architecture. Moreover, the proximity of this region to the United States, a major global player, renders any escalation in the Latin American nuclear landscape a matter of substantial concern for the international community.

The third level: non-nuclear states

The third level of the future nuclear arms race encompasses countries that presently lack nuclear programs but have expressed their intentions to construct their inaugural nuclear power plants. This emerging stage in the arms race is marked by the ambitions of non-nuclear nations such as Saudi Arabia,[91] Türkiye,[92] UAE and Algeria to venture into the realm of nuclear energy generation. The pursuit of such programs introduces significant geopolitical implications, entailing potential shifts in the global power dynamics, intricate technological challenges and implications for nuclear non-proliferation regimes.[93]

As these countries seek to build their first nuclear plants, they enter into a complex landscape in which the acquisition of nuclear technology entails strategic, economic and diplomatic considerations. Navigating this terrain requires careful deliberation and engagement with multiple stakeholders, including international entities, regional powers and domestic actors.[94] By embracing nuclear energy, these countries seek to diversify their energy portfolios, enhance domestic security, meet increasing energy demands and reduce dependence on fossil fuel resources.[95]

However, their entry into the nuclear arena also raises concerns regarding proliferation risks and the potential for a shift in the global balance of power. The acquisition and development of nuclear technology can bestow significant leverage and influence on a nation, amplifying its standing in the international community. It is essential to recognise that the decision to pursue nuclear power installations not only has far-reaching consequences on energy policies but also reverberates through the broader geopolitical landscape.

Moreover, the successful establishment of nuclear power programs necessitates robust technological capabilities, considerable financial investments and strong institutional frameworks. These countries must address technical challenges related to reactor design, fuel cycle management, nuclear waste disposal and safety measures to guarantee responsible and sustainable utilisation of nuclear energy. Collaboration with more experienced nuclear powers, engagement with relevant international agencies and adherence to established safety protocols and non-proliferation norms are vital in mitigating potential hazards associated with nuclear technology development.

Conclusion

This study presented four principal domains in which AI can contribute to the nuclear industry and nuclear proliferation cycles: production, targeting, testing and safeguarding. In the production cycle, AI can optimise performance, innovate and reduce costs associated with the development and production of nuclear material. In the targeting domain, AI can create an autonomous nuclear weapon system, augmenting ISR capabilities; automated target recognition and terminal guidance technology; and delivery and defence systems used against nuclear attacks. In testing, it can simulate and evaluate nuclear explosions to reduce the risk of nuclear tests and nuclear radiation. Finally, in terms of safeguards, AI can detect technical problems in the enrichment and production process through its collaborative analysis platform, therefore, lowering the dangers associated with the development of nuclear warheads.

The convergence between nuclear proliferation and AI serves as a unique challenge to international security. AI-powered improvements in targeting and autonomous precision guidance, leading to even lower CEP, can further erode deterrence. At the same time, the unequal rate of diffusion of AI technology, if kept on the theoretically expected trajectory, has the potential to increase the power disparity in the international system. Being aware of such challenges, policymakers can shape the international system by deliberately creating agreements with strong enforcement mechanisms to minimise the risks of nuclear catastrophes. Moreover, using sanctions and military force to curb proliferation can also be an option. Finally, the potentially asymmetric diffusion of AI technology can be a bulwark against the proliferation of advanced, AI-powered nuclear weapons if the leading states weaponise patents, software control and components to restrict the access of nuclear aspirants to AI-powered nuclear technology.

Some possible pathways of future research may include establishing historical parallels between the diffusion of certain commercial technologies exploited for military purposes in the past and how that led to a more militarised world and the diffusion and integration of AI into military technology. What factors allowed previous technologies to be diffused and taken advantage of by regional powers to develop their military capabilities? Were there any mistakes made by the pioneers of such technologies that could be avoided with a better management of the diffusion of AI? For example, up until the late 1980s, accurate cruise missiles needed sophisticated guidance and navigation technology. Key to the effectiveness of these systems were highly accurate inertial navigation systems (INS) and navigational updates provided by terrain contour matching (TERCOM) and digital scene matching correlation (DSMAC). The role of TERCOM is to deliver a cruise missile close enough to its target to allow DSMAC to sense it, perform a correlation and provide terminal guidance.[96] As long as TERCOM and DSMAC remained state-of-the-art technologies, there were barriers to acquiring cruise missiles. The increasing commercial availability of signals from GPS constellations and its non-American counterparts (GLONASS and BeiDou) has considerably reduced the barriers to entering the cruise missile competition and is allowing cruise missiles to strike targets accurately at long ranges.[97]

By delving into these questions, scholars can produce new innovative research as well as policy-oriented insights to grasp the underlying empirics of the diffusion of commercial and military technology.

Notes

1 Rose Gottemoeller, 'Rethinking nuclear arms control', *The Washington Quarterly* 43:3 (2020), 139–159. https://doi.org/10.1080/0163660X.2020.1813382
2 Benjamin Zala, 'How the next nuclear arms race will be different from the last one', *Bulletin of the Atomic Scientists* 75:1 (2019), 36–43. https://doi.org/10.1080/00963402.2019.1555999
3 Jon Brook Wolfsthal, 'Why arms control?', *Daedalus* 149:2 (2020), 101–115. https://doi.org/10.1162/daed_a_01792; Dmitri Trenin, 'Stability amid strategic deregulation: Managing the end of nuclear arms control', *The Washington Quarterly* 43:3 (2020), 161–175. https://doi.org/10.1080/0163660X.2020.1813401
4 James Johnson, 'Artificial intelligence & future warfare: Implications for international security', *Defense & Security Analysis* 35:2 (2019), 147–169. https://doi.org/10.1080/14751798.2019.1600800
5 Mohammad Eslami, Alena Vieira, Arshin Adib-Moghaddam, Lauro Borges, Maria Papageorgiou, Fabio Cristiano, Ibrahim Al-Marashi, Tom Sauer and Christian Kaunert, 'The geopolitics of AI-driven arms races', *Geopolitics* (2025), 1–43.

6 Maria Papageorgiou, Muhammed Can and Alena Vysotskaya Guedes Vieira, 'China as a threat and balancing behavior in the realm of emerging technologies', *Chinese Political Science Review* 9:4 (2024), 441–482. https://doi.org/10.1007/s41111-024-00248-0

7 James Johnson, 'Catalytic nuclear war in the age of artificial intelligence & autonomy: Emerging military technology and escalation risk between nuclear-armed states', *Journal of Strategic Studies* (2021), 1–41. https://doi.org/10.1080/01402390.2020.1867541

8 James Johnson, 'Deterrence in the age of artificial intelligence & autonomy: A paradigm shift in nuclear deterrence theory and practice?', *Defense & Security Analysis* 36:4 (2020), 422–448. https://doi.org/10.1080/14751798.2020.1857911

9 Matthijs M. Maas, 'How viable is international arms control for military artificial intelligence? Three lessons from nuclear weapons', *Contemporary Security Policy* 40:3 (2019), 285–311. https://doi.org/10.1080/13523260.2019.1654954

10 We acknowledge the fact that some claim that acoustic homing torpedoes have been AI assisted 'autonomous' munitions. However, we consider them the early generations of 'automatic' weapons.

11 István Szabadföldi, 'Artificial intelligence in military application – opportunities and challenges', *Land Forces Academy Review* 26:2 (2021), 157–165. https://doi.org/10.2478/lfar-2021-0022

12 Chang Eun Lee, Jin Ho Son, Hyeon Seok Park, Seung Yong Lee, Seung Jun Park and Young Taek Lee, 'Technical trends of AI military staff to support decision-making of commanders', *Electronics and Telecommunications Trends* 36:1 (2021), 89–98. https://doi.org/10.22648/ETRI.2021.J.360108

13 Peter Svenmarck, Linus Luotsinen, Mattias Nilsson and Johan Schubert, 'Possibilities and challenges for artificial intelligence in military applications', in *Proceedings of the NATO Big Data and Artificial Intelligence for Military Decision Making Specialists' Meeting* (2018), 1–16.

14 Maria Glenski, Ellyn Ayton, Sannisth Soni, Emily Saldanha, Dustin Arendt, Brian Quiter, Ren Cooper and Svitlana Volkova, 'Learning global proliferation expertise evolution using AI-driven dnalytics and public information', *IEEE Transactions on Nuclear Science* 69:6 (2022), 1375–1384.

15 Nina Tannenwald, 'The vanishing nuclear taboo?' *Foreign Affairs* 97:6 (2018), 16–24; Michal Smetana, 'The Prague agenda: An

obituary?', *New Perspectives* 26:1 (2018), 16–22. https://doi.org/10.1177/2336825X1802600102

16 Mohammad Eslami and Alena Vysotskaya Guedes Vieira, 'Iran's strategic culture: The "revolutionary" and "moderation" narratives on the ballistic missile programme', *Third World Quarterly* 42:2 (2020), 312–328; Mohammad Eslami and Alena Vysotskaya Guedes Vieira, 'Shi'a principles and Iran's strategic culture towards ballistic missile deployment', *International Affairs* 98:2 (2022), 675–688.

17 Daniel Wertz, 'The US, North Korea, and nuclear diplomacy', *Washington: National Committee on North Korea* (2018). https://ncnk.org/resources/briefing-papers/all-briefing-papers/u.s.-north-korea-and-nuclear-diplomacy (accessed 5 February 2026).

18 Rose Gottemoeller, *Negotiating the New START Treaty* (New York: Cambria Press, 2021); Gottemoeller, 'Rethinking nuclear arms control'.

19 Alexander Lanoszka, 'Nuclear blackmail and nuclear balance in the Baltic Region', *Scandinavian Journal of Military Studies* 2:1 (2019), 84–94. https://doi.org/10.31374/sjms.22

20 Hans M. Kristensen, Matt Korda and Eliana Reynolds, 'Chinese nuclear weapons, 2023', *Bulletin of the Atomic Scientists* 79:2 (2023), 108–133. https://doi.org/10.1080/00963402.2023.2178713; Caitlin Talmadge, 'Would China go nuclear? Assessing the risk of Chinese nuclear escalation in a conventional war with the United States', *International Security* 41:4 (2017), 50–92. https://doi.org/10.1162/ISEC_a_00289

21 Nick Ritchie and Benoît Pelopidas, 'European nuclear nationalism: UK and French perspectives on nuclear disarmament', in Nik Hynek and Michal Smetana (eds), *Global Nuclear Disarmament* (London: Routledge, 2015), 225–250.

22 Łukasz Kulesa, 'Strategic arms control deadlock and the possible ways out', in Adérito Vicente, Polina Sinovets and Julien Theron (eds), *Russia's War on Ukraine: The Implications for the Global Nuclear Order* (Cham: Springer Nature Switzerland, 2023), 109–119.

23 Mohammad Al-Saidi and Mehran Haghirian, 'A quest for the Arabian atom? Geopolitics, security, and national identity in the nuclear energy programs in the Middle East', *Energy Research & Social Science* 69 (2020). https://doi.org/10.1016/j.erss.2020.101582

24 Dalia Dassa Kaye and Frederic M. Wehrey, 'A nuclear Iran: The reactions of neighbours', *Survival* 49:2 (2023), 111–128.

25 Leila Hennaoui and Marzhan Nurzhan, 'Dealing with a nuclear past: Revisiting the cases of Algeria and Kazakhstan through a decolonial lens', *The International Spectator* 58:4 (2023), 91–109.
26 James Jonson, 'AI, autonomy, and the risk of nuclear war', *War on Rocks* (2022). https://warontherocks.com/2022/07/ai-autonomy-and-the-risk-of-nuclear-war/ (accessed 5 February 2026).
27 *Arms Control Negotiation Academy*, 'How artificial intelligence is revolutionizing nuclear material production' (2023). https://www.armscontrolnegotiationacademy.org/insights (accessed 1 October 2025).
28 Jean-Marc Rickli, 'The strategic implications of artificial intelligence for international security', in Al Naqvi and J. Mark Munoz (eds), *Handbook of Artificial Intelligence and Robotic Process Automation: Policy and Government Applications* (London: Anthem Press, 2020), 41–54.
29 On hypersonic missile technology: Dean Wilkening, 'Hypersonic weapons and strategic stability', *Survival* 61:5 (2019), 129–148. https://doi.org/10.1080/00396338.2019.1662125; Shannon Bugos and Kingston Reif, *Understanding Hypersonic Weapons: Managing the Allure and the Risks* (Washington, DC: Arms Control Association, 2021).
30 The development of nuclear bombs by terrorist groups has been at the centre of attention in both academic and political debates for years. However, there has been no evidence of any non-state actor or terrorist organisation attempting to build them, as acquiring materials and delivery systems would still pose significant obstacles. Notably, there have been several non-state actors and terrorist organisations in the Middle East and Africa that have access to both nuclear material and delivery systems, such as sophisticated missile systems.
31 Anja Kaspersen and Chris King, 'Mitigating the challenges of nuclear risk while ensuring the benefits of technology', in Vincent Boulanin (ed.), *The Impact of Artificial Intelligence on Strategic Stability and Nuclear Risk: Euro-Atlantic Perspectives* (Stockholm: SIPRI, 2019), 53–62. https://www.sipri.org/publications/2019/research-reports/impact-artificial-intelligence-strategic-stability-and-nuclear-risk-volume-i-euro-atlantic (accessed 5 February 2026).
32 Avin Shahar and Sonja Michelle Amadae, *Autonomy and Machine Learning at the Interface of Nuclear Weapons, Computers and People* (Stockholm: SIPRI, 2019), 1–14.

33 Michael Horowitz, *Artificial Intelligence and Nuclear Stability: The impact of Artificial Intelligence on Strategic Stability and Nuclear Risk* (Stockholm: SIPRI, 2019), 79–83.

34 Edward Geist and Andrew J. Lohn, *How Might Artificial Intelligence Affect the Risk of Nuclear War?* (Santa Monica, CA: RAND Corporation, 2018). https://www.rand.org/pubs/perspectives/PE296.html (accessed 5 February 2026).

35 Linda Jaeck, *Assessing Challenges and Opportunities in the Age of Artificial Intelligence: Views of Non-Western Experts in the Debate on Nuclear Security* (Prague: Peace Research Center Prague, 2021), 1–25.

36 *Arms Control Negotiation Academy*, 'How artificial intelligence is revolutionizing nuclear material production'.

37 We affirm that the employment of nuclear bombs is not a routine event, and, as previously mentioned, typical nuclear strategy calls for the use of weapons as a retaliatory/deterrent measure rather than a tactical approach in which surveillance and intelligence might be relevant. Accordingly, it is unlikely that armies would give full autonomy to AI in controlling their nuclear arsenals.

38 Geist and Lohn, *How Might Artificial Intelligence Affect the Risk of Nuclear War?*

39 Vincent Boulanin, 'The future of machine learning and autonomy in nuclear weapon systems', in Vincent Boulanin (ed.), *The Impact of Artificial Intelligence on Strategic Stability and Nuclear Risk: Volume 1, Euro-Atlantic Perspectives* (Stockholm: SIPRI, 2019), 53–62.

40 Geist and Lohn, *How Might Artificial Intelligence Affect the Risk of Nuclear War?*

41 James Johnson, 'Automating the OODA Loop in the age of intelligent machines: Reaffirming the role of humans in command-and-control decision-making in the digital age', *Defence Studies* 22:3 (2022), 1–25. https://doi.org/10.1080/14702436.2022.210248; James Johnson, 'Delegating strategic decision-making to machines: Dr. Strangelove redux?', *Journal of Strategic Studies* 45:3 (2022), 439–477. https://doi.org/10.1080/01402390.2020.1759038; Johnson, 'Catalytic nuclear war'.

42 Johnson, 'Deterrence in the age of artificial intelligence & autonomy'.

43 Yuna H. Wong, John Yurchak, Robert W. Button, Aaron B. Frank, Burgess Laird, Osonde A. Osoba, Randall Steeb, Benjamin N. Harris and Sebastian Joon Bae, *Deterrence in the Age of Thinking Machines* (Santa Monica, CA: RAND Corporation, 2020). https://

www.rand.org/pubs/research_reports/RR2797.html (accessed 5 February 2026).

44 Wong et al., *Deterrence in the Age of Thinking Machines.*

45 Arthur Holland Michel, *The Black Box, Unlocked: Predictability and Understandability in Military AI* (Geneva: United Nations Institute for Disarmament Research, 2020). https://doi.org/10.37559/SecTec/20/AI1

46 Lena Trabucco, 'What is meaningful human control, anyway? Cracking the code on autonomous weapons and human judgment', *Modern War Institute* (2023). https://mwi.westpoint.edu/what-is-meaningful-human-control-anyway-cracking-the-code-on-autonomous-weapons-and-human-judgment/ (accessed 5 February 2026).

47 Ingvild Bode and Tom Watts, *Meaning-Less Human Control: Lessons from Air Defence Systems for Lethal Autonomous Weapons* (Oxford: Drone Wars UK, 2021). https://dronewars.net/wp-content/uploads/2021/02/DW-Control-WEB.pdf (accessed 5 February 2026).

48 Michael C. Horowitz and Erik Lin-Greenberg, 'Algorithms and influence: Artificial intelligence and crisis decision-making', *International Studies Quarterly* 66:4 (2022). https://doi.org/10.1093/isq/sqac069

49 Linda J. Skitka, Kathleen L. Mosier and Mark Burdick, 'Does automation bias decision-making?', *International Journal of Human-Computer Studies* 51:5 (1999), 991–1006. https://doi.org/10.1006/ijhc.1999.0252

50 Basil Wahn, Laura Schmitz, Frauke Nora Gerster and Matthias Weiss, 'Offloading under cognitive load: humans are willing to offload parts of an attentionally demanding task to an algorithm', *PLOS ONE* 18:5 (2023), e0286102. https://doi.org/10.1371/journal.pone.0286102

51 Juan-Pablo Rivera, Gabriel Mukobi, Anka Reuel, Max Lamparth, Chandler Smith and Jacquelyn Schneider, 'Escalation risks from language models in military and diplomatic decision-making', *arXiv Preprint* (2024), arXiv:2401.03408.

52 Rivera et al., 'Escalation risks'.

53 Harold L. Beck, Steven L. Simon, André Bouville and Anna Romanyukha, 'Accounting for unfissioned plutonium from the Trinity atomic bomb test', *Health Physics* 119:4 (2020), 504–516. https://doi.org/10.1097/HP.0000000000001291

54 Anna Heise, 'AI, WMD and arms control: The case of nuclear testing', in Thomas Reinhold and Niklas Schörnig (eds), *Armament, Arms Control and Artificial Intelligence: The Janus-Faced Nature of Machine Learning in the Military Realm* (Cham: Springer International Publishing, 2022), 117–127.
55 Laura Rockwood, Noah Mayhew, Artem Lazarev and Mara Pfneisl, *IAEA Safeguards: Staying Ahead of the Game* (Vienna: Vienna Center for Disarmament and Non-Proliferation, 2019). https://vcdnp.org/wp-content/uploads/2019/09/201914-iaea-safeguards-staying-ahead-of-the-game.pdf (accessed 5 February 2026).
56 *IAEA*, 'Strengthening the effectiveness and improving the efficiency of agency safeguards: Report by the Director General, GC(62)/8' (2018), paras 40–41. https://www.iaea.org/sites/default/files/gc/gc62-8_en.pdf (accessed 5 February 2026).
57 *Arms Control Negotiation Academy*, 'How artificial intelligence is revolutionizing nuclear material production'.
58 Melanie Reuter-Oppermann and Peter Buxmann, 'Introduction into artificial intelligence and machine learning', in Thomas Reinhold and Niklas Schörnig (eds), *Armament, Arms Control and Artificial Intelligence: The Janus-faced Nature of Machine Learning in the Military Realm* (Cham: Springer International Publishing, 2022), 11–26.
59 United Nations Conference on Trade and Development, *Technology and Innovation Report 2023* (New York: United Nations Publications, 2023), 15; Kezia Grace Jungco, '100 Top AI companies trendsetting In 2024', *Datamation* (2024). https://www.datamation.com/featured/ai-companies/ (accessed 5 February 2026).
60 Jeffrey Ding, 'The diffusion deficit in scientific and technological power: Reassessing China's power', *Review of International Political Economy* 31:1 (2024), 173–198. https://doi.org/10.1080/09692290.2023.2173633
61 Stephen B. Johnson, 'Systems integration and the social solution of technical problems in complex systems', in Andrea Prencipe, Andrew Davies and Michael Hobday (eds), *The Business of Systems Integration* (Oxford: Oxford University Press, 2005), 35–55.
62 Andrea Gilli and Mauro Gilli, 'Why China has not caught up yet: Military-technological superiority and the limits of imitation, reverse engineering, and cyber espionage', *International Security* 43:3 (Winter 2018–19), 141–189. https://doi.org/10.1162/isec_a_00337

63 Sangbae Kim and Jeffrey A. Hart, 'Technological capacity as fitness: An evolutionary model of change in the International Political Economy', in William R. Thompson (ed.), *Evolutionary Interpretations of World Politics* (Abingdon: Routledge, 2001), 285–314.

64 When China achieved the breakthrough of domestically producing a suitable engine for the fifth-generation fighter jet J-20 in 2023, thus breaking free from dependence on Russian engines or less reliable domestic ones, the US had already mastered stealth technology. In 2023, the US possessed B-2s, F-22s and F-35s, thereby being ahead of China in stealth aircraft. See The International Institute for Strategic Studies, *The Military Balance 2023* (London: The International Institute for Strategic Studies, 2023), 35–49; Rick Joe, 'What a 19-year-old study tells us about China's J-20', *The Diplomat* (2022). https://thediplomat.com/2022/02/what-a-19-year-old-study-tells-us-about-chinas-j-20/ (accessed 5 February 2026); Rick Joe, 'China's J-20 gets another upgrade', *The Diplomat* (2023). https://thediplomat.com/2023/08/chinas-j-20-gets-another-upgrade/ (accessed 5 February 2026).

65 Peter Layton, 'Fifth generation air warfare', *Royal Australian Air Force, Air Power Development Centre:* Working Paper 43 (2017); David A. Deptula, Lawrence A. Stutzriem and Heather R. Penney, 'Ensuring the common defense: The case for fifth generation airpower', *Mitchell Institute Policy Papers* 20 (2019).

66 Franz-Stefan Gady, 'Mauro Gilli: Selling the F-35 to countries operating the S-400 is a bad idea', *The Diplomat* (2019). https://thediplomat.com/2019/07/mauro-gilli-selling-the-f-35-to-countries-operating-the-s-400-is-a-bad-idea/ (accessed 5 February 2026).

67 James Johnson, 'The end of military-techno Pax Americana? Washington's strategic responses to Chinese AI-enabled military technology', *The Pacific Review* 34:3 (2021), 351–378. https://doi.org/10.1080/09512748.2019.1676299

68 A circular error probable (CEP) is the radius of a circle within which half of a missile's projectiles are expected to fall. A weapon possessing a CEP of five hundred feet will find half of those weapons landing within five hundred feet of the target and the other half landing farther away. See Andrew F. Krepinevich, *The Origins of Victory: How Disruptive Military Innovation Determines the Fates of Great Powers* (New Haven, CT: Yale University Press, 2023), 41.

69 Keir A. Lieber and Daryl G. Press, 'The new era of counterforce: Technological change and the future of nuclear deterrence', *International Security* 41:4 (2017), 9–49. https://doi.org/10.1162/ISEC_a_00273

70 Robert O. Work, *Principles for the Combat Employment of Weapons Systems with Autonomous Functionalities* (Washington, DC: Center for a New American Security, 2021), 8–9.

71 Nuno Monteiro, *Theory of Unipolar Politics* (New York: Cambridge University Press, 2014), 14–15.

72 Benjamin Zala, 'How the next nuclear arms race will be different from the last one', *Bulletin of the Atomic Scientists* 75:1 (2019), 36–43; William J. Perry and Tom Z. Collina, *The Button: The New Nuclear Arms Race and Presidential Power From Truman to Trump* (Dallas, TX: BenBella Books, 2020); Brendan Rittenhouse Green, *The Revolution That Failed: Nuclear Competition, Arms Control, and the Cold War* (Cambridge: Cambridge University Press, 2020).

73 David Carlton and Carlo Schaerf (eds), *The Dynamics of the Arms Race* (London: Routledge, 2020); Ernest J. Moniz and Sam Nunn, 'The return of doomsday: The new nuclear arms race-and how Washington and Moscow can stop it', *Foreign Affairs* 98 (2019), 150–161; Michael T. Klare 'AI arms race gains speed', *Arms Control Today* 49:2 (2019), 35. https://www.jstor.org/stable/26633411 (accessed 5 February 2026).

74 Götz Neuneck, 'The deep crisis of nuclear arms control and disarmament: The state of play and the challenges', *Journal for Peace and Nuclear Disarmament* 2:2 (2019), 431–452; Matthew Evangelista, *Innovation and the Arms Race: How the United States and the Soviet Union Develop New Military Technologies* (Ithaca, NY: Cornell University Press, 2023).

75 Ejaz Hussain, 'India–Pakistan relations: Challenges and opportunities', *Journal of Asian Security and International Affairs* 6:1 (2019), 82–95; Devin T. Hagerty, 'The power of suggestion: Opaque proliferation, existential deterrence, and the South Asian nuclear arms competition' in Zachary S. Davis and Benjamin Frankel (eds), *The Proliferation Puzzle: Why Nuclear Weapons Spread (and What Results)* (London: Routledge, 2020), 256–283; Owen B. Toon, Charles G. Bardeen, Alan Robock, Lili Xia, Hans Kristensen, Matthew McKinzie, Roy J. Peterson, Cheryl S. Harrison, Nicole S. Lovenduski and Richard P. Turco, 'Rapidly expanding nuclear arsenals in

Pakistan and India portend regional and global catastrophe', *Science Advances* 5:10 (2019), eaay5478.

76 Ankit Panda, *Kim Jong Un and the Bomb: Survival and Deterrence in North Korea* (Oxford: Oxford University Press, 2020).

77 Mohammad Eslami and Alena Vysotskaya Guedes Vieira (eds), *The Arms Race in the Middle East: Contemporary Security Dynamics* (Cham: Springer International Publishing, 2023). Mohammad Eslami and Alena Vysotskaya Guedes Vieira, 'Introducing the arms race in the Middle East in the twenty first century: A "powder keg" in the digital era?', in Mohammad Eslami and Alena Vysotskaya Guedes Vieira (eds), *The Arms Race in the Middle East: Contemporary Security Dynamics* (Cham: Springer International Publishing, 2023), 3–13; Mohammad Eslami, 'Exploring the driving forces behind Iran's nuclear deterrence strategy: A novel methodological approach', *Journal for Peace and Nuclear Disarmament* (2024), 1–25.

78 Edward Ifft, 'Lessons for negotiating with North Korea', in The International Institute for Strategic Studies (ed.), *Survival: Global Politics and Strategy (February–March 2020): Deterring North Korea* (London: Routledge, 2023), 89–106.

79 John J Mearsheimer, 'Back to the future: Instability in Europe after the Cold War', in Michael Sheelan (ed.), *National and International Security* (London: Routledge, 2018), 107–158; Trevor McCrisken and Maxwell Downman, '"Peace through strength": Europe and NATO deterrence beyond the US Nuclear Posture Review', *International Affairs* 95:2 (2019), 277–295.

80 James Johnson, 'The AI-cyber nexus: Implications for military escalation, deterrence and strategic stability', *Journal of Cyber Policy* 4:3 (2019), 442–460. https://doi.org/10.1080/23738871.2019.1701693

81 Mark Fitzpatrick, 'Can Iran's nuclear capability be kept latent?', *Survival* 49:1 (2019), 33–57.

82 José Goldemberg, Carlos Feu Alvim and Olga Y. Mafra, 'The denuclearization of Brazil and Argentina', *Journal for Peace and Nuclear Disarmament* 1:2 (2018), 383–403.

83 Kjølv Egeland and Benoît Pelopidas, 'European nuclear weapons? Zombie debates and nuclear realities', *European Security* 30:2 (2021), 237–258; Josef Joffe, 'The "Scandilux" connection: Belgium, Denmark, the Netherlands, and Norway in comparative perspective', in Gregory Flynn (ed.), *NATO's Northern Allies: The*

National Security Policies of Belgium, Denmark, the Netherlands, and Norway (London: Routledge, 2021), 224–257; Gabriela Rosa Hernandez, 'Poland reignites nuclear sharing conversation', *Arms Control Today* 52: 9 (2022), 29–30.

84 Perry and Collina, *The Button*.

85 Tiwi Gustria Ningsih, 'Nuclear powered warship, does Indonesia need it?', *Jurnal Strategi Pertahanan Laut E-ISSN* 2830 (2022), 2338.

86 Ramesh Thakur, 'Japan and the nuclear weapons prohibition treaty: The wrong side of history, geography, legality, morality, and humanity', in *The 2017 Nuclear Ban Treaty* (London: Routledge, London, 2020), 194–214.

87 Lami Kim, 'South Korea's nuclear hedging?' *The Washington Quarterly* 41:1 (2018), 115–133.

88 Mohammad Eslami, Nasim Sadat Mosavi and Muhammed Can, 'Sino–Iranian cooperation in artificial intelligence: A potential countering against the US hegemony', in Paulo Duarte, Francisco Leandro and Enrique Galán (eds), *The Palgrave Handbook of Globalization with Chinese Characteristics: The Case of the Belt and Road Initiative* (Singapore: Springer Nature, 2023), 543–559; Mohammad Eslami and Joel Anthony Kemie, 'China–Iran's 25-year deal: The implication for the Belt and Road Initiative and Joint Comprehensive Plan of Action (JCPOA)', in Paulo Duarte, Francisco Leandro and Enrique Galán (eds), *The Palgrave Handbook of Globalization with Chinese Characteristics: The Case of the Belt and Road Initiative* (Singapore: Springer Nature Singapore, 2023), 575–589.

89 Gawdat Bahgat, 'A nuclear arms race in the Middle East: myth or reality?', *Mediterranean Quarterly* 22:1 (2011), 27–40; Richard L. Russell, 'Off and running: The Middle East nuclear arms race', *Joint Force Quarterly* 58 (2010), 94–99.

90 Luis J. Rodriguez and Elizabeth Mendenhall, 'Nuclear weapon-free zones and the issue of maritime transit in Latin America', *International Affairs* 98:3 (2022), 819–836.

91 Ibrahim Al-Marashi, 'Saudi petro-nukes? Riyadh's nuclear intentions and regime survival strategies', in William Potter and Gaukhar Mukhatzhanova (eds), *Forecasting Nuclear Proliferation in the 21st Century: Volume 2 – A Comparative Perspective* (Redwood City, CA: Stanford University Press, 2010), 76–99. https://doi.org/10.1515/9781503627420-005

92 Ibrahim Al-Marashi and Nilsu Goren, 'Turkish perceptions and nuclear proliferation', *Strategic Insights* 8:2 (2009), 1–18.
93 Green, *The revolution That Failed;* Evangelista, *Innovation and the Arms Race.*
94 Naomi Egel and Steven Ward, 'Hierarchy, revisionism, and subordinate actors: The TPNW and the subversion of the nuclear order', *European Journal of International Relations* 28:4 (2022), 751–776.
95 Leslie-Anne Duvic-Paoli and Priska Lueger, 'A democratic nuclear energy transition? Public participation in nuclear activities', *Review of European, Comparative & International Environmental Law* 31:2 (2022), 199–209.
96 On TERCOM and DSMAC, see Frederick W. Riedel, Shannon M. Hall, Jeffrey D. Barton, James P. Christ, Brian K. Funk, Thomas D. Milnes, Peter E. Neperud and David R. Stark, 'Guidance and navigation in the global engagement department', *Johns Hopkins APL Technical Digest* 29:2 (2010), 118–132. https://secwww.jhuapl.edu/techdigest/content/techdigest/pdf/V29-N02/20-02-Riedel.pdf (accessed 5 February 2026).
97 Thomas G. Mahnken, *The Cruise Missile Challenge* (Washington, DC: Center for Strategic and Budgetary Assessments, 2005), 20–21; Jeff Kueter and Howard Kleinberg, *The Cruise Missile Challenge: Designing a Defense Against Asymmetric Threats* (Washington, DC: George C. Marshall Institute, 2007), 2.

6

AI in the military domain: experimentation, regulation and the role of private companies in the Gaza and Ukraine wars

Bassant Hassib and Fatimah Ayad

Introduction

The use of artificial-intelligence-powered military capabilities in the War on Gaza (2023) and the Russian invasion of Ukraine (2022) marked a significant milestone in the use of such technologies in warfare. The unprecedented scale of destruction and civilian casualties caused by artificial-intelligence-based weapons revived the debate among policymakers, academics and strategists on the ethics of the use of artificial intelligence (AI) in warfare.[1] This revived debate developed further to include issues pertaining to an international regulatory framework on the sale and use of AI for miliary purposes and the unresolved question of accountability.

These technologies are considered revolutionary and instrumental in deciding the 'fate of nations'.[2] The benefits that AI delivers in terms of security, commerce and geostrategic incentives is compelling for many states and private multi-national companies seeking to acquire or maintain their share in this sector in regard to use, development and deliverable results, not just for great powers but even for small states that are increasingly joining the game. As such, there is no rolling back the development, sale and use of AI, not only in the military but also in the security and economic domains at large. Therefore, regulating AI in a manner that truly takes into consideration international humanitarian law and human rights law seems increasingly complicated when it is being heralded as a potential equaliser in terms of military capabilities. In particular, this stems from the difficulty in reaching a shared perception between states, private technology companies and civil society actors on what constitutes a 'red-line' during conflict scenarios.[3]

This chapter explores the interplay between private technology companies and states in the challenge of establishing a global regulatory framework for the use and sale of AI in military contexts and the implications of this challenge for safeguarding human rights and ensuring accountability. It uses the recent cases of the Gaza and Ukraine wars, as they have proven to emblematic of how the rapid pace of AI development continues to raise unprecedented ethical concerns, especially as it pertains to the responsibility of states and private companies. The chapter then concludes by giving recommendations on how a multi-stakeholder governance could lead to a global consensus over an effective regulatory framework on the use of such technologies.

The 'red-line' in the use of AI in warfare

The use of AI in the military domain raises concerns regarding how AI makes calculations about consequences and what is the 'red-line' in terms of 'acceptable' losses, considering that, increasingly, the role of human decision-makers is diminishing, as AI-powered military technology continues to develop.[4] In addition, threat assessments made by AI might be exaggerated and inadvertently lead human commanders to escalate conflicts, assuming greater threats for national security, potentially causing catastrophic results. This is especially detrimental in warfare in which risk calculations already carry their own inherent risks in terms of uncertainty, unpredictability and issues related to human bias. The problem of human bias is that it may transfer into the AI system by the human engineers who encode it, as a reflection of their own biases.[5] Some believe that this should discourage militaries from deploying such autonomous weapons in the field and ask them to make life-or-death evaluations.[6]

Autonomous weapons could be classified are 'fire-and-forget' weapons that allow human decision-makers to figuratively keep their hands clean without having to worry about the consequences of the decision to kill.[7] Advocates of AI, whose main argument stems from the idea that there is no turning back time on this military development, claim that critics of AI fail to take into account the actual circumstances of modern warfare, in which insurgents and terrorists often use 'human shields' to protect themselves or to conceal themselves among civilians as a tactic to manipulate drones. Additionally, they claim that AI can help enhance targeting precision, owing to their higher level of situational awareness (supposedly surpassing that of a human), which would further protect innocents, an argument that has been debunked, considering how often drones have been found to misidentify targets and create false alarms.[8] This is also attributed to the cyber security vulnerabilities of

AI-powered systems, which makes them subject to manipulation through cyber attacks for function disruption and carrying out unwanted attacks, espionage or misuse.[9] These shortcomings would lead to a total destabilisation of conflict areas if deployed at large scale. Moreover, these errors are caused by AI's inability to grasp contextual reasoning in terms of intentions and motivations of subjects due to their lack of empathy. Thus, although they are better and faster at monitoring threats, they lack human common sense, which is essential in unfamiliar or new circumstances in which they have no guidelines for in the first place.[10]

Here, the problem with AI is that while human soldiers would possibly accept more risks to themselves in order to avoid creating further damage – more than what would already be considered necessary in times of war – as part of their duty to adhere to the principles of international humanitarian law, autonomous weapons – unless directed to by human commanders – would not necessarily make the same consideration. Robert Quinn, vice president of TALON Robot Operations for Foster-Miller,[11] said, 'the big advantage of moving to armed robots is that you take the emotion, the fear factor out of the decision to shoot'.[12] Autonomous weapons are programmed to prioritise the achievement of the target mission and are not prone to trauma. Detractors of autonomous weapons often claim that rather than seeking to minimise war-related traumas, these technologies are designed to reduce culpability and accountability, a sort of 'moral off-loading' or 'outsourcing of our consciences' to non-humans that are poorly equipped to make these choices.[13]

The question of accountability and the responsibility gap should be central to any discussion of human versus AI as, technically, robots cannot be held accountable for their own design, and yet advocates of AI argue that 'if a system performs outside its tolerance level, no one is blameworthy for resultant harms',[14] positing that if a piece of technology performs outside of the expected parameters rendering it unreliable, no person bears the accountability for this unexpected malfunction to which all technology is susceptible. Additionally, as AI continues to make strides, the accountability of humans and their involvement is increasingly pushed aside the further they are from the military theatre. While proponents of AI argue heavily in favour of developing such technologies, claiming that they reduce the risk to enemy combatants and civilians,[15] the responsibility gap continues to be an issue of contention. On the one hand, some researchers claim that AI cannot bear the responsibility because 'it is not a full moral agent, as it does not have autonomy',[16] at least not at the same level of humans. On the other hand, there are groups that view autonomous weapons and robot armies as 'artificial agents' or a 'class of combatants'. For all intents and purposes, as Coker stated, 'we are trying to "moralise" weapons, an elegant term for abdicating control over our own ethical decision-making [to intelligent machines]'.[17]

With AI becoming progressively more of an unavoidable certainty of modern warfare, the role of humans becomes more uncertain, and the realities of war, which would ignite a rejection of such technologies, fade in favour of national security considerations. In effect, rather than trying to force AI development and use to accord with existing international norms, norms are being reframed to make way for autonomous weapons to be used with minimal consequence.[18]

Barriers to governance: the role of private companies and state dynamics in regulating AI in the military domain

Considering the frequently discussed challenges and ongoing debates surrounding responsible AI development and deployment in the military domain, efforts to establish a cohesive and enforceable governance regime for AI-powered warfare are continuously impeded by the stakeholders' lack of political will and the proper incentive to expedite consensus-building to keep up with AI's rapid pace of progress. While the lack of regulation for states means that developing or acquiring AI to bolster their defence capabilities and, by extension, their national security is easier, they may not necessarily be the sole hinderance to efforts to establish international AI regulation. These efforts are further complicated by tech and defence companies, whose financial interests could be adversely affected by the implementation of such regulations. However, the absence of a unified governance framework based on consensus between state and non-state actors has led to lack of coordination in the field of AI-powered military capabilities, which poses significant risks to international peace and security.

Since the implications of using AI in the military domain extend beyond national boundaries and impact international security, efforts by states to engage with non-state actors at the national level are insufficient to address the international dimension of the issues related to AI-powered warfare. This necessitates that policymakers and regulators work towards establishing a shared understanding that transcends national interests. Achieving this requires the development of a global governance framework grounded in a multi-stakeholder approach. Indeed, only recently have states begun to recognise the importance of such an approach to shaping policy responses and governance frameworks, which is essential for fostering trust and addressing challenges posed by geopolitical tensions, industrial competition and state rivalries. In addition to including members of their own armed forces, who are primarily charged with acquiring and using these technologies and, as such, whose experiences may contribute significant insight to the realities surrounding the deployment of AI during conflict, states are increasingly engaging with non-state actors. These include epistemic communities of tech experts, researchers, think tanks and academics, as well as civil society organisations that provide invaluable insights, expertise and evidence on the technological, policy, humanitarian, legal and ethical dimensions of AI-powered warfare. The active participation of civil society organisations and epistemic communities will further enhance public confidence and legitimacy while promoting transparency and accountability in the ethical development, deployment and use of AI in the military domain. Most significantly, states are also engaging with the private sector in the form of the aforementioned tech and defence companies that can contribute to shaping governance approaches and solutions, particularly in regard to compliance with any proposed regulation, as much of the research, development and financial investment in military AI resides within the private sector. This will allow companies to demonstrate their commitment to responsible innovation, thereby building trust among shareholders, policymakers and users. As such, the international community recognises that there is an urgent need to establish, promote and support an independent, neutral and trusted platform that facilitates multi-stakeholder dialogue and fosters the development of governance pathways and solutions for the responsible development, acquisition and deployment of AI in the military domain.

There have been several attempts to establish such platforms, chief among them was the United Nations Institute for Disarmament Research (UNIDIR) Expert Network on the Governance of Artificial Intelligence in the Military Domain that brought together experts from academia, governments, international organisations and civil society as well as companies from the tech and defence industries. In early 2024, UNIDIR, in collaboration with Microsoft, launched the Roundtable for AI, Security, and Ethics (RAISE) to promote multi-stakeholder dialogue on the use of AI in security and defence.[19]

Similar platforms emerged, such as the Summit on Responsible AI in the Military Domain (REAIM), which was held at the Hague in February 2023 and in Seoul in September 2024. During REAIM 2023, the Political Declaration on Responsible Military Use of Artificial Intelligence and Autonomy was launched and later issued by the United States in November 2023 and endorsed by sixzty-two states, including Israel.[20] REAIM 2024 similarly resulted in a Blueprint for Action endorsed by sixty-one states.[21] Unlike the previous year, Israel did not endorse this document, as, at the time of the Summit, it was engaged in the war on Gaza. However, despite the promising picture portrayed by the Declaration in terms of the measures that should be implemented by states in the development, deployment, or use of military AI capabilities, it does not specify how these commitments would be ensured through specific enforcement mechanisms. Even the Blueprint reiterated many of the same commitments, including a call for each state to develop its own national strategies, policies and legislation, however, with no clear guideline on enforcement. In effect, no true measures to ensure accountability were articulated in either document.

Impediments remain in reaching a consensus among stakeholders to establish a global regulatory framework. Based on the policy report of the recently launched UNIDR-RAISE,[22] we identified three main impediments. The first impediment arises from the lack of universally agreed-upon definitions that takes into account each state's policy environment, strategic objectives, values, aspirations, cultural norms, legal frameworks and historical context. This issue was especially apparent during discussions of Group of Governmental Experts (GGE) on lethal autonomous weapons systems (LAWS) under the Convention on Certain Conventional Weapons (CCW) and during the China–United States Track II Dialogue on AI and International Security led by Tsinghua University's Center for International Security and Strategy and the Brookings Institution. Furthermore, there was no common understanding of what constitutes a 'red line' or what could be considered as unlawful use cases. This lack of consensus in regard to definitions continues to lead to a divided policy environment on the global level, obstructing effective multi-lateral governance dialogues and contributing to a lack of trust among states.

The second impediment relates to confidence-building in both the people developing, deploying and using AI-enabled capabilities and the technology itself. Confidence must be established in the technology throughout its life-cycle from the beginning, starting with the contractors and vendors responsible for developing these technologies and ensuring their responsible use, particularly those from the private sector, and in the later stages, particularly as it pertains to its deployment during conflict and the operators who are responsible for providing oversight. This highlights a complex moral issue regarding the human element for responsible use of AI in the military domain. For example, in the development stage, the engineers building the interface must consider several factors. First, they must ensure that their own biases are not reflected on to the technology. Second, that the parameters in which AI conducts its decision-making abides by established international humanitarian law (IHL). Both of these factors require that the datasets being used to train the AI comply with the relevant international law and ensure that the biases that result from cultural variations are accounted for. Third, and perhaps most importantly, that operators of the technology will continue to have sufficient oversight over the AI's decision-making to prevent catastrophic damage. Another important aspect to consider when evaluating the human element is that confidence must extend to the user or operator and include assurance regarding the commander's intent when deciding to deploy and utilise specific AI-enabled capabilities in military scenarios. This is contingent upon their level of technical literacy as well as their understanding of the legal, ethical and moral issues that arise when using these technologies, which require both training and capacity-building.

The third impediment stems from AI-enabled weapons' potential to act as both a force-multiplier and a threat-multiplier. AI-enabled weapons enhance the effectiveness, efficiency and operational capabilities of military forces, especially for small states and malevolent non-state actors. This amplifies the power and impact of an actor's military capabilities, allowing it to gain ground in any conflict with fewer resources or personnel. At the same time, these weapons also magnify risks and threats. As such technologies become widely available or fall into the hands of malevolent non-state actors, rogue states or adversaries, it could destabilise international security, increase the likelihood of asymmetrical warfare, intensify the proliferation of such weapons and provoke an arms race,[23] further exacerbating regional – as in the case of the Middle East – and global tensions – especially between superpowers. Given their significant destabilising effects, it is crucial to determine appropriate international or regional responses to such threats. However, this task is complicated by the lack of consensus on what constitutes a 'red line' or unlawful use cases as previously mentioned. The main concern stems from the extent to which there is no unified understanding of the extent to which civilian casualties can be deemed acceptable, especially amid intensifying competitive dynamics. This ambiguity adds further complexity to preexisting security challenges, such as ensuring accountability and establishing effective international governance on dual-use technologies.

In addition to the above three impediments, we are highlighting a fourth impediment concerning the ambiguity surrounding the extent to which existing export control instruments, particularly those addressing military technologies, may also apply to dual-use technologies employed in AI-powered weapons. For example, unlike post-Cold War export controls aimed at promoting transparency and preventing destabilising arms buildups there are currently no specific bans, regulations or requirements concerning the degree of human control in autonomous weapons systems (AWS). Despite this, weapons systems must comply with international humanitarian law. This lack of clarity enables developers – both states and private companies – to expand production and enhance proficiency in such technologies without significant constraints. Additionally, in the absence of robust safeguards, some actors may resort to irresponsible technology transfers as a means of offloading systems, exacerbating non-proliferation risks, such as the unconditional sale of technology to states with a history of undemocratic or unethical use of dual-use technologies. Existing mechanisms and ongoing discussions in national and multilateral forums highlight the potential need for additional export controls and explore what form such measures should take. One of the main issues highlighted in regard to being able to establish effective export control regimes for AI is that, like other emerging technologies, it goes beyond the traditional boundaries of non-proliferation governance instruments, institutions and regimes. This fragmented approach causes overlaps in control lists across regimes, highlighting the need for coordination to address redundancies. These challenges prompt broader questions about the overall effectiveness, adaptability and relevance of the current non-proliferation governance frameworks in addressing dual-use technologies such as AI. To improve implementation, harmonised practices and unified guidance are needed. However, the independent handling of these technologies by each regime creates inefficiencies and undermines the system's overall effectiveness.[24]

From the existing arms control treaties, the most relevant is the Wassenaar Arrangement (WA), despite not being legally binding. This is due to its focus on conventional arms and dual-use technologies. Its guidelines and control lists serve as the foundation for most national export control frameworks, including those in the European Union (EU) and the US. Recently, several national and multi-lateral initiatives have been launched to review and propose enhancements to export controls and strategic trade management tools for emerging technologies, including AI.[25] Currently, the WA consists of forty-two members, mostly consisting of NATO member states and excluding Russia, China and Israel. The WA engages in informal technical dialogues with other arms export control regimes as part of its outreach efforts, collaborating with the Missile Technology Control Regime (MTCR), the Nuclear Suppliers Group (NSG) and the Arms Trade Treaty (ATT) on matters related to control lists. Nevertheless, the universalisation of regime export controls remains difficult. This is, in large part, because some supplier states have intentionally opted to stay outside certain regimes. This decision is often driven by a desire to avoid restrictions and scrutiny of their export practices. For instance, China and Israel, two of the largest exporters of military drones, have not joined the MTCR.[26] This issue is further complicated by the fact that even member states of the aforementioned agreements with established national strategies, such as the United States and the EU, continue to export these technologies sometimes in contradiction to their own stated ideals. The EU's dual-use regulation (currently Regulation (EU) 2021/821), which directly applies to its member states, integrates the control lists from four multi-lateral export control regimes (the Australia Group, the WA, the NSG and the MTCR) into a single list.[27] In the US, export control systems implement WA guidelines, though some regulations extend beyond them.[28]

Once again, the difficulty in establishing a coherent export control regime occurs largely due to the absence of a clear consensus on what constitutes a red line or an unlawful use case. The United States and its companies are continuing to supply AI-enabled capabilities to allies, despite criticism from various sources, including advocacy groups, academics, social movements and even its own citizens. This is particularly evident in the context of Israel, where such technologies have been associated with actions perceived as oppressive and contributing to the ethnic cleansing of Palestinians.

The absence of regulation underscores the pivotal role private tech companies play in the development, sale and deployment of AI for military purposes. Many states heavily rely on these companies to supply advanced capabilities, including AI and other services that can be used in conjunction, such as cloud platforms, drones, cyber defence systems and advanced logistics networks, to bolster their security and geopolitical standing. This dependency not only enhances national power but also reinforces economic and strategic dominance on a global scale. Geopolitical competition among states, especially the US, China and Russia, to develop cutting-edge technologies, coupled with rivalry among tech companies and a pervasive fear of missing out, exacerbates the situation.[29] States often turn a blind eye to violations of international norms for strategic gains, while companies prioritise commercial benefits over ethical considerations. This dynamic feeds into the lack of consensus and political will to establish regulations or impose meaningful limitations, perpetuating the unregulated expansion of AI-enabled military capabilities. Furthermore, as technology advances, militaries increasingly rely on complex systems that often require expertise beyond their personnel's capabilities, creating a demand for private contractors to fill critical skill gaps.[30] While these contractors provide essential support, overreliance raises concerns about accountability and transparency. Essentially, the absence of international regulatory control and enforcement reinforces these state-industry dynamics, allowing them to operate without too much attention given to accountability.

Gaza and Ukraine wars: testing grounds for AI development and the question of accountability

The ethical concerns raised by recent developments in the Russia–Ukraine war and especially Israel's war on Gaza bring into focus the debates regarding how the development of AI technology is contingent upon the continued experimentation in conflict disrupting the possibility of having effective governance regimes. Israel ranks among the top countries worldwide in terms of its AI-driven advancements in cyber warfare, intelligence and AWS. Not only was it one of the first countries in the Middle East to deploy military drones, but it also continues to be unmatched in terms of AI and cyber capabilities, to the extent that it is now one of the most prolific exporters of such technologies globally. Its lightweight and cost-effective drones, such as the highly advanced Golden Eagle drone, were instrumental in Israel's military AI capabilities, reshaping the conduct of warfare. The Golden Eagle drone is exceptional in terms of its tracking and targeting of objects, demonstrating a high level of precision regardless of whether the object is on the ground or in the air, even if the lighting conditions are unfavourable. The Israeli offensive 'Operation Guardian of the Walls' on Gaza in 2021 – often referred to as the world's 'first AI war' – witnessed the utilisation of reconnaissance autonomous drones.[31] These drones acted as a force multiplier dramatically enhancing the scope of Israel's military capabilities.[32] Israel has also managed to develop its own army of military robots, which has been operational since 2012. Such robots were used in guard towers in the Occupied West Bank and are even capable of attacking Palestinians with tear gas and sponge-tipped bullets.[33]

There is a growing concern among scholars, journalists and activists who argue that Israel uses the occupied Palestinian territories as a laboratory to test its own technologies.[34] In his most recent book, Lowenstein expounds on the 'laboratory thesis' in which he traces the development of Israel's military and digital surveillance technologies from when they were first used against the Palestinians in the occupied territories to their eventual export worldwide.[35] The Israeli newspaper *Haaretz* has reported that during the Gaza war, Israel has been using Gaza as a 'testing ground' for its military robots.[36] In fact, there is a growing recognition that the occupation and subjugation of the Palestinian territories is crucial to Israel's national identity as a tech superpower.[37] Mhajne clarified that, 'we cannot separate Israel's achievements in AI from its occupation of Palestinians'.[38] This is the case not just in Gaza, Ukraine has also become a testing ground for AI-powered weapons. The concern among critics stems from the perception that civilian populations are being used in experimental settings, with security officials providing moral justifications for such actions. They argue that these tragic outcomes are necessary to understand how AI weapons function in war and to develop better regulatory frameworks to address ethical considerations.[39] The idea that this experimentation is ongoing is treated as matter of fact, and quite often taken for granted, despite growing ethical concerns. Private technological companies also play a role in this experimentation, particularly in Ukraine. As providers of AI-technologies, they act as drivers for the testing of AI weapons in battlefields by creating 'war labs'. Alex Karp, the CEO of Palantir Technologies who collaborated with Ukrainian armed forces during the war,[40] and Mykhailo Fedorov, Ukraine's Minister of Digital Transformation, both contended that wars like Ukraine are the best testing grounds for new technologies, as they cannot be tested in domestic contexts. Jorritt Kaminga, the director of the AI defence company RAIN,[41] stated that 'Ukraine is a living laboratory in which some of these AI-enabled systems can reach maturity through live experiments and constant, quick reiteration'.[42]

The extreme consequences that result from such testing on the ground is subject to errors, malfunction, mistargeting and unwarranted attacks on civilians, increasing the number of unnecessary 'accidental' civilian deaths. Even if the end benefit of such testing leads to improvements of the technology, the absence of international regulation on the use and export of these weapons raises concerns about the lack of mechanisms to ensure accountability and prevent collateral damage.

October 7 marked a significant landmark in terms of AI warfare. Hamas's attacks raised questions regarding Israel's cyber security and cyber intelligence capabilities, while magnifying the capabilities of Iran-backed non-state actors. This prompted Israel to respond with overwhelming force in order to assert its dominance, regardless of global ethical and legal concerns.

The course of the war revealed Israel's unprecedented military capability in deploying a combination of advanced AI-based surveillance, targeting and combat systems, particularly the Gospel or the Habsora, which is a system that accelerates the selection of targets in Gaza for bombing and provides an estimate of the number of deaths in advance. This AI system was proudly referred to by a former Israeli intelligence officer as a 'mass assassination factory'.[43] The system uses traffic light colours to indicate an estimation of casualties: red indicates too many casualties to justify an attack and green indicates less casualties, which signals a go ahead. In this system, the algorithms depend on the quality and amount of data they process, from which they base their predictions or suggestions. Raids can be quickly organised using another AI system known as 'Fire Factory', which determines munition requirements, ranks and allocates thousands of targets to aircraft and drones and suggests a timeline for execution.[44] The problem is that Gospel can falsely label an individual as a combatant if he shares the same characteristics of those identified as combatants. Such a system frames its analysis of information as absolute certainty, despite the fact that its analysis is inherently flawed due to the fact that it is working from biased information. Many Palestinians mentioned that numerous residential buildings were targeted where no members of Hamas resided.[45] In point of fact, Israel has repeatedly stated that civilian structures, such as hospitals and schools are acceptable targets because their systems have identified Hamas targets and weapons in these buildings, which has been proven to be categorically false by journalists covering the war. This prompted human rights activists and groups in the Middle East – including Israeli groups – to request transparency on the safeguards of Israel's AI weapons, as they describe such weapons as 'the most nefarious threat to Palestinians'.[46] The ethical concerns were further compounded when the Israel Defense Forces (IDF) revealed that the final decision of attack is always made by humans and approved by at least another person of command.[47] This suggests that Israel was certainly able to avoid civilian casualties, indicating that collateral damage from drone strikes is intentional, and Israel should be held accountable for every civilian death and injury, especially as it is well known that Israel has a variety of precision munitions in addition to its highly sophisticated surveillance and geospatial intelligence technology. Ron Reiter, the co-founder and Chief Technology Officer of the Israel-based cyber firm Sentra and a former Israeli intelligence officer, confirmed that Israel's targeting systems are designed to be very accurate to minimise civilian casualties.[48] In a report by RUSI, Noah Sylvia further clarified that there is a rigorous legal procedure that is followed inside the IDF, in which 'lawyers must sign off on every target – human or AI-generated – even if there are hundreds in a single day […] every single target is generated, approved, ordered and struck with the full knowledge and consent of human IDF operators'.[49] For many, this revelation validated the argument that states must be held accountable for the collateral damage caused as a result of the deployment of AWS. The case of Israel dispels the back and forth on the issue of the 'responsibility gap'. The lengthy confirmation process that Israel requires for each and every use of its AI military capabilities confirms that the supposed autonomy of these machines does not negate the moral and legal responsibility of the state, even in the event of an 'unintended' malfunction. As such, it is increasingly apparent that it is unrealistic to claim that we are facing a 'responsibility gap' issue because it is clear where the blame lies. Human rights activists' insistence on blaming Israel's decision to target civilians and civilian infrastructure, regardless of the technology used, cited multiple incidents in which Israel targeted aid organisations that provide food or medical services to Palestinians in Gaza, 'even after their GPS coordinates were provided to Israeli authorities'.[50] When an Israeli drone bombed the charity organisation World Central Kitchen, their founder and head chef José Andrés stressed that it wass a deliberate attack, as he clarified, 'they were targeting us in a deconflicting zone, in an area controlled by IDF […] the airstrikes on our convoy I don't think were an unfortunate mistake […] it was really a direct attack on clearly marked vehicles whose movements were known by everybody at the IDF'.[51] Israel's use of AI-powered weapons demonstrates how such technology became a tool to facilitate violence against Palestinians, while reducing the IDF's human cost in warfare. The intention to cause harm is evident in most of Israel's attacks on Gaza, which renders their actions morally reprehensible. The sale of such technology to other governments worldwide extends such impact beyond Palestinian territories, as Israel exports these lethal technologies to Chile, China, India, South Korea and Türkiye.[52] By selling these technologies, Israel widens responsibility, as other countries indirectly benefit from their use in the conflict with Palestinians. This dynamic further complicates the establishment of an international legal framework that regulates the use and exportation of such weapons. As multiple states and tech companies benefit from unrestrained development – complicated by their interdependence as previously mentioned

– reaching a global consensus on such a regulatory framework would be challenging.

This was evident in Israel's heavy investments in new AI technologies, often in partnership with US companies. Microsoft's cloud platform, Azure, was reportedly utilised by Unit 8200, an elite Israeli intelligence division, to operate an AI-driven database for identifying potential targets associated with Hamas and Palestinian Islamic Jihad (PIJ).[53] Similarly, Google has been a significant contractor for the Israeli government since 2021, after being awarded, along with Amazon, the multi-billion-dollar Nimbus cloud computing contract to modernise Israeli government technology infrastructure. The Nimbus contract has sparked protests among employees at both Google and Amazon, who argue against collaborating with the Israeli government due to its treatment of Palestinians, as they were concerned that the contract could allow Israeli military and intelligence agencies to use Google's AI technology. Google, however, expressed concern that delays in providing access might lead the IDF to favour its competitor, Amazon. In response to the dissent, and despite its stated AI policies that commit the company to refraining from using the technology in ways that could cause harm to individuals, Google dismissed more than fifty employees last year for protesting the contract. Gaby Portnoy, the director general of Israel's National Cyber Directorate, hinted at the Nimbus contract's contribution to military operations, stating that the platform facilitated remarkable developments during combat, which he described as playing a crucial role in achieving victory.[54]

The Gaza war has also demonstrated the scale of Israel's deployment of their combat and surveillance robots, particularly 'robodogs'. Israel is using robodogs, manufactured by the US-based company Ghost Robotics, in tunnels to spot traps and identify enemy locations. Another example is the deployment of the Rooster, manufactured by the Israeli company Robotican, which has the ability to jump and fly, overcoming obstacles such as steps and enabling it to fly through windows.[55] As in Israel, the war in Ukraine continues to prompt massive developments in robotics. Samuel Bendett, a Russia analyst at the US think tank Center for Naval Analyses, has been tasked with tracing military drone and robotics technology use and has stated that Ukraine is increasingly developing small robots, specifically unmanned ground vehicles (UGVs), because they are harder to track by Russian drones.[56] Taras Ostapchuk, the owner of the Ukrainian tech company Stolb.com.ua, with support from Ukraine's military technology cluster Brave1, has developed three kinds of robots, all called Ratel. The robots range from logistics robots charged with carrying supplies to the frontlines, evacuation robots to evacuate the injured and combat robots that carry and deploy landmines and are equipped with explosives and weapons. However, these robots are not fully autonomous, as they are remote-controlled by humans. According to Ostapchuk, UGVs serve to supplement some of the more dangerous missions that would traditionally be carried out by human soldiers while maximising the damage inflicted on adversaries.[57]

The increase in the deployment of AI in military contexts highlights the responsibility of both states and private companies when designing, assessing and deploying technologies such as autonomous weapons and robot soldiers. In fact, Israel's military–technology complex is uniquely characterised by a close synergy between its security establishment and high-tech sector. Each year, tens of thousands of discharged soldiers transition from the Israeli military to the high-tech industry, bringing with them specialised skills and a high level of motivation, as highlighted by venture capitalist Jon Medved. According to Itamar Yaar, a former deputy head of Israel's National Security Council, 'there's a sort of ping-pong between a tech company and the IDF'. He adds that, 'long before there's a marketable product, the tech companies offer it to the IDF, the police, or the intelligence agencies, and they try it out, sometimes in ongoing operations, to test and to improve it. If it is good, then it is procured fairly quickly'. This approach accelerates procurement and bypasses the delays commonly experienced in product development, known as the 'valley of death'.[58] While in Gaza, Israel is the most readily culpable; in Ukraine, culpability also extends to private technological companies such as the German Quantum Systems, the Japanese Rakuten, the US Clearview and Palantir Technologies and the Turkish Baykar. Such tech companies consider these battlefields as marketplaces to sell and test their technologies, which gives companies independent state-like powers in wars mainly dependent on AI weapons, in which most of the algorithmic-based targeting relies on their technologies.[59]

In the absence of a global regulatory framework, this comes with the risk of flouting international norms, as the company would claim no accountability when errors emanate from decisions made by AI-weapons and used by states. The recent cases of deploying autonomous weapons and robots in the Gaza and Ukraine wars highlight the need for international frameworks to regulate the use of such technologies in armed conflicts. Relying on national regulation of AI is insufficient to guarantee the safeguards in using such technology, especially when multi-national companies are involved and when such technologies are exported to other states. A lack of international frameworks for AI – that clearly delineates the scope and responsibility of their use – will only result in facilitating war crimes by technology rather than limiting it.

Conclusion: the way forward

In the past decades, and most recently with Ukraine and Gaza, the development of AI-powered military technologies has revealed itself, particularly for states such as Israel, as a driver for conflict. This chapter has demonstrated the role of AI weapons in the escalation of violent conflicts while addressing the ethical and legal controversies surrounding their use. However, despite all the apparent drawbacks of these technologies, the purpose of this chapter is not to suggest that military applications of AI do not have their place but that their unchecked use in conflicts have greatly damaged the perception of such technologies. In and of themselves, there are many potential benefits, such as avoiding excessive casualties; however, states and companies in their zeal to develop and use autonomous weapons, rather than err on the side of caution, have allowed the presence of these technologies to inspire some truly heinous acts, while divorcing themselves from responsibility. As mentioned previously, turning back the clock on AI is not feasible; states will not readily concede to the heavy restriction of such a transformative technology; nevertheless, it remains imperative that there should be an attempt to build the widest possible consensus between global regulators. Every actor – whether states, technology companies, human commanders or others – understands their duty to minimise harm, avoid intentionally causing damage to innocents and prioritise the welfare of both combatants and non-combatants in every stage of designing, assessing and deploying AI military technology.

Based on the above, any legal principle would have to address two central questions. First, how does AI make decisions? Second, who should be held accountable for the actions of these increasingly autonomous machines? Rather than this worrisome trend in which actors increasingly attempt to abrogate their responsibility, there should be an attempt to centre global regulation on these two principles. In doing so, we may be able to overcome one aspect of the challenges of achieving a consensus on AI regulation while addressing concerns that a global regulatory framework may result in more harm than good. These concerns, highlighted by human rights activists, global civil society actors and even tech companies, stem from the idea that even if some sort of consensus is reached, it might result in regulation that is 1) open for misuse by states, is highly politicised and is non-inclusive and, as such, may selectively be implemented or have a futile enforcement mechanism, and 2) restrictive, prompting tech companies to focus on compliance rather than on advancing the learning capabilities of the technology to improve threat and security assessments. As such, in reference to the first question, global regulation must recognise that machine learning has its own inherent biases stemming from the biases of those that designed the technology; for example, Israel's lack of respect for Palestinian lives is evident in its technology. This bleeds into the second question regarding accountability. By regulating who is responsible, as evidenced by the cases of Gaza and Ukraine, both tech companies and states should be held accountable. This may guarantee that states will take responsibility for civilian casualties but also that weapons manufacturers will make their sale of weapons conditional on respect for international humanitarian legal and ethical standards. This will encourage tech companies to avoid selling to states that will misuse their technology, and states will avoid buying technologies from manufacturers that do not uphold rigorous procedures for assessing the learning capabilities of their machines, perhaps even encouraging these companies to innovate a more 'ethical AI', whose supposed agency is not taken for granted due to the assumption of 'rationality'.

If we are to have any sort of effective regulation, this must be accompanied by a strict enforcement mechanism that does not differentiate between small or great powers, Western or Eastern, North or South, which is sorely lacking in several aspects of international humanitarian law. Gaza and Ukraine are currently test cases that will either help or hinder the future of AI regulation. The international community, in which we include multiple stakeholders and not just states, is currently calling for a precedent to be set and for accountability and punishment for international crimes to be decided.

Notes

1 Elise Vincent, 'Israel's use of AI in bombings raises questions over rules of war', *Le Monde* (2023). https://www.lemonde.fr/en/opinion/article/2023/12/15/israel-s-use-of-ai-in-bombings-raises-questions-over-rules-of-war_6345351_23.html (accessed 5 February 2026).

2 Agnes Callamard and James Rogers, 'We need a new international accord to control drone proliferation', *Bulletin of the Atomic Scientists* (2020). https://thebulletin.org/2020/12/we-need-a-new-international-accord-to-control-drone-proliferation/ (accessed 5 February 2026).

3 Mohammad Eslami, Alena Vieira, Arshin Adib-Moghaddam, Lauro Borges, Maria Papageorgiou, Fabio Cristiano, Ibrahim Al-Marashi, Tom Sauer and Christian Kaunert, 'The geopolitics of AI-driven arms races', *Geopolitics* (2025), 1–43.

4 Bassant Hassib and Fatimah Ayad, 'The challenges and implications of military cyber and AI capabilities in the Middle East: The geopolitical, ethical, and technological dimensions' in Mohammad Eslami and Alena Vysotskaya Guedes Vieira (eds), *The Arms Race in the Middle East: Contemporary Security Dynamics* (Cham: Springer International Publishing, 2023), 49–66.

5 James Johnson, 'Artificial intelligence in nuclear warfare: A perfect storm of instability?', *The Washington Quarterly* 43:2 (2020), 197–211. https://doi.org/10.1093/oso/9780192858184.003.0002

6 Aaron M. Johnson and Sidney Axinn, 'The morality of autonomous robots', *Journal of Military Ethics* 12:2 (2013), 129–141. https://doi.org/10.1080/15027570.2013.818399; Duncan MacIntosh, 'Fire and forget: A moral defense of the use of autonomous weapons systems in war and peace', in Claire Finkelstein and Jens David Ohlin (eds), *Lethal Autonomous Weapons: Re-Examining the Law and Ethics of Robotic Warfare* (Oxford: Oxford University Press, 2021), 1–23; Massimiliano Lorenzo Cappuccio, Jai Christian Galliott and Fady Shibata Alnajjar, 'A taste of armageddon: A virtue ethics perspective on autonomous weapons and moral injury', *Journal of Military Ethics* 21:1 (2022), 19–38. https://doi.org/10.1080/15027570.2022.2063103

7 MacIntosh, 'Fire and forget'.

8 James Johnson, 'Artificial intelligence in nuclear warfare: A perfect storm of instability?', *The Washington Quarterly* 43:2 (2020), 197–211. https://doi.org/10.1093/oso/9780192858184.003.0002

9 Mohammad Eslami and Alena Vysotskaya Guedes Vieira (eds), *The Arms Race in the Middle East: Contemporary Security Dynamics* (Cham: Springer International Publishing, 2023).

10 Johnson, 'Artificial intelligence in nuclear warfare'.

11 A US-based military robotics manufacturer, a subsidiary of QinetiQ a multi-national defence technology company.

12 Peter W. Singer, *Wired for War: The Robotics Revolution and Conflict in the 21st Century* (New York: Penguin, 2009).

13 MacIntosh, 'Fire and forget'; Duncan MacIntosh, 'PTSD weaponized: A theory of moral injury', paper presented at the Center for Ethics and the Rule of Law at the University of Pennsylvania Law School (2015), December 3–5; Cappuccio et al., 'A Taste of Armageddon'; James Johnson, 'The AI commander problem: Ethical, political, and psychological dilemmas of human-machine interactions in AI-enabled warfare', *Journal of Military Ethics* 21:3–4 (2023), 246–271. https://doi.org/10.1080/15027570.2023.2175887

14 Erich Riesen, 'The moral case for the development and use of autonomous weapon systems', *Journal of Military Ethics* 21:2 (2022), 132–150. https://doi.org/10.1080/15027570.2022.2124022

15 Riesen, 'The moral case for the development and use of autonomous weapon systems'.

16 Ross W. Bellaby, 'Can AI weapons make ethical decisions?' *Criminal Justice Ethics* 40:2 (2021), 86–107. https://doi.org/10.1080/0731129X.2021.1951459

17 Christopher Coker, *Warrior Geeks: How 21st-Century Technology Is Changing the Way We Fight and Think About War* (London: Hurst & Company, 2013).

18 Bellaby, 'Can AI weapons make ethical decisions?'; Johnson, 'The AI commander Problem'.

19 Yasmin Afina and Giacomo Persi Paoli, *Governance in Artificial Intelligence in the Military Domain: A Multi-Stakeholder Perspective on Priority Areas* (Geneva: UNIDIR, 2024).

20 US Department of State, *Political Declaration on Responsible Military Use of Artificial Intelligence and Autonomy* (2023). https://www.state.gov/bureau-of-arms-control-deterrence-and-stability/political-declaration-on-responsible-military-use-of-artificial-intelligence-and-autonomy (accessed 5 February 2026).

21 The Readable, *REAIM Blueprint for Action* (2024). https://thereadable.co/reaim-blueprint-for-responsible-ai-use-military/ (accessed 11 September 2024).

22 Afina and Paoli, *Governance in Artificial Intelligence in the Military Domain.*

23 Mohammad Eslami and Alena Vysotskaya Guedes Vieira, 'Introducing the arms race in the Middle East in the twenty first century: A "powder keg" in the digital era?', in Mohammad Eslami and Alena Vysotskaya Guedes Vieira (eds), *The Arms Race in the Middle*

East: Contemporary Security Dynamics (Cham: Springer International Publishing, 2023), 3–13.

24 Kolja Brockmann, 'Applying export controls to AI: Current coverage and potential future controls', in Thomas Reinhold and Niklas Schörnig (eds), *Armament, Arms Control and Artificial Intelligence: The Janus-faced Nature of Machine Learning in the Military Realm* (Cham: Springer International Publishing, 2022); Kolja Brockmann, 'Challenges to multilateral export controls: The case for inter-regime dialogue and coordination', *SIPRI* (2019). https://www.sipri.org/sites/default/files/2019-12/1912_regime_dialogue_brockmann.pdf (accessed 5 February 2026).

25 Wassenaar Arrangement, 'List of dual-use goods and technologies and munitions list' (2019), WA-LIST (19) 1. Wassenaar Arrangement Secretariat. https://www.wassenaar.org/app/uploads/2019/12/WA-DOC-19-PUB-002-Public-Docs-Vol-II-2019-List-of-DU-Goods-and-Technologies-and-Munitions-List-Dec-19.pdf (accessed 5 February 2026).

26 Brockmann, 'Challenges to multilateral export controls'.

27 Council of the European Union (2021) *Regulation (EU) 2021/821 of the European Parliament and of the Council of 20 May 2021 setting up a community regime for the control of exports, transfer, brokering and transit of dual-use items.* Official Journal of the European Union, L206.

28 Brockmann, 'Applying export controls to AI'.

29 Antonio Calcara 'Contractors or robots? Future warfare between privatization and automation', *Small Wars & Insurgencies* 33:1–2 (2021), 250–271. https://doi.org/10.1080/09592318.2021.1957534; Bassant Hassib and James Shires, 'Digital recognition: Cybersecurity and internet infrastructure in UAE–Israel diplomacy', *International Affairs* 100:6 (2024), 2399–2418. https://doi.org/10.1093/ia/iiae233

30 Calcara, 'Contractors or robots?'.

31 Mohammad Eslami, 'Iran's drone supply to Russia and changing dynamics of the Ukraine war', *Journal for Peace and Nuclear Disarmament* 5:2 (2022), 507–518. https://doi.org/10.1080/25751654.2022.2149077

32 Anwar Mhajne, 'Israel's AI revolution: From innovation to occupation', *Carnegie Endowment for International Peace* (2023). https://carnegieendowment.org/sada/2023/11/israels-ai-revolution-from-innovation-to-occupation (accessed 5 February 2026).

33 The New Arab Staff, '"Robodogs" part of Israel's "army of robots" in Gaza war', *The New Arab* (2024). https://www.newarab

.com/news/robodogs-part-israels-army-robots-gaza-war#:~:text =Vision%2060%20units%2C%20which%20are,surveillance%20of %20alleged%20enemy%20positions (accessed 5 February 2026).

34 Darryl Li, 'The Gaza Strip as laboratory: Notes in the wake of disengagement', *Journal of Palestine Studies* 35:2 (2006), 38–55; Eyal Weizman, *Hollow Land: Israel's Architecture of Occupation* (Brooklyn, NY: Verso Books, 2012); Naomi Klein, 'Laboratory for a fortressed world', *The Nation* (2007). https://www.thenation.com/article/archive/laboratory-fortressed-world/ (accessed 5 February 2026); Jonathan Cook, '"The lab": Israel tests weapons, tactics on captive Palestinian population', *Washington Report on Middle East Affairs* (2013), 16–17; Jonathan Cook, *Disappearing Palestine: Israel's Experiments in Human Despair* (London: Bloomsbury Publishing, 2008); Stephen Graham, 'Laboratories of war: Surveillance and US–Israeli collaboration in war and security', in Elia Zureik, David Lyon and Yasmeen Abu-Laban (eds), *Surveillance and Control in Israel/Palestine* (London: Routledge, 2010), 157–176; Charlotte Silver, 'Israel gets a kick (back) out of conflict', *Al Jazeera English* (2012). http://www.aljazeera.com /indepth/opinion/2012/12/20121224133753129619.html (accessed 5 February 2026); Who Profits, *Proven Effective: Crowd Control Weapons in the Occupied Palestinian Territories* (Tel Aviv: Who Profits Research Center, 2014). https://rb.gy/vcl6ku (accessed 5 February 2026).

35 Antony Lowenstein, *The Palestine Laboratory: How Israel Exports the Technology of Occupation around the World* (London: Verso Books, 2023).

36 Sagi Cohen, 'Gaza becomes Israel's testing ground for military robots', *Haaretz* (2024). https://www.haaretz.com/israel-news/2024 -03-03/ty-article-magazine/.premium/gaza-becomes-israels-testing -ground-for-remote-control-military-robots/0000018e-03ed-def2 -a98e-cfff1e640000 (accessed 5 February 2026).

37 Leila Stockmarr, 'Beyond the laboratory thesis: Gaza as transmission belt for war and security technology', in Jana Hönke and Markus-Michael Müller (eds), *The Global Making of Policing: Postcolonial Perspectives* (London: Routledge, 2016).

38 Mhajne, 'Israel's AI revolution'.

39 Joseph Gedeon and Maggie Miller, 'Israel under pressure to justify its use of AI in Gaza', *Politico* (2024). https://www.politico.com/news/2024 /03/03/israel-ai-warfare-gaza-00144491 (accessed 5 February 2026).

40 Palantir Technologies is an American company specialising in AI software platforms for big data analytics.

41 RAIN+ Ethics, a division of the RAIN Research Group, a Washington, DC based international research firm working on the nexus between AI and defence.
42 Vera Bergengruen, 'How tech giants turned Ukraine into an AI war lab', *Time* (2024). https://time.com/6691662/ai-ukraine-war-palantir/ (accessed 5 February 2026).
43 Jonathan Fenton-Harvey, 'The Gospel: Israel's controversial AI used in the Gaza war', *The New Arab* (2023). https://www.newarab.com/analysis/gospel-israels-controversial-ai-used-gaza-war (accessed 5 February 2026).
44 Marissa Newman, 'Israel quietly embeds AI systems in deadly military operations', *Bloomberg* (2023). https://www.bloomberg.com/news/articles/2023-07-16/israel-using-ai-systems-to-plan-deadly-military-operations (accessed 5 February 2026).
45 Newman, 'Israel quietly embeds AI systems'.
46 Gedeon and Miller, 'Israel under pressure'.
47 Gedeon and Miller, 'Israel under pressure'.
48 Gedeon and Miller, 'Israel under pressure'.
49 Noah Sylvia, 'Israel's targeting AI: How capable is it?', *RUSI* (2024). https://www.rusi.org/explore-our-research/publications/commentary/israels-targeting-ai-how-capable-it (accessed 5 February 2026).
50 Gedeon and Miller, 'Israel under pressure'.
51 Holly Williams, Erin Lyall and Tucker Real, 'World Central Kitchen boss José Andrés accuses Israel of "Direct Attack" on Gaza aid convoy', *CBS News* (2024). https://www.cbsnews.com/news/israel-gaza-world-central-kitchen-strike-jose-andres-direct-attack-aid-workers/?intcid=CNI-00-10aaa3a (accessed 5 February 2026).
52 Mhajne, 'Israel's AI revolution'.
53 Harry Davies and Yuval Abraham, 'Revealed: Microsoft deepened ties with Israeli military to provide tech support during Gaza war', *The Guardian* (2025). https://www.theguardian.com/world/2025/jan/23/israeli-military-gaza-war-microsoft (accessed 5 February 2026).
54 Gerrit De Vynck, 'Google rushed to sell AI tools to Israel's military after Hamas attack', *The Washington Post* (2025). https://www.washingtonpost.com/technology/2025/01/21/google-ai-israel-war-hamas-attack-gaza/ (accessed 5 February 2026).
55 The New Arab Staff, '"Robodogs" part of Israel's "army of robots" in Gaza war'.

56 Mohammad Eslami and Lauro Borges, *The Drones Race and International Security* (Cham: Springer International Publishing, 2025).
57 Matt Burgess, 'Robots are fighting robots in Russia's war in Ukraine', *Wired* (2024). https://www.wired.com/story/robots-are-fighting-robots-in-russias-war-in-ukraine/ (accessed 5 February 2026).
58 Anchal Vohra, 'Israel's military-technological complex is one of a kind', *Foreign Policy* (2019). https://foreignpolicy.com/2023/12/19/israels-military-technology-complex-is-one-of-a-kind/ (accessed 5 February 2026).
59 Bergengruen, 'How tech giants turned Ukraine into an AI war lab'.

Concluding reflections: the monstrosity of AI warfare

Alena Vysotskaya Guedes Vieira, Arshin Adib-Moghaddam and Mohammad Eslami

There is something eerily uncomfortable about artificial intelligence (AI) and the emerging modes of warfare. The horror of this inevitable trend is already witnessed by the civilians engulfed by the ever-expanding battlefields of Gaza, Ukraine and elsewhere. The integration of AI into the fabric of contemporary warfare marks not merely a technological evolution but a profound transformation in the ontology of conflict. This is why our emphasis on the various angles of AI attempted to situate the future of warfare within broader discourses of power, ethics and global security as well as its implications for cyber warfare, quantum computing and nuclear security. We acknowledge and further the notion developed by critical AI scholars that, beyond its tactical and operational dimensions, the militarisation of AI raises deeper questions about the nature of power, the erosion of human agency and the ethical limits of technological innovation in the pursuit of security.[1] These concluding reflections extend these critiques, offering a more radical comment about the AI-driven arms race and its implications for the future of global order and human societies.[2]

Perfecting death

The contemporary qualitative arms race,[3] driven by AI, can be framed by a broader (neo)liberal logic of efficiency, optimisation and market-driven innovation. In this paradigm, warfare is increasingly framed as a problem of data management, in which the goal is not merely to destroy the enemy but to outthink, outmanoeuvre and outpace them through superior algorithms and computational power. This is also referred to as a new form of 'hybrid warfare' – a form of psycho-techno-politics, in which power operates not only through overt coercion but also through the subtle manipulation of information, perception and decision-making. In the context of warfare, this manifests itself as a shift away from traditional forms of kinetic violence towards an ever-more destructive form of cognitive warfare, in which the battlefield is as much about controlling narratives and perceptions as it is about severe material destruction.

This (neo)liberal logic is intensely deceptive. It reduces warfare to a technical problem, obscuring the human and ethical dimensions of military conflict. The emphasis on efficiency and precision, often sold to the public as a means to minimise collateral damage, has already normalised violence by framing contemporary warfare as a rational and calculated activity. This technocratic framing of war erodes the moral and emotional dimensions of conflict, the pain and suffering of the targeted population, transforming the representation of conflict into a sterile and dehumanised process. For instance, the use of AI-powered drones or prepped personal devices allow operators to kill from a distance in a cheap and disastrously efficient way.[4] This physical and psychological distance to the target not only desensitises actors to the consequences of their actions, but also undermines the legal, moral and ethical frameworks that have historically constrained the use of force.

Undoubtedly, the autonomy of AI systems is increasing, challenging the foundations of international law and notions of *jus ad bellum* – the conditions under which states may resort to war or use armed force in general – and *jus in bello* – the law that governs the way in which warfare is conducted. Can an autonomous system be said to have 'intention' to cause harm? Can it differentiate between combatants and civilians in line with the principles of distinction and proportionality? Some of these questions expose the limits of our legal and ethical frameworks, which were designed for an international system in which human beings, not machines, were the primary agents in war.[5]

Furthermore, the so called 'black box' problem can be seen as an opportunity by states and rogue actors to lower the threshold of war and to evade culpability. When an AI system decides, it is often impossible to trace both the chain of decision-making and the reasoning behind that decision, making it that much more difficult to assign responsibility in cases of error or misconduct. This lack of transparency undermines the principles of justice and accountability that are central to international humanitarian law (IHL). Already, all of this has created dangerous precedents, in which states, private and/or non-governmental actors deploy AI systems with minimal oversight, knowing that the opacity of these systems will shield them from scrutiny. This increasing confinement of human agency is not merely a technical or legal problem. At its core, it is a deeply philosophical issue, as it must be seen as a part of a wider trend towards the dehumanisation of life, in which we are reduced to data points and algorithms.[6]

This dehumanisation, critical AI studies reveals, is not a coincidence. In fact, it is inherent to the logic of AI warfare, which operates by abstracting from human experience and emotions. In this context, the use of AI in warfare represents a new form of 'geo-techno-politics', which disperses war into every sphere of life, even turning our personal devices into potential weapons.

The killing dividend

The dehumanisation of warfare as a function of (neo)liberalism also points to a broader tendency towards the commodification of warfare, i.e., the nexus between war and profit. The collaboration between governments and the so-called tech-giants, so vividly expressed at the time of writing by the current companionship between the US president Donald Trump and tech-entrepreneur Elon Musk, underlines the various ways in which perfecting the methods of death comes with a dividend. The case studies highlighted in our study, from the use of increasing numbers of AI-powered drones in Ukraine to the vast deployment of autonomous systems in Gaza, demonstrate the ways in which battlefields are already laboratories for the testing and refinement of AI-powered weaponry. This instrumentalisation of war as a site of experimentation reflects a disturbing convergence of militarism and techno-capitalism, in which human lives are reduced to algorithmic calculations and datafied decisions in the pursuit of technological advancement and profit.

This 'killing dividend' is not merely a question of ethics in warfare. It points to the immense influence of corporate interests in determining the trajectory of international security, further galvanising a military–industrial AI complex that is premised on profit and market competition. This creates an insidious incentive structure, a 'death capitalism' in which the monstrosity of war is furthered to maximise profit margins and technological advancement. The dual use applicability of AI further complicates this problem, as technologies developed for civilian purposes can be rapidly and relatively cheaply weaponised, transcending the boundaries between peaceful deployment and weaponisation. This creates an immensely destructive feedback loop, in which the same technologies that are marketed as tools for human progress or social development can also be used to further violence, war and oppression. The result is a form of 'techno-imperialism', in which the benefits of AI are unevenly distributed, while the risks and harms are borne primarily by the most vulnerable strata of (international) society.[7]

Thus, the AI-driven arms race represents more than a merely technical or strategic challenge but an explicitly politico-philosophical one. It is a cruel reminder of a form of technological development in which the pursuit of profit supersedes the demands of society for more human security and emancipation from various private and governmental mechanisms of techno-power. However, the techno-capitalistic dehumanisation of the current modes of AI warfare in the name of 'progress' is not inevitable. All over the world, various forms of techno-resistance are emerging, and they are initiating a dialogue about the deployment of AI in society and warfare more specifically.[8] As the authors who contributed to this study demonstrate clearly, addressing the technological challenges of the future goes beyond finding technological solutions, as it demands a fundamental rethinking of the nexus between power, profit, war and ethics.

The primary aim of these countermovements must be to interrogate and condemn the new forms of hybrid AI warfare and to resist a new epistemology of war, in which power and knowledge are primarily mediated by algorithms and data. By virtue of the awesome potential of AI technology, this new quest for techno-supremacy is a real and present danger to the future of the planet and an existential threat to humanity.[9] By flagging and interrogating these pivotal themes, the present book has highlighted the need for a new approach that prioritises human security over a discourse of dominance and suppression. What we need is more poetry for peace and no more drumbeats for war. This compassionate approach to the world requires human understanding, empathy and, first and foremost, the political and cultural vigilance of the critics and activists, whose dedication and self-sacrifice for the cause of humanity is needed today – more than ever before.

Notes

1 See further Arshin Adib-Moghaddam, *The Myth of Good AI: A Manifesto for Critical Artificial Intelligence* (Manchester: Manchester University Press, 2025).

2 Mohammad Eslami, Alena Vieira, Arshin Adib-Moghaddam, Lauro Borges, Maria Papageorgiou, Fabio Cristiano, Ibrahim Al-Marashi, Tom Sauer and Christian Kaunert, 'The geopolitics of AI-driven arms races', *Geopolitics* (2025), 1–43.

3 Mohammad Eslami and Alena Vysotskaya Guedes Vieira, 'Introducing the arms race in the Middle East in the twenty first century: A "powder keg" in the digital era?', in Mohammad Eslami and Alena Vysotskaya Guedes Vieira (eds), *The Arms Race in the Middle East: Contemporary Security Dynamics* (Cham: Springer International Publishing, 2023), 3–13.

4 Mohammad Eslami, 'Iran's drone supply to Russia and changing dynamics of the Ukraine war', *Journal for Peace and Nuclear Disarmament* 5:2 (2022), 507–518. https://doi.org/10.1080/25751654.2022.2149077

5 See further Ingvild Bode and Hendrik Huells, *Autonomous Weapons Systems and International Norms* (Montreal: McGill-Queen's University Press, 2022).

6 See Roberto J. González, *War Virtually: The Quest to Automate Conflict, Militarize Data, and Predict the Future* (Berkeley, CA: University of California Press, 2022).

7 See further Michael Kwet, 'Digital colonialism: US empire and the new imperialism in the Global South', *Race and Class* 60:4 (2019), 3–26; Nick Couldry and Ulises A. Mejias, 'Data colonialism: Rethinking Big Data's relation to the contemporary subject', *Television and New Media* 20:4 (2019), 336–349.

8 See further Rachel Adams, 'Can artificial intelligence be decolonised?', *Interdisciplinary Science Reviews* 46:1–2 (2021), 176–197.

9 See further Arshin Adib-Moghaddam, *Is Artificial Intelligence Racist? The Ethics of AI and the Future of Humanity* (London: Bloomsbury, 2023).

Index

Index

EU authorised representative for GPSR:
Easy Access System Europe, Mustamäe tee 50,
10621 Tallinn, Estonia
gpsr.requests@easproject.com

www.ingramcontent.com/pod-product-compliance
Ingram Content Group UK Ltd.
Pitfield, Milton Keynes, MK11 3LW, UK
UKHW021828100926
8556IPUK00004B/227
* 9 7 8 1 5 2 6 1 9 6 1 6 3 *